Achim Hescher
Reading Graphic Novels

Narratologia

Contributions to Narrative Theory

Edited by
Fotis Jannidis, Matías Martínez, John Pier,
Wolf Schmid (executive editor)

Editorial Board
Catherine Emmott, Monika Fludernik, José Ángel García Landa, Inke Gunia,
Peter Hühn, Manfred Jahn, Markus Kuhn, Uri Margolin, Jan Christoph Meister,
Ansgar Nünning, Marie-Laure Ryan, Jean-Marie Schaeffer, Michael Scheffel,
Sabine Schlickers, Jörg Schönert

Band 50

Achim Hescher

Reading Graphic Novels

Genre and Narration

DE GRUYTER

ISBN 978-3-11-057770-9
e-ISBN (PDF) 978-3-11-044594-7
e-ISBN (EPUB) 978-3-11-044539-8
ISSN 1612-8427

Library of Congress Cataloging-in-Publication Data
A CIP catalog record for this book has been applied for at the Library of Congress.

Bibliographic information published by the Deutsche Nationalbibliothek
The Deutsche Nationalbibliothek lists this publication in the Deutsche Nationalbibliografie;
Detailed bibliographic data are available on the Internet at http://dnb.dnb.de.

© 2016 Walter de Gruyter GmbH, Berlin/Boston
This volume is text- and page-identical with the hardback published in 2016.
Typesetting: Lumina Datamatics GmbH, Griesheim
Printing: CPI books GmbH, Leck

♾ Printed on acid-free paper
Printed in Germany

www.degruyter.com

Für Uli, meine geliebte Frau

Acknowledgements

Many special thanks go out to Anke Uebel, long-standing friend and colleague, for sharing many thoughts that have entered this book and for editing the manuscript. Also, I sincerely thank my colleague and friend Bernd Engelhart for his contribution in the editing process.

Contents

1	**Introduction** —— 1	
2	**Beginnings, Periods, Movements, and Developments** —— 8	
2.1	Underground Roots —— 8	
2.2	Alternative Comics and the First Hype of the Graphic Novel —— 12	
2.3	The 1980s and 1990s: Significant Changes on the (Comic) Book Market —— 19	
2.4	From 2000 on: the Second Hype of the Graphic Novel —— 23	
2.5	Graphic Novels and *bandes dessinées* —— 26	
3	**Graphic Novels and the Problem of Categorization** —— 30	
3.1	Academic Interest in Comics and Graphic Novels —— 30	
3.2	General Categorization Criteria for Graphic Novels —— 32	
3.2.1	Lengthiness and Serialization —— 32	
3.2.2	Seriousness and Authenticity —— 33	
3.2.3	Cartoonicity —— 37	
3.2.4	Complexity —— 38	
3.3	From Prototypes to a Typology of Complexity —— 39	
3.3.1	Format, Medium, Mode, and Genre —— 39	
3.3.2	From Classical Categories to Family Resemblances —— 43	
3.3.3	Fuzzy Boundaries: From Family Resemblances to Prototypical Categories —— 45	
3.3.4	From Prototypes to a Typology —— 52	
3.3.4.1	Multilayered Plot and Narration —— 57	
3.3.4.2	Multireferential Use of Color —— 61	
3.3.4.3	Complex Text/Image Relation —— 64	
3.3.4.4	Meaning-Enhancing Panel Design/Layout —— 66	
3.3.4.5	Structural Performativity —— 73	
3.3.4.6	Multiplicity of References to Texts/Media —— 77	
3.3.4.7	Self-Referential Narration and Metafictional Devices —— 81	
3.3.5	A Short Parenthesis on Autobiography —— 83	
3.4	Critical Approaches to Comics and Graphic Novels —— 85	
3.4.1	Will Eisner's Practical Sequentiality —— 87	
3.4.2	Scott McCloud's (Mis)Understanding of Comics —— 87	
3.4.3	Charles Hatfield's Alternatives to Sequentiality —— 92	
3.4.4	Thierry Groensteen's Visual Arthrology —— 95	
3.4.5	Martin Schüwer's Comprehensive Intermedial Approach —— 100	
3.4.6	Hannah Miodrag's *Langue* vs. *Parole* in the "Web" of Comics —— 102	
3.4.7	Conclusion —— 106	

4	**Verbal and Pictorial Narration in Graphic Novels** —— 108	
4.1	Preliminary Reflections: Why Graphic Narratives Have no Transmitting Communication System and not Necessarily a Narrator —— 108	
4.2	The Pictorial Track and Problems Concerning 'Focalization' —— 116	
4.3	Showing and Seeing in the Pictorial Narration —— 122	
4.3.1	What Is Shown and What Is (not) Seen: Mise en Scène vs. Character Vision —— 126	
4.3.1.1	Showing Taken to the Extreme: Cross-Cutting Strands of Action/*Montage* —— 132	
4.3.1.2	Mise en Scène and Ocularization —— 137	
4.4	Words and Text as Showing and Narrating —— 144	
4.4.1	Paratext —— 145	
4.4.2	Narratorial Captions —— 148	
4.4.3	Balloons and Balloon Speech —— 149	
4.4.4	An Excess of Showing: Sounds and Lettering —— 150	
4.4.5	Texts in the Fictional World —— 152	
4.4.6	Tags —— 155	
4.5	Of Authors, Artist-Writers, and Narrators —— 156	
4.6	Narratorial and Pictorial Representation in Graphic Memoirs and Fictional Biographies —— 162	
4.7	Why the Narrating and Experiencing I Should Not Be Used on the Graphic Memoir —— 170	
4.8	Focalization Revisited: What Is Known and What Is Shown —— 171	
4.9	Representations of Subjectivity —— 181	
4.9.1	Styles and Their Makers —— 181	
4.9.2	The Subjectivity of Characters —— 183	
4.9.3	Character Imagination —— 184	
4.9.4	The Subjectivity of Narrators —— 189	
4.9.5	Signs and Metaphors of Subjectivity —— 190	
4.10	Layout Revisited: Classification and Critical Efficiency —— 192	
5	**Taking Stock: The Graphic Novel as a Narrating Genre** —— 195	
6	**Works Cited** —— 203	
6.1	Primary Verbal and Graphic Works —— 203	
6.2	Secondary Works —— 206	
7	**Index of Primary Works** —— 218	

1 Introduction

In the last ten to fifteen years, no book format other than e-books has had a bigger boom than graphic novels, which have recently also started to come out in electronic form. It has even been argued that graphic novels have ensured the survival of bookstores in the electronic age (cf. Platthaus 2010). However, the popularity of graphic novels has certainly not been solely due to clever marketing ploys. After the void left by literary postmodernism (in verbal narrative fiction, that is), graphic novels have been the field or genre most prone to experimenting with form(s) and subject matters. If I apply paradigms such as 'historiographic metafiction' or 'self-referentiality,' for example,[1] I find postmodernist features in graphic novels of the 1980s and 90s, when postmodernist narrative fiction was still in fashion, as in Alan Moore and Dave Gibbons' *Watchmen* (1986–1987), Alan Moore and Eddie Campbell's *From Hell* (1999), Art Spiegelman's *Maus* (1986/92), and in Marc-Antoine Mathieu's *Julius Corentin Acquefacques, prisonnier des rêves* (6 vols., 1990–2013). But even nowadays, works like Bryan Talbot's *Alice in Sunderland* (2007), Mana Neyestani's *Une métamorphose iranienne* (2012), or Chris Ware's *Building Stories* (2012) are strikingly self-referential in their makeup: Talbot and Neyestani frequently employ metalepsis, which has also been found in the exemplarily postmodern novel by John Fowles, *The French Lieutenant's Women* (1969); and Ware's *Building Stories*, coming in a box as a loose leaf or booklet collection, strongly remind me of B.S. Johnson's 'book in the box' *The Unfortunates* (1969), which, like Fowles' novel, has also been viewed as exemplary of postmodernism.[2] And as an experiment with layout, Ware's *Building Stories* may be traced back to Julio Cortázar's postmodern trailblazer *Rayuela* (1963), in which the author suggests

---

[1] The term was created by Linda Hutcheon (1988). For a critical assessment of 'historiographic metafiction' and of other such paradigms in the context of the 'postmodern novel,' see Hescher 1996: 76–81 et passim. Drawing back on this concept, Seamus O'Malley, for example, asserts that Moore and Campbell underscore the constructedness of the historiographical process in *From Hell* by adding two appendixes: endnotes undercutting the main text by explaining "how arbitrary many of the choices Moore made truly were" (O'Malley 2012: 176) and a kind of epilogue suggesting that "history is more made up of (and by) historians than it is by history itself" (ibid. 177).

[2] In contrast to European literary criticism, postmodernism in the U.S. is normally used as a period term signifying the 1960s and 70s, in which U.S.-American authors like John Barth, Donald Barthelme, Raymond Federman, Richard Brautigan, William Gass, Ronald Sukenick, or the British writers B.S. Johnson and Christine Brooke-Rose, intensively experimented with the form of the novel (cf. Hescher 1996: 43).

two different orders to read the individual chapters. In this respect, postmodernism has survived in the graphic novel – in fact, the graphic novel openly celebrates the revival of postmodernism, as in *City of Glass* (2004), Paul Karasik and David Mazzucchelli's graphic adaptation of Paul Auster's eponymous 1985 novella.

A considerable share of graphic novels are autobiographically motivated. The so-called graphic memoirs (see chapter 3.3.3), however, are not just graphic autobiographies; they rather thematize the making of the work itself and/or the factuality and fictionality of the self and other, as seen in Lynda Barry's *One Hundred Demons* (2002), David B.'s *Epileptic* (2005), Alison Bechdel's *Fun Home* (2006), Julie Doucet's *Ciboire de Criss!* (1996), Fabrice Neaud's *Journal* (1996–2002), or Lewis Trondheim's *Approximativement* (1995). Not every graphic memoir, though, is self-referential or metafictional, as Ulli Lust's *Heute ist der letzte Tag vom Rest deines Lebens* (2009), Marjane Satrapi's *Persepolis* (2000–2003) or David Small's *Stitches* (2010).

Like graphic memoirs, reportage comics (also called travelogues or graphic journalism) are concerned with fact and fiction and display an explicit awareness of the problems at work in their narratives. Thus, Joe Sacco's *Palestine* (1993–2001) and Emmanuel Guibert, Didier Lefèvre, and Frédéric Lemercier's *Le photographe* (2003–2006) make an increased use of irony, employ eye-catching layouts, and incorporate different media like photographs and contact prints. Although cartoonistic images seem at first to jar with the journalistic demand for objectivity, upon closer inspection, they allow for a critical presentation of 'facts' and the involvement of the journalists' self in their presentation: Sacco, for example, drawn like a Crumbian underground hero, makes ironic and sarcastic comments about himself, his desire for fame, and his journalistic methods; also, he uses a layout that is reminiscent of a storyboard and underscores the subjectivity involved in the choice of his material; Guibert, Lefèvre, and Lemercier also occur as drawn characters, whereas the Afghanis, objects, and the (beautiful) countryside are often shown in photographs or on a strip of contact prints. The mixing of the different media and their layout on the page seem to highlight the dubiousness and difficulty of the journalistic undertaking, and it seems at times that *Le photographe* is at least as much about the author Didier Lefèvre himself as about his mission in Afghanistan. The crossing of genre borders (from graphic journalism to the graphic memoir, as in Sacco and Lefèvre, from the postmodern superhero story to the apocalyptic novel in Moore and Gibbons' *Watchmen*, or from graphic metafiction to graphic intermedial fantasy as in Mathieu's *Julius Corentin Acquefacques*) is a specific feature of the graphic novel that has made it interesting to a new and growing audience apart from adult males that have outgrown the comic books of their youth.

Only a couple of years ago, insisting upon the comic book/graphic novel distinction was widely looked at as pedantic (and, although the winds have changed, it is still partly frowned upon). Starting around 2010, the term graphic novel has increasingly figured in the titles of articles, monographs, and essay collections. Before, with few exceptions, graphic novels were either tacitly subsumed under comics, or they were simply not subject to investigation. This considered, Roger Sabin's *Comics, Comix, and Graphic Novels* (1996) and Hans Baetens' *The Graphic Novel* (2001) must be looked at as pioneers in the field.

In general, the classification terminology is oriented toward comics and implies that graphic novels are a subcategory to them. Chapter three starts out with the first criteria brought up to distinguish graphic novels from comics, that is length (which concerns the page numbers in traditional American comic books compared to their Franco-Belgian peers), serialization (many but not all graphic novels first appeared in installments before they were rounded up in one volume), seriousness or authenticity (regarding the subject matter, for example, in autobiographical works), the cartoonicity of the characters, and, last but not least, complexity (which has been referred to aspects of form and the subject matter). In the end, however, these criteria have proved as too blurry and therefore inappropriate to uphold viable pertinence: there were always too many 'exceptions' from the rule, if the rule is to be the distinguishing criterion. Take the serialization issue: a good many graphic novels first came out in installments, and many others were immediately published in book format. An 'either/or' decision for or against membership in the category 'graphic novel' on the basis of serialization would be dubious. And take length: where is the cut-off point? Are Karasik and Mazzucchelli's *City of Glass* and Jason's *The Left Bank Gang* (2005) not graphic novels because of their relative brevity (though they do exceed the Franco-Belgian 48-page limit)? Here again, as with respect to other possible distinguishing criteria, an either/or seems out of place. Reflections of this kind led me to the conclusion that firstly, there should not be one single major criterion but several distinguishing criteria and secondly, those criteria should be *graded* to be of critical pertinence.

In fact, precisely because it was less precise than the other criteria brought up in the critical literature, *complexity* seemed most promising, presupposing that it was, first of all, graded, and that it came with a clear-cut set of subcategories graded in their own right. Such a terminological construction can only be realized in a *prototype approach*, which admits "fuzzy boundaries" (Dittmar 2008: 25) in – and overlap between – the categories and which is based on a well-defined set of core features to be completed by peripheral distinguishing features. A prototype approach thus admits categorizations based on 'both … and' as well as 'x rather than y' in addition to 'either/or' decisions. Moreover, it has one more considerable advantage: unlike classical categories, it is not exclusive regarding whether an object is or is not a member of a category; its flexible categories thus forestall the necessity typical of classical categories to add new categories over time when a new object does not fit in the old ones. In other words: it provides systemic stability.

Yet before that approach can take hold, the basic terms 'format,' 'medium,' and 'mode,' which have been so heterogeneously employed, need to be (re)defined. First, I take 'comics' to signify a medium rather than a genre. As a second step, I shall set up a general, prototypical, genre classification in which graphic novels figure as a (twice removed) subgroup of graphic narratives, the counterpart to verbal narratives (see chapter 3.3.3, Fig. 3.2). With this, I shall consolidate the graphic novel as a genre, that is a historical text group. To conclude chapter three, I shall assess what I think have been the most significant approaches to comics and graphic novels, historically and with respect to critical pertinence.

In chapter four, I shall elaborate on the process of narration in graphic narratives in general and graphic novels in particular. In comparison with drama and verbal narrative fiction, I hold that there is no narrator in graphic narratives unless it is marked on both the verbal-narratorial and the pictorial plane. Graphic narratives lack the mediating and transmitting communication system of verbal narrative fiction; there is no fictional entity that would solely bring forth the whole discourse of the work, that is, the verbal-narratorial and the pictorial track. As in drama, *showing* is the dominating mode in graphic narratives, despite the possibility of narratorial caption script. Showing here is defined as visual-pictorial in terms of the *mise en scène* and *point of view*. In graphic narratives, showing is set against *seeing*, which relates primarily to character vision and secondarily to what the reader-observers see (chapter 4.1).

Only recently have comics critics started to increasingly write about narratorial representation and particularly focalization. The latter, however, is too infused with connotations from classical narratology, which strongly stand against its application to the pictorial track in graphic narratives. To problematize the pertinence of focalization in practice, I shall demonstrate with examples from James Vance and Dan Burr's historical graphic novel *On the Ropes* (2013) that focalization accounts neither for point of view switching nor for unattributable points of view and that the novel's protagonist is not a narrator but a narrating character. As a result, I shall abandon the focalization concept from classical narratology and focus instead on the relation between 'what is shown' – the mise en scène and *point of view* – and 'what is seen,' or character vision, to the extent that it is displayed in the image (chapter 4.2).

The focus of section 4.3 is therefore on the pictorial track. When the point of view of an image is not attributable to a subject in the story world, it is referred to as an objective image; and if it is attributable, it is either subjective, as the point of view image, or half-subjective (such as, for example, the over-the-shoulder or reaction image). However, in half-subjective images (the great majority of comics images), the characters often see something else from what the implied observer (or projection center of the image) is supposed to see, and that in turn may be different from what the empirical reader-observer sees. I shall demonstrate these points in detail with a page from Daniel Clowes' *Ghost World* (1993–1997, see chapter 4.3.1.2).

What is shown in terms of point of view is subordinate to the mise en scène, which pertains to the external communication system, or the artist-writer (team). That the mise en scène shows something else from what characters see, I shall demonstrate with examples from Alan Moore and David Lloyd's *V for Vendetta* (1988–1989) and Moore and Gibbons' *Watchmen* (see chapter 4.3.1). *Montage* and cross-cutting also pertain to the artist-writer and represent above all a specific case of showing in which point of view and character vision are of secondary importance. They add complexity to the pictorial track and the plot, either in the form of two parallel strands of action or two strands of action of which one is delayed in time so that the other anticipates the upcoming events. Alan Moore and Eddie Campbell's historical novel *From Hell* (1999) contains examples of both types of cross-cutting (see chapter 4.3.1.1).

The crucial relation between what the single image shows and what the characters see is best accounted for in François Jost's term *ocularization* and its subtypes: primary internal, secondary internal, and zero ocularization. I have extended the definitional scope of ocularization to include the parameters of the mise en scène such as angle, framing, lighting, coloring, etc. and the perspective construction, in other words everything that the image visually and pictorially displays (chapter 4.3.1.2).

Until now, the focus of investigation has been on the pictorial track. In chapter 4.4, I shall elaborate on the different types of text in the verbal track: paratext, narratorial captions, speech and thought balloons, sounds and lettering, texts in the story world, and tags. It is noteworthy in this context that all these types of text are to some extent pictorial, which is most obvious with regard to sound lettering or speech balloons.

At the beginning of chapter four, I put forth the thesis that graphic narratives lack the mediating/transmitting communication system reified in the fictional narrator, who solely generates the whole narrative. In subchapters 4.5–4.7, the question concerning the (im)possibility of a fictional narrator shall be readdressed, and reasons are given why teachers of graphic novels need not worry that their students draw biographical conclusions about author-writers. Apart from that, fictional narrators may exist in graphic novels under the condition that they possess a spatio-temporal identity and that they are marked as narrators on both the narratorial and pictorial plane (captions and images), as distinct from the intradiegetic story world (chapter 4.5). This is not at all different in graphic memoirs or biographies. Neither one necessarily comes with a default narrator and thus, unless otherwise marked, the 'voice' speaking in the captions is no one else than the artist-writer's (chapter 4.6). Why the terms 'narrating I vs. experiencing I' should not be used on graphic memoirs concludes my investigations about (im)possible narrators (chapter 4.7).

Whereas ocularization is an efficient tool for pictorial track and particularly single-image analysis, its visual-pictorial parameters are inappropriate for the assessment of a sequence, episode, or a whole work. On that plane, we need to rely on cognitive parameters which again result, at least in part, from the assessment of the ocularizations. This applies to focalization as defined by Jost. Like ocularization, it is a relational term and assesses character as opposed to viewer *knowledge* with regard to plot: not everything readers/viewers perceive in an image sequence or episode is important for the plot or gives them a cognitive advantage over the characters (and vice versa). What is more, contrary to ocularization, focalization also accounts for the verbal-narratorial track (speech balloons and narratorial captions). After pinpointing the concept's problem spots and making the necessary definitorial adjustments, I shall use Jost's three focalization types (external, spectatorial, and internal) on several examples from graphic novels in chapter 4.8.

Focalization is only one aspect of subjectivity or subjective bending in graphic narratives. In chapter 4.9, I shall elaborate on other forms of subjectivity that exclusively pertain to the pictorial track: styles specific to artist-writers, character and narrator subjectivity and other signs of subjectivity like emanata.

The final reflections in this book relate to a parameter which has already been subject to scrutiny (see chapter 3.3.4.4). In graphic novels, artist-writers tend to be more experimental with panel design and layout than in other books of comics, which results in an increase in complexity, especially when there is cross-cutting or *montage*. Contrary to the layout of the chunks of text, on which little has been written, some attempts at classification have been made about the spreading of the panels on the page. In chapter 4.10, I shall elaborate on how useful or efficient those classifications are with regard to the meaning production across the pictorial plane.

Now first things first. In the following chapter two, I shall elaborate on the historical roots of the graphic novel and the development of (a certain strand of) comics from the 1960s and 70s until now. Steeped in underground comix (with an 'x'), the first decisive step toward current forms and subject matters was taken with the so-called alternative comics from the 1980s and 90s. This was also the period in which the first long-form books of comics appeared which belong to what I called the "first hype" of the graphic novel (cf. Hescher 2012). Graphic novels as they are nowadays published belong to the "second hype" (ibid.), which started to build around the turn of the millennium. A discussion of graphic novels in the context of Francophone *bandes dessinées*, which had comparable developments in the 1980s and 90s, will conclude part two. – I have included nothing on the aspect of fandom, which is usually found in overviews on 'comics,' simply because for graphic novels, this aspect is of no relevance: their readers are a rather mixed, adult clientele and unlike comic books, graphic novels have never been collectors' items.

Note: Unless otherwise indicated, all quotes from sources other than English have been translated by myself, AH.

Note: chapter 2.4 appeared in a shorter version in Hescher 2014b; several sections in chapter three appeared in less elaborate form in Hescher 2012 and 2014a. – All illustrations are used in accordance with 'faire use.'

2 Beginnings, Periods, Movements, and Developments

For several reasons, it is virtually impossible to situate the beginnings of the graphic novel (as it is with comics, depending upon the criteria to be applied). Besides its status of an artistic phenomenon, the graphic novel is subject to marketing and distributing on the book market and, more recently, to academic assessment. Yet labels, formats, bindings, and technical terms, for example, are outward appearances and often misleading. – I might go back to the 1920s and 30s and find similarities to graphic novels in Frans Masereel's expressionist *Die Stadt* (1925), in Lynd Ward's woodcuts *God's Man* (1929), or in Milt Gross' *He Done Her Wrong* (1930, labeled, ironically enough, "The Great American Novel"), all of which are wordless picture narratives and considered forerunners to the graphic novel. Their creators, of course, could not care less about the label. Beginnings, it must be said, are often constructs serving to back up other constructs in pragmatic, commercial, or institutional frameworks.

2.1 Underground Roots

I tend to see the 'roots' of the graphic novel in underground comics,[1] or comix with an *x*, as they were spelled to distinguish them from mainstream or traditional comic books, whose readers were predominantly juvenile.[2] By the 1960s, the mainstream U.S. comic market, cornered by the publishers Marvel Comics and DC Comics,[3] consisted of superhero, action, and adventure comics – the genre I call traditional comic books (see ch. 3.3.4): *Action Comics* (featuring Superman), *Detective Comics* (featuring Batman), *The Amazing Spider-Man, Captain America, The*

---

[1] Actually, underground comics should be referred to as 'new underground' – I deliberately leave out what came to be known as Tijuana bibles, kinky comics, or the notorious eight-pagers, i.e. pornographic comic books that circulated from the 1920s to the 1960s (cf. Daniels 1971: 166, among others). Apart from this decade-spanning clandestine literature, Gabilliet sees two forerunners to the new underground: Harvey Kurtzman (1924–1993) and his satirical magazines *Mad* (1952–) and *Help!* (1960–1965), to the latter of which contributed the young Robert Crumb, Gilbert Shelton, and J. Lynch, who would later become underground heroes in their own right (cf. Gabilliet 2010: 62).

[2] Cf. Rhoades 2008a, 95: "The notion of comic books outside the mainstream was suggested by the headline 'Comics Go Underground' on the October 1954 cover of *Mad*."

[3] DC Comics was founded in 1934. The initial DC goes back to *Detective Comics*, featuring the Batman series, started in Detective Comics #27 in 1939.

Fantastic Four, The Hulk, X-Men, etc., and of mystery and horror: *Tower of Shadows, House of Secrets, Vampirella*, etc., and Gilberton's *Classics Illustrated* comics, action-oriented adaptations of classic novels like *Treasure Island, The Last of the Mohicans*, and romances such as *Wuthering Heights* (cf. Sabin 1996: 76). Interestingly enough in the context of graphic novels, "Gilbertson maintained that its adaptations of literary classics were not comic books" (Nyberg 1998: 117). Obviously, and excepting only the classics adaptations of romances, the publishers' programs were geared toward young boys or male adolescents. Only in Britain did publishers also aim at young female readers: from the 1950s on, a respectable number of girls' comic books were available, *Jackie* (DC Thomson, 1973–1993) being the most prominent and "final major success of the British boom" (Sabin 1996: 84).

Fig. 2.1: Seal of the Comics Code Authority

In this environment of the late 1960s, underground comics emerged, "a new wave of humorous, hippie-inspired comic books that were as politically radical as they were artistically innovative" (Sabin 1996: 92). They were also extremely sexual, violent, and drug-infused (cf. Lopes 2009: 78), which necessitated particular ways of distribution. It is noteworthy that at that point, comic book publishers had agreed for about 15 years to submit their comic productions to the Comics Code Authority (CCA),[4] who censored U.S. comic books according to the

---

4 The CCA was founded in 1954 as a body of the Comics Magazine Association of America in response to hearings held in the spring of that year before the Senate Subcommittee to Investi-

Comics Code, stipulating that "'all scenes of horror, excessive bloodshed [...], lust, sadism [and] masochism shall not be permitted'" (Duncan/Smith 2009: 40). From 1954 on until well into the 1980s, comic books would bear the seal of the CCA on the top right of their covers (Fig. 2.1). "It's a sign that this comic book is meant for children and safe for them, and that if by chance it had struggled against being safe for children, its errors had been corrected" (Wolk 2007: 4–5). Although underground comics violated the Code in principle, they were not really affected by the pressure from the local boards and authorities since their target readership was adult. A lot of underground material in the 1960s and 70s sold and circulated – albeit in very limited numbers, compared to the distributors of main stream comic books – through record stores and the so-called head shops: little shops emerging first in the underground boom town of San Francisco and specializing in cannabis paraphernalia such as pipes or bongs, recreational drugs, and other counterculture equipment (cf. Nyberg 1998: 137).[5]

Underground's most outstanding creator and the icon of counterculture is, of course, Robert Crumb (*1943), however, there were other very original artist-writers like Bill Griffith, S. Clay Wilson, Gilbert Shelton, Victor Moscoso, Rick Griffin, and Manuel "Spain" Rodriguez, all of whom contributed to Crumb's comics magazine *Zap*, which started out as a comic book and developed into an anthology when Crumb opened it later to other contributors. *Zap* became the epitome of the late 1960s counterculture and had sold over one million copies by 1972 (cf. Lopes 2009: 78). However, Crumb was often reproached for his own material being sexist and misogynist. Indeed, when we look at *Zap* issues, we find explicit sexuality – including, for example, sadism, rape, and incest – and demeaning portraits of women and African Americans. Yet I should add that Crumb was not the only creator whose works were ethically controversial; the same holds true for the works of Wilson, Shelton, and Rodriguez (cf. Lopes 2009: 81–82). To sum up, violence and drug culture, ethically dubious sexuality,

---

gate Juvenile Delinquency in the U.S. When the CCA approved of a work, it would bear their seal on its cover (see Fig. 2.1). The issue of comic books being bad for children was brought up in the late 1940s by diverse articles in popular magazines like *Reader's Digest* and *Collier's*. Fredric Wertham's book *Seduction of the Innocent: the Influence of Comic Books on Today's Youth* (New York: Rinehart, 1954) represents the peak of the anti-comics movement in an era which had been seeing McCarthyism. 'The Code' would drive several publishers out of business, among whom William Gaines' EC comics, which were renowned for their line of horror (cf. Nyberg 1998: 117). The Code was modified in 1971 and 1989, giving the creators and publishers larger scope with respect to titles and content (for details, see Nyberg 1998: 140–151 and 170–179).

5 May I here recall the often quoted anecdote about Robert Crumb selling issues out of a pram on street corners in Haight Ashbury, a district of San Francisco (cf. among others Sabin 1996: 95).

and horror – another bestselling genre in the movement (featured in publications like *The Skull* or *Bogeyman*) – found ample representation in underground comics of the late 1960s and early 70s.[6]

Underground seems to have been an all-male society – which begs the question: Was there actually a women's underground? The answer is yes. To start with, very few women worked in the comics business, and if they did, they worked in mainstream comics. Trina Robbins (*1938), one of the leading figures of the women artists, formed the Women's Comix Collective and launched the famous anthology *Wimmen's Comix* (1972–1992, cf. Chute 2010: 21), which featured stories about marriage and work life – there were other magazines to follow with related themes. Before *Wimmen's Comix*, Robbins had set up the first comic book entirely created by women (*It Ain't Me Babe: Women's Liberation*, 1970), by which, according to Hillary Chute, she "effectively created women's underground comics" (ibid. 20). As a matter of course, it was the feminist underground artists who fought back against demeaning sexuality in their colleagues' works: Robbins publicly expressed her outrage over Crumb (cf. Lopes 2009: 82), and so did Lyn Chevely, co-editor of and contributor to *Tits and Clits Comix* (1972, together with Joyce Farmer, cf. Chute 2010: 21). Apart from the feminists, Bill Griffith, cofounder of the anthology *Young Lust* (1970), "denounced the proliferation of pornographic and horror titles that he felt had no link to the original project of freedom of expression that the underground movement had embodied" (Gabilliet 2010: 81).

This is not to say that there was no explicit or 'kinky' sexuality in women's underground comics. In fact, it was in *Wimmen's Comix* that Aline Kominsky-Crumb (*1948), the equally controversial wife of the controversial Robert Crumb, published her first five-page story "Goldie" in 1972, which "picks up from [Justin] Green in its unflinching, and unglamorous, depiction of sexuality" (Chute 2010: 21). It is noteworthy that Kominsky-Crumb was heavily influenced by Green's *Binky Brown*, whose outspoken representations of (traumatized) sexuality had also shaped Robert Crumb's styles in "The Confessions of R. Crumb" (1972, and in a lot of works following up). Yet after falling out over several issues with the Women's Comix Collective, Kominsky-Crumb started her own comic book *Twisted Sisters* in 1976 (together with Diane Noomin). Although virtually unknown to a wider public – much unlike her husband – she strongly inspired contemporary graphic

---

[6] "In 1968 and 1969, Apex Novelties came out with pornographic comix including *Snatch Comics* and *Jiz Comics*, while Rip Off Press published the pornographic *Big Ass Comics*" (Lopes 2009: 82), the first issue of which (July 1969) was illustrated by Robert Crumb. The maybe most notorious comic of that time was *Cunt Comics*, created by Rory Hayes.

novel artists like Lynda Barry, Phoebe Gloeckner, and Alison Bechdel (cf. Chute 2010: 30).

As opposed to the mainstream comics readership, underground readers were distinctly older, at least college student age until up into their thirties. Charles Hatfield even speaks of a "sea change" suffered by the comics readership: "It was through the underground comix that comic books per se became an adult medium" (Hatfield 2005: 7).

Around 1970,

> [t]here were comix communities all over America, mainly based in the big cities, producing hundreds of titles each month. Certainly, most were small beer: typical print runs were in the hundreds – smaller still would be their distribution. Yet there were also a few major publishers – Krupp Comic Works (later Kitchen Sink), Rip Off, The Print Mint, The San Francisco Comic Book Company and Last Gasp – which between them had the power to take things to a new level of commercialism. With their help, [...] Crumb and Shelton, could hope to sell hundreds of thousands per issue. (Sabin 1996: 107)

Little later, in 1973, the underground comic market crashed due to a Supreme Court decision decreeing the 'community standard' doctrine, according to which "local communities were given greater power to decide what was obscene and what was not" (Lopes 2009: 85). This decision would allow any police officer to arrest shop owners for selling obscene material.[7] Thus, a lot of small publishers were forced out of business, and the underground market shrunk remarkably. The main underground publishers switched to a new form of distribution called the direct market system, which was to dominate the whole comic book market until the early 1990s (see ch. 2.3).

2.2 Alternative Comics and the First Hype of the Graphic Novel

The reason why I have elaborated in some detail on underground is that there, I find the first forerunners to graphic novels leading the way in terms of subject matters, styles and narrative structure – and readership, as just referred to. Crumb's solo publication from 1972, the four-page story "The Confessions of R. Crumb," included in the 28-page one-shot *The People's Comics*, may be considered a forerunner to what critics today call "autobiographical memoirs"

---

7 "In June, with the Miller v. California (413 U.S. 15) decision, the Supreme Court stated that it was not competent to define obscenity and as a result, the responsibility for doing so was returned to local authorities" (Gabilliet 2010: 82).

(Gardner 2008: 1), in which the author-protagonist is the subject of the narrative throughout. Charles Hatfield writes about underground comics that "the self-contained nature of these 'books,' [...] made the medium an ideal platform for kinds of expression that were outrageously personal and self-regarding" (Hatfield 2005: 7). Autobiographical traits, though not as preponderant as in Crumb's "Confessions," also exist in two other comic books often quoted in the historical context of the graphic novel: Justin Green's surreal *Binky Brown Meets the Holy Virgin Mary* (also from 1972) and Will Eisner's *A Contract with God* (1978), supposedly the first graphic novel, although actually a comic book featuring four short narratives.[8] Let me anticipate here that graphic memoirs (that is autobiographical graphic novels) will follow later, from the 2000s on, with increased frequency. For now, let me briefly stick with Green and Eisner.

In the preface to *Binky Brown*, Green admits that his youth alter ego Binky bears autobiographical traits (cf. Green 2009: 55–56) with regard to a compulsive neurosis (obsessive-compulsive disorder or OCD, as which it is known today), which is due to his strict, Catholic upbringing and a guilt trauma: playing ball in his parents' house, he smashes a statue of the Virgin Mary; in the narrative that follows, Binky tries through the years to come to terms with this traumatic experience by developing a number of obsessions. *Binky Brown* deeply influenced both comics artists Robert Crumb and Art Spiegelman (the latter of whom will be my subject below). This becomes obvious in the prefatory "Confession," a kind of narrative frame which Green put around Binky's story and in which he introduces an author figure – very similar to the beginning of Crumb's "Confessions" – informing the readers about and legitimizing his OCD (such meta-referential statements or frames can be found in a number of contemporary graphic novels, either at the beginning or the end or in particular spots in the middle of the narrative).

Eisner also added a preface to his 1978 volume *A Contract with God*: the setting, a caricature of a street in the Bronx, is "the biography of the street itself [...]"[9] Similarly, the story's Jewish protagonist, Frimme Hersh, is Will Eisner's alter ego and so is "Willie", the young boy in the story "Cookalein",[10]

---

8 Merino holds that "Héctor Germán Oesterheld invented the graphic novel [...]. He preceded both Will Eisner and Art Spiegelman in labeling the genre, which arose with such literary force in Argentina. He called it 'the new comic' " (Merino in Tabachnick 2009: 272).
9 "[...] through the physical evolution of the block, the rise and fall of the tenement building at No. 55 [Dropsie Avenue] and the ethnic and social changes of its stream of occupants" (Eisner 2006: x).
10 " 'Cookalein' is a combination of invention and recall. It is an honest account of my coming of age" (Eisner 2006: xiv).

and the apartment house in "Super" is "the house where I [W.E.] lived as a young boy" (ibid.). Apart from "The Street Singer", which concerns, according to Eisner, a phenomenon of the Depression years, the volume *A Contract with God*, like *Binky Brown*, is to a certain extent autobiographic. Unlike *Binky Brown*, Eisner's 1978 volume represents no continuous, not one longer story; it is four stories united in one volume, very different in content and depth from *Binky Brown* or other underground comic books. Although Eisner's readers at the time were mostly not Crumb's nor Green's, I observe one similarity with regard to reader age: in Eisner's case also, reader age is distinctly higher, the work demanding maturer minds compared to readers of mainstream comic books.

Heavily influenced by Crumb, Green, and Eisner, another comics heavyweight appeared on the scene: Art Spiegelman (*1948), the future creator of the epitome of the graphic novel, *Maus* (I + II, 1986/92). Spiegelman started out in the 1970s with his comics magazine *Arcade, the Comics Revue* (1975), which is said to represent 'the last whimper of the underground movement'.[11] To work more experimentally, Spiegelman and Françoise Mouly, his future wife, started a new comics magazine called *Raw* (1981), and employed artist-writers like Bill Griffith (*1944, co-founder of *Arcade*, founder of the anthology *Young Lust*, 1970, and creator of the comic strip *Zippie*, 1971), illustrator Gary Panter (*1950), and Charles Burns (*1955), who was to become world-famous with his graphic novel *Black Hole* (2005). It was in *Raw* #2 that Spiegelman started to publish the first mini-installments of what was to become *Maus: A Survivor's Tale* in 1986 *(Maus II* was to follow in 1992).[12] In this groundbreaking work, Spiegelman narrates his father Vladek's WWII ordeal and how he survived the Holocaust. The characters are depicted as anthropomorphic animals: the Nazis as cats, the Jews as mice, and the Polish as pigs. As its precursors from underground and later Eisner, *Maus* is (auto)biographical, featuring a metareferential frame story with an author as narrator (Art), who tells Vladek about the comic book he wants to write and instigates him to tell about his "life in Poland, and the war" (Spiegelman 2003: 14).[13] *Maus* has had world-wide success and has been known as an example of postmodern storytelling and as the epitome of the graphic novel per se.

---

[11] Gary Groth quoted in Duncan/Smith 2009: 67.
[12] Actually, the origins of *Maus* go back to 1972, when Spiegelman published a three-page prototype story called "Maus" in Robert Crumb's one-shot *Funny Aminals* [sic].
[13] Metareferential episodes thematizing Art's book in the making or cartooning in general reoccur throughout the narrative, cf. Spiegelman 2003: 14, 25, 134–135, 171–172, 176, 205–207.

Spiegelman, although very experimental, and the older contributors to *Raw* were still more or less steeped in underground. The new generation of artists like Gary Panter, Charles Burns, Peter Bagge, and Daniel Clowes were also influenced by underground, yet even more so by punk. Artists like Bagge also worked for the big mainstream publishers DC and Marvel. Many artists of the new generation were published by Fantagraphics Books (founded in 1976) under the label of 'alternative comics,' whose readers were predominantly adults (cf. Round 2010: 23) or young adults, as Clowes' readers.

By reviewing underground and its successor, alternative comics,[14] one important step is taken on the way to the roots of the graphic novel. *Maus* inevitably represents a corner stone among all the works mentioned, yet the graphic novel was given its label about ten years later: by marketing experts on the one hand and academic critics on the other. There are two other cornerstones that I see as constitutive for a genre that should not be based solely on the kind of stories told therein (like autobiographic stories): *Batman: The Dark Knight [Returns]*[15] (DC Comics, 1986), created by Frank Miller (*1957), a darker and pluckier four-issue sequel to the Batman of the 1960s and 70s, and *Watchmen* (DC Comics, 1986–1987, originally twelve issues, later united in one volume), written and drawn by the British Alan Moore (*1953) and Dave Gibbons (*1949), a parody of vigilanteism as well as an apocalyptic narrative with a postmodern twist. With restrictions, one more outstanding work of the period could be added: Neil Gaiman's series *The Sandman*,[16] with its main character Dream/Morpheus and its scripting method that Gaiman had picked up from Alan Moore (cf. Round 2010: 21). The success of the trailblazers Spiegelman, Miller, Moore and Gibbons, the growth of the trade paperback format – the binding together of "entire stories structured over six or eight consecutive issues" – and "its wide distribution in libraries" certainly increased the popularity of *The Sandman* (Gabilliet 2010: 100).

The reason why *The Dark Knight* and *Watchmen* are important for the graphic novel is twofold: firstly, they "reoriented the industry's energies dramatically towards older readers"[17] – this, of course, is also due to the fact that the child and adolescent readers from the past had meanwhile become adults. Moreover,

---

14 "[...] 'alternative' more often denotes satirical, political, and autobiographical elements inherited from underground comix" (Hatfield 2005: 26).
15 Originally, the series was called *The Dark Knight*. Little later, when the four issues were compiled in one volume, the title of the first issue was used for the compilation.
16 Published by DC Comics (1989–1996), actually a revival of the eponymous series from 1974–1976, featuring, among others, the art of Jack Kirby.
17 Cf. Sabin 1996: 162 and Rhoades 2008a: 124.

there has been a distinct increase in complexity with regard to their pictorial and narrative design: *The Dark Knight* ties up with an until then unattained host of characters and respective subplots known to adherents of the Batman issues of the 1960s and 70s; also, Miller introduced the foregrounding and visualizing of different media (print and TV) in terms of panel and caption styles, hitherto unknown.[18] *Watchmen* consists of more than 20 cross-cut subplots and more than 25 characters, not counting what in cinematic terms is called the extras. Apart from that, it engrosses readers by the sophisticated and humorous ways text and images relate to each other; as in Miller, *Watchmen* foregrounds the mediality of information through the pictorial design of the captions and panels (cf. Hescher 2013). In short, both works feature a complexity in the comics medium unknown until then. And complexity, as I shall explain below (ch. 3), is one core feature of graphic novels which distinguishes them from traditional comic books, whose target clientele was essentially juvenile. In this sense, the origin of graphic novels lies in comics becoming complex in their makeup.

Secondly, the publication of *The Dark Knight* and *Watchmen* marks the beginning of an extraordinary comics boom to be followed not even ten years later by a major crash because of a dramatically dwindling collector and speculator market. After the 1986 publication of Miller's and Moore and Gibbons' magna opera, publishers increased their number of titles, raised cover prices on a regular basis, and placed special issues. Hoping to get rich, collectors and speculators would often buy multiple copies of one and the same issue (one to read, one or more to keep or sell). By early 1993, prices had risen by almost 100 percent, compared to 1985, and most fans could not afford anymore to buy the enormous amount of publications by the whole line, for example the whole DC or Marvel line. Therefore, many quit collecting altogether (cf. Rhoades 2008a: 128–130). And with the comic market crash of the mid-1990s ended what I call the *first hype* of the graphic novel, developing from underground through Eisner to Spiegelman on the one hand and Miller, Moore and Gibbons on the other. To use a graphic representation (Fig. 2.2):

---

[18] Cf. Mitchell 2009: 117: "*The Dark Knight* [...] is highly cinematic and televisual, employing the full repertoire of motion picture and video rhetoric while continually breaking frames and foregrounding the apparatus of visual representation."

2.2 Alternative Comics and the First Hype of the Graphic Novel — 17

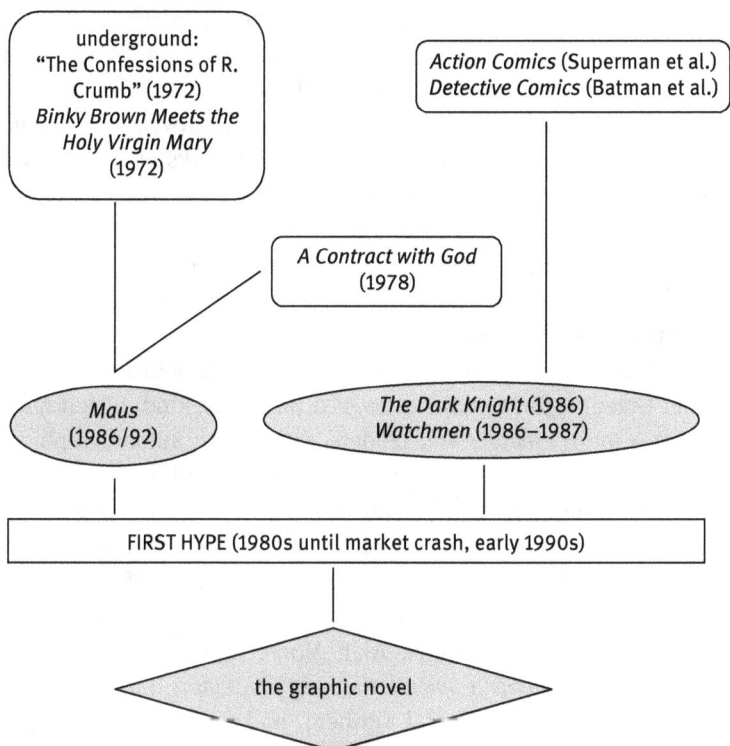

Fig. 2.2: The first hype of the graphic novel

The coloring in the schema indicates that *Maus*, *The Dark Knight*, and *Watchmen* are considered graphic novels and what came before them trailblazers, making them possible. With the publication of these three works, the idea of the graphic novel moved beyond comic shops and into the book trade (cf. Hatfield 2005: 29). – Not few experts see the graphic novel in terms of a label and as a marketing trick (cf. Sabin 1996: 165). The fact, as I emphasized above, that a different, adult, readership was addressed certainly helped that move because "it was believed that this was where the sales would be in the future" (Sabin 1996: 167). This tendency was fostered by mainstream publishers such as Penguin, Gollancz, Pantheon, and others launching graphic novel lines (cf. ibid. and Round 2008a: 188). It is also interesting to note that in 1986, *The Dark Knight* came out in a hitherto unusual, prestigious binding format, as would many others, following through the years.[19]

---

[19] Cf. Hoppler in Ditschke et al. 2009: 63–64 and Gabilliet 2010: 92.

All things reconsidered, it is impossible to ignore the ties of what was sold as graphic novels with the comics and book market, but this is only one side to the coin. On the other side, I see art works that differ absolutely or by degrees from traditional or merely lengthy comic books. Graphic novels and comic books share the same (comics) medium, yet as narrative works of art they are subject to a literary history (accounting for socio-economic and reception-oriented factors marking them as particular), genre theory, as well as to literary and semiotic analysis. These disciplines account for the specific contexts and structures (or parameters) of graphic novels and enable readers to establish connections with and tell them apart from traditional comic books.

In the underground of the early 1970s, Alina Kominsky-Crumb, Robert Crumb, and Justin Green began to tell stories of a particular kind, which have been engrossing to a lot of creators and readers until today: autobiographical stories. The difference is that today, they mostly come in the longer format of the graphic novel or memoir, whereas in the 1970s they used to have comic book length. One touchstone of the post-underground market crash period was Harvey Pekar's serial comic book *American Splendor* (1976–2008).[20] Having no talent to draw, Harvey Pekar (1939–2010) collaborated with many artists of great or recent fame, such as Alison Bechdel, Alan Moore, Spain Rodriguez, Joe Sacco, to name but a few. *American Splendor*'s main character, Harvey, is a an unobtrusive working class man, a typical antihero, and author-narrator Pekar tells mostly about Harvey's daily life in Cleveland, Ohio, but also about jazz musicians, artists, or friends collaborating with him on the series – which was sold until Pekar's death in 2010. Pekar's stories, like Green's and Crumb's, are often self- (or meta-)referential in that Harvey thematizes cartooning (among other things, the selling of cartoons, being an artist, etc.) and the possibility of an authentic self in representation. In his own way, of course, Harvey is a caricature of the author's self, like R. Crumb and Binky Brown before him. In fact, a large row of autobiographical comics emerged during the 1980s and 90s, whose underground influences were still clearly visible. They represented the new school that "tended to stress the abject, the seedy, the anti-heroic, and the just plain nasty. [...] the dominant narrative modes have been tragedy, farce, and picaresque. In the wake of Pekar, these scarifying confessional comics have in fact reinvented the comic book hero" (Hatfield 2005: 111). In fact, the "wake of Pekar", that is the 1980s and 90s, saw a considerable number of artists/writers of autobiographical or 'slice-of-life' comics. There were, for example, the Her-

---

[20] Also, see the movie *American Splendor*, USA 2003, dir. Shari Springer Berman & Robert Pulcini. Pekar and his last wife Joyce Brabner participated in the script writing.

nandez brothers, Dave Sim, Chris Ware, Daniel Clowes, Peter Bagge, Seth (aka Gregory Gallant), Adrian Tomine, Terry Moore, Jessica Abel, Julie Doucet, Diane di Massa, Mary Fleener, Roberta Gregory, Megan Kelso. This new generation was probably at least as much inspired by punk or grunge as by underground, and they often produced self-published comic book series, some of which were compiled and later sold as trade paperbacks, however, with moderate success. All in all, alternative comics remained largely unknown to a wider public:

> The constant lament of alternative rebels was the inability to expand their readership. And the two main culprits usually presented were fanboys and low regard toward comics outside comic book culture. [...] The alternative comics movement struggled with its marginality in comic book culture. (Lopes 2009: 127/8)

In the context of lagging reader numbers, it may be interesting to note a survey commissioned by Marvel Comics in 1983, in which it was found that of all comics readers, 63% were aged 6 to 18, 13 on average; and of these 63%, 94% were male readers (Gabilliet 2010: 205). These figures may explain why there was not a promising market for alternative comics. Even ten years later, male adolescents still represented the big bulk of readers preferring superheroes, adaptations of television series and feature films over alternative comics. Those few who did discover alternative or independent comics (I will elaborate on the *indies* in the following) were frequently older and female, and they would read the more 'sophisticated' series like Neil Gaiman's *The Sandman* (1988–1996) or manga.[21]

Although there was a certain number of 'minority' creators in the 1990s – gays, lesbians, African Americans (who did not identify with the Caucasian-dominated movement of alternative comics) – the number of minority readers was not big enough to incite mainstream publishers to cater to such a "niche market."[22]

2.3 The 1980s and 1990s: Significant Changes on the (Comic) Book Market

In order to fully understand the 'rise' of the graphic novel, one must also account for changes in both the comic book and the book market. Throughout the 1960s

---

[21] Cf. Gabilliet 2010: 100 and Round 2010: 23. According to Gabilliet, figures about adult readers were generally difficult to be had because 1) the data gathered would refer to comic book stores only, and 2) studies of adults' reading habits did not include comic books in the categories offered (ibid. 207–208).

[22] For more detailed information about minority authors and readers, cf. Lopes 2009: 139f.

and 70s, the big mainstream publishers Marvel and DC sold their comic books mostly to newsvendors, running newsstands on street corners, where newspapers and mainstream comic books, among other formats, were on display (underground comics, in contrast, were bought in particular head shops or circulated secretly, see above). The newsvendor would place a comic book order consisting of more copies than could be sold. S/he would return the unsold copies to the publisher for the number of which s/he would be reimbursed. This, of course, was highly inefficient since the risk of unsold comic books was entirely on the side of the publisher.

By the 1980s, and through some clever business ploys, the tables had turned: now the big publishers sold their comic books to special *comic shops* – "nasty little holes in the ground" (Wolk 2007: 43) – which were usually run by comic fans who wanted to do business on their part. The risk of unsold copies, although to a lesser extent because of a higher discount to be had from their main distributor, was now on the side of these shops, where unsold copies would just be destroyed. That kind of distribution from the publishers to retail or comic shops was called the *direct market* system.[23] The comic shops catered to both the demands of the publishers and the fans: the number of comic books produced would more precisely match the number of copies actually sold, which resulted in larger profits for the publishers; the fans, in turn, were now able to buy the sequels to their favorite comics at one place – and in due time (the newsstands had, as a matter of fact, often proved unreliable in offering particular comics series or follow-ups on time, especially when newsstand sales declined in the late 1970s). And of course, the comic shops would also offer a broader choice of comics than the newsstand.

Besides the big publishers, *independent publishers* started to sprout, although small at first, who wanted to have their piece of the comic market pie (Fantagraphics, Drawn & Quarterly, Top Shelf, Pacific Comics, etc.). They would use the direct market structures and cater to "comics specialty shop retailers" (Duncan/Smith 2009: 94). As competitors to the big publishers (Marvel and DC), they would have to distinguish themselves by their products sold, that is by the talent of the authors and the kind of comic books they published. This was when another great change was taking place on the comic market of the time: the independent publishers would credit their creators on the covers (and pay them due royalties,

---

[23] I decided not to elaborate in too great detail on the direct market system (which, among other things, would bring about the whole comic market crash 20 years later) because of the good and already existing accounts, e.g. in Duncan/Smith 2009: 68–70, 94–96, Hatfield 2005: 20–31, Lopes 2009: 110–117, 129–135, or in Gabilliet 2010: 143–152.

respectively), which slowly but surely forced the 'big two' to do alike: DC by the mid-1980s and Marvel by the 1990s. The independents' scheme, however, would work out only because the fans increasingly demanded comics by their favorite creators.[24]

It is before this background that *Watchmen*, *The Dark Knight*, and also *Sandman* made their claim to fame. Firstly because of their creators' newly gained rights: formerly, comics had been marketed on the basis of their characters, not their authors, like on the conventional book market; secondly, because the conventional book market would now sell exactly those works under the graphic novel label:

> [...] as a result of the publicity given to the form in 1987, graphic novels were taken up in high-street bookshops and public libraries, where special shelves were devoted to them. At the same time, the many reviews in the literary sections of newspapers meant that the names of Alan Moore and Frank Miller became widely recognized. This was a cue for mainstream book publishers to enter the fray. In time, Penguin, Gollancz, Mandarin, Boxtree and many others launched graphic novel lines. [...] In Britain, this strategy was finely honed. In particular, Titan Books, who repackaged *Dark Knight* and *Watchmen* (among others) for the British market, went so far as to hire a PR specialist to push adult comics. (Sabin 1996: 165/175, footnote #8)

As Julia Round has it,

> the star artist ha[d] given way to the star *writer*. [...] This new emphasis on narrative further redefined comics as literature. Fuller scripting may also have contributed to reemphasizing narrative elements in contemporary comics, such as Neil Gaiman's detailed panel descriptions [...] in *The Sandman: Dream Country* trade paperback and *The Absolute Sandman* series. It was a scripting method Gaiman picked up from Alan Moore [...] (Round 2010: 21)

Obviously, Moore and his creator colleagues' success was not merely due to the clever marketing strategies of the big publishers or high-street book shops. Through the 1980s, the fan clientele and their preferences had started to change, which would create a particular demand for *auteurs*, for example Dave Sim (*Cerebus*), the brothers Hernandez (*Love Rockets*), Peter Bagge (*Hate!*), Chris Ware (*Acme Novelty Library*), Seth (*Palookaville*), Daniel Clowes (*Eightball*), or Terry Moore (*Strangers in Paradise*, cf. Gabilliet 2010: 169 and Round 2010: 27). By the 1990s, readers of these works were older and frequently female; on the other hand, there was a large adolescent readership consuming superhero comics, adaptations of TV series, films, or Japanese comics (cf. Gabilliet 2010: 100). Yet adolescents were not interested in the

---

24 Indeed, the "growing fandom" is essential to the direct market and the alternative/independent comic culture of the 1980s and 90s (cf. Hatfield 2005: 26).

above authors – whose works were now considered avant-garde *literature* rather than comics (cf. Round, loc. cit.).

Had alternative or independent comics now become a mass product? – Not yet, but the 1990s marked the onset of a period in which graphic works had become presentable and had a non-negligible stock of readers who would appreciate more sophisticated characters, plots, and stylistic devices, one more reason that precluded the survival of the comic book from the newsstand of twenty years before. In fact, in the mid-1990s,

> […] it became possible for retailers to order single copies of books published by DC Comics. This change allowed retailers to special-order books to meet customer demand without the risk of graphic novels going unsold […] This new system of ordering made it possible for bookstores and public libraries to order graphic novels directly from a vendor, whereas previously libraries had been forced to order graphic novels through a comic book shop. This now made it possible for public libraries to collect graphic novels. Drawn to the readability of the books, librarians promoted them heavily. Graphic novels circulated with alarming frequency […] These books infused the public library with a new energy and hipness – and as a result, graphic novel collections have become the fastest-growing print component of public library collections since 2002. (Weiner in Williams 2010: 3–13)

One more time, the distribution system which had put the graphic novel on its track in the mid-1980s (then still under the label alternative or independent) had evolved in its own way: away from the retailer (the comic or comics specialty shop) and directly to the vendor or publisher. Graphic novels were becoming a public good and educational tool: "The movement among librarians and teachers to promote graphic novels has unquestionably had a major impact on the comic book field. […] In terms of the new graphic novel market, purchases from libraries by 2007 accounted for 10 percent of this market" (Lopes 2009: 169). Considering the limited budgets of public libraries, this number is rather huge. In this context, it should be noted that reader preferences had definitely changed by the end of the 1990s: "At the start of the twenty-first century, outside of the context of newspapers, comics were no longer a mass medium as they had been from the Second World War to the beginning of the 1950s" (Gabilliet 2010: 207). In a survey commissioned by Smartgirl.com and The American Library Association (ALA) in 1999, only 33 percent of the 11 to 18-year-olds read comic books or graphic novels, and of these 42% were boys and 27% girls. For boys, comic books ranked 7th, for girls 11th on the scale of their favorite reading material. In a 2001 survey by the same commissioners, only 2 % of the girls and 4 % of the boys claimed that their most read item were comic books (cf. ibid.). It could be hazardous, however, to conclude that since the turn of the twentieth century, the preferred comic book has been the graphic novel because little is known about today's adults' buying and reading habits (see above): those who read comics from the 1950s to the 1970s as children and adolescents have probably not all stopped reading comic books today; they might have just switched the series or type. – In this context, note that the surveys mentioned above were conducted one and a half decades ago; until the present day, it seems to me, comics literacy has been drastically declining. When I teach graphic novels, I am always somewhat sadly reminded that my (German) students have not or rarely read comics when they were children – the occasional didactic encounter with comics in high school notwithstanding. The present student generation has to be taught not only comics analysis but, above all, comics reading skills.

2.4 From 2000 on: the Second Hype of the Graphic Novel

In fact, if I keep on looking at numbers, I learn that from 2004 on, mainstream book publishers started publishing graphic novels and that in 2005, according to Publishers Weekly, estimated sales of graphic novels figure between 200 and 245 million dollars – which marks a 35 % increase over 2003.[25] "By 2006, overall sales for comic books and graphic novels were 640 million dollars, with manga accounting for 170 to 200 million dollars. Sales of non-manga comic books [...] had never been better since 1995, two years after the collapse of the direct market boom" (Lopes 2009: 165). These numbers suggest that at least one third of the comic books sold are graphic novels, although I ignore, of course, what exactly was sold under this label. It cannot be denied, however, that graphic novel reader numbers have reached wuthering heights and represent a sizable given for mainstream book publishers.

From 2000 on, I would hold, there has been a *second hype* of graphic works that differ from the works of the 1980s and 90s by their sheer length and by the fact that they bear little or no visible influence from underground or alternative comics. A considerable share of the best-selling graphic novels was, at least partly, (auto)biographical in nature: Chris Ware's *Jimmy Corrigan, the Smartest Kid on Earth* (2000), Marjane Satrapi's *Persepolis* (4 vols., 2000–2003, originally published in French), Lynda Barry's *One Hundred* Demons (2002), Craig Thompson's *Blankets* (2003), Guibert, Lefèvre & Lemercier's *Le photographe* (three volumes: 2003/4 and 2006,), David B[eauchard].'s *Epileptic* (2005, originally serialized in French as *Ascension du haut-mal*), Alison Bechdel's *Fun Home* (2006), Doxiadis & Papadimitriou's *Logicomix* (2009), and, more recently, Reinhard Kleist's *Der Boxer,* Mana Neyestani's *Une métamorphose iranienne* and

---

[25] Cf. Lopes 2009: 160, Matz in Tabachnick 2009: 328, and Dean 2005: 18–22.

Mary and Bryan Talbot's *The Dotter of Her Father's Eyes* (all three published in 2012), or Jean-Michel Dupont and Mezzo's *Love in Vain* (2014). The list could certainly be extended, yet the above works represent the best-known or best-selling ones – that is, from a Western European view. What is noteworthy about the second hype, if I consider the time span from 2000 until now, is that a good number of what has been sold as graphic novels were not simply repackaged or remarketed comic books (like Marvel's *Ultimate* series: *Ultimate Spiderman/X-Men/Fantastic Four*, launched in 2000/2001, *Black Hole*, 1995–2004, *Ghost World*, 1993–1997, etc.) but were immediately published in book format (cf. Hatfield 2005: 161). This is certainly true about the lion's share of the so-called graphic memoirs (cf. Gardner 2008: 21), but also for a number of non-(auto)biographic works such as Spiegelman's *In the Shadow of No Towers* (2004), Bryan Talbot's *Alice in Sunderland* (2007), David Mazzucchelli's *Asterios Polyp* (2009), Thompson's *Habibi* (2011), or Miller's *Holy Terror* (2011).

Another type of the long-form comic book – different and yet not so different in the end – emerged during the second hype of the graphic novel with the so-called reportage, docu or travel comics, practically all of which are autobiographical, or at least to a certain extent. They usually present an author figure, who is not seldom a journalist or war correspondent, and thematize the author's travel experiences or his reportages through countries or war zones outside of Europe or the United States. The most prominent of those reportage cartoonists are the American Joe Sacco and his books about the Gaza strip and the war in Bosnia (*Palestine*, 2003, serialized from 1993–2001, *Safe Area Goražde*, 2000 and 2001), the Canadian Guy Delisle's reportage or travel comics about Shenzhen, Pyongyang, Burma, and Jerusalem (2000, 2003, 2007, and 2011), the Frenchmen Emmanuel Guibert, Didier Lefèvre, & Frédéric Lemercier's (photo)graphic novel about the Afghan resistance to the Russian invasion, *Le photographe* (three vols., 2003, 2004, and 2006), or the American David Axe's book on the war in Iraq, *War Fix* (2006), to name the most prominent.[26] These works problematize the reportage as a whole and the reported subject(s), truth/authenticity and

---

[26] I may add Brendan Burford's 'picto-essays' *Syncopated* (2009); K. Thor Jensen's *Red Eye, Black Eye* (2007) and Josh Neufeld's *A Few Perfect Hours* (2004) render their authors' travels in the U.S., Central Europe, or Southeast Asia; Craig Thompson's *Carnet de Voyage* (2006) presents stories about the author's travels through Europe and Morocco during a promotion tour for his graphic novel *Blankets* (2003); the Austrian Ulli Lust's youthful meanderings in Italy, *Heute ist der letzte Tag deines Lebens* (2009), or the German artist and creator group Montagatari (Jap.: story telling), consisting of six art school graduates from Berlin-Weißensee (among whom Ulli Lust, Tim Dinter, Markus Witzel ("Mawil"), Kai Pfeiffer, Jens Harder, Kathi Käppel) and their works on Berlin and Basel, *Alltagsspionage* (2001) and *Operation Läckerli* (2004).

representation, addictions to extreme experiences as they occur in the daily life or on the job, extreme violence including torture, rape, or abuse, war politics, etc. In fact, except their claim to (or problematization of) authenticity, they share virtually all the rhetorical means and devices with what is exemplarily known as graphic novels. This is why a lot of readers, including experts, subsume them under graphic novels or just 'long-form comics'. – Graphic reportage or travel writing is, of course, not really new under the sun. The French romantic painter Eugène Delacroix (1798–1863), who strongly influenced generations of painters and movements after him, accompanied a diplomatic mission to Morocco in 1832, from which resulted a sketchbook with illustrations and comments on what he perceived "as a world unchanged since ancient times" (Walker 2010: 73); or the American illustrator Lester Hornby (1882–1956), who "took his sketchbooks behind the lines of World War I having been given a pass by General Pershing in 1917 to travel with American forces in France [... . His] *Balkan Sketches* [1926] contain a mix of illustration and prose" (ibid.), however, it does not render image sequences – which constitutes a big difference when I compare them to contemporary reportage comics. Finally, it is interesting to note that the American reportage or travel comics came out with publishers known as 'indies' (see above, chapter 2.3), such as Fantagraphics (Sacco), Top Shelf (Thompson, Jensen), Alternative Comics (Neufeld), or NBM Publishing, formerly known as Flying Buttress Publications, founded in 1976, who carry the caption "America's First Publisher of Graphic Novels" in their logo. Such evidence prompts me to see reportage or travel comics (or travelogues, as they are also called) as a subgroup or particular form of graphic novels.

Similarly to authors of reportage comics, the big majority of women graphic novel authors from the 1990s until now – although not all as popular as the best-selling authors Marjane Satrapi (*Persepolis*, 2000–2003) and Alison Bechdel (*Fun Home*, 2006) – have been published by independent houses.[27] Their works are often autobiographic, and not rarely are they classified as feminist or lesbian literature; some few works among them are very extreme in the choice of their subjects and, above all, they show the seduction, (near-)rape, and sexual abuse of their author-protagonists, which made the books subject to censorship as in Phoebe Gloeckner's case (*A Child's Life and Other Stories*, 2000) or restricted sales at first to the specialty shops (as Debbie Drechsler's *Daddy's Girl*, 1996/2008).

---

27 For example, Drawn & Quarterly (Julie Doucet, Miriam Katin, Rutu Modan), Fantagraphics (Lynda Barry, Lilli Carré, Sophie Crumb, Debbie Drechsler, Mary Fleener, Ellen Forney, Roberta Gregory, Miss Lasko-Gross, C. Tyler), Four Walls Eight Windows (Sue Coe), Cleis Press (Diane DiMassa), and Soft Skull Press (Megan Kelso), Seal Press (Erika Lopez); Doris Seda was published by one of the few surviving underground publishers, Last Gasp.

2.5 Graphic Novels and *bandes dessinées*

Although their authors did not produce such trailblazing specimens as *Maus*, *Watchmen*, or *The Dark Knight*, Francophone long form comics and graphic novels must not be excluded from the body of works I have set out to write on in this book. In fact, there has been one or the other feature specific to the works themselves or to their production and marketing on the Franco-Belgian comic (book) market that makes the Francophone works somewhat comparable to their Anglo-American peers. Nowadays, in France, *roman graphique* has undoubtedly also become a marketing label although, as of yet, it still rather stands for a niche within the overwhelmingly large and diversified sector of comics. Even in the larger and more diversified French book stores, there rarely is a *rayon roman graphique*, not excepting large department stores with vast *bande dessinée* sections such as the FNAC.[28] In this context, it is indicative of a certain attitude, popular and academic, that an exceptional work published by the end of 2014 has been classified by the French press as a *BD* (speak: /bede/, *bande dessinée*, originally signifying 'drawn strip' and later applied to books of comics in general) – and not as a graphic novel or biography: Jean-Michel Dupont and Mezzo's *Love in Vain* has been elected "La BD de la rentrée" (the comic book of the beginning of the school year) by Le Grand Journal and Canal+. *Love in Vain*, originally the title of one of his most famous songs, thematizes the dramatically short life of the blues legend Robert Johnson (1911–1938), *ab ovo* until his untimely death at age 27. Besides Mezzo's wonderful drawings, which bear influences of the woodcuts by Lynd Ward and Frans Masereel, another specific feature of the work is its narrator, the devil himself, who speaks in serrated captions (as the legend has it, Johnson, who was said to have poorly played the guitar, concluded a pact with the devil on a crossroads near Clarksdale, Mississippi, after which he became a blues guitar whiz).

In Francophone comics criticism – as in Anglophone criticism of Francophone comics – distinguishing the graphic novel as a genre different from the 'comic book' or *bande dessinée* has not really been a big issue either. If you browse the *MLA International Bibliography*, you will almost always come across references to graphic or cinematic adaptations of *bandes dessinées* or classic verbal fiction. Only two major publications from the first decade of this

---

28 As opposed to the FNAC Strasbourg, for example, FNAC Paris (Châtelet les Halles) had a small yet respectable *roman graphique* section integrated in the comics/best-selling novelties of the medium on my last visit in spring 2015. In fact, two years before, in the FNAC Strasbourg, I had asked a store clerk if there was a *rayon roman graphique*; in return, he asked me what that signified before telling me that there was no such section.

millennium bring up 'graphic novel' in their title (Baetens 2001, McKinney 2008). Bart Beaty (2007), Thierry Groensteen (2007), Ann Miller (2008), Benoît Peeters (1993), mention graphic novels more or less in passing or not at all; in the meantime, Francophone critics also refer to Francophone long form comics and graphic novels, although in a body together with primary works of diverse proveniences (as in Groensteen 2013 or in Baetens/Frey 2015).

Today, *Persepolis* (Marjane Satrapi, 2000–2003), *Le photographe* (Emmanuel Guibert, Didier Lefèvre, and Frédéric Lemercier, 2003–2006), *Shenzhen* (Guy Delisle, 2000), *L'Ascension du haut mal* (David B., 1996–2004), and *Une métamorphose iranienne* (Mana Neyestani, 2012) are internationally renowned works by Francophone authors or authors publishing in French. Some ten years ago, Anglophone comics critics started to label them graphic novels and underscored their status as 'complex' or 'experimental' narratives. In this context, however, it is important to also account for the numerous less known complex and experimental Francophone specimens from the recent and more remote past that did not bear the graphic novel label: as early as the 1970s, with the foundation of the alternative publisher Futuropolis,[29] Francophone artists started to experiment with form/layout. In 1978, the Belgian publisher Casterman issued the magazine *(À Suivre)*, in which authors were able to go beyond the Franco-Belgian standard of 48 pages, with translations of Auclair's *Bran Ruz*, Hugo Pratt's *Corto Maltese in Siberia*, and Tardi and Forest's *Ici même* (cf. Miller 2008: 27). Yet the main boost of works similar in length and complexity to (mainly) American graphic novels from the late 1980s[30] on was provided by the alternative publisher L'Association, created in 1990, which served as a springboard to success for its founders Jean-Christophe Menu, David B., Lewis Trondheim, and subsequently for comics artists like Joann Sfar, Jean-Claude Forest, Edmond Baudoin, Guy Delisle, and, of course, Marjane Satrapi (cf. Beaty 2007: 17–43).

---

29 Futuropolis was founded in 1974, sold to Gallimard in the late 1980s, and shut down in 1994; since 2004, and with a new marketing set-up, they have been publishing comics artists like Blutch, David B., or Étienne Davodeau. For a more thorough account, cf. Beaty in McKinney 2008: 69 et passim. and Miller 2008: 51 et passim.
30 The first hype of graphic novels (see ch. 2.2 and Fig. 2.2) set in with Alan Moore and David Gibbons' dystopic superhero pastiche *Watchmen* (12 vols., 1986–1987), Frank Miller's *The Dark Knight Returns* (1986), Art Spiegelman's *Maus I+II* (1986/92), and Neil Gaiman's *Sandman* series (1989–1996, in collaboration with the artist Dave McKean et al.). "[J]ust about every new comics series was commissioned on the basis that it would eventually be collected into a graphic novel, while at the same time there was a rush to repackage runs of four, six or eight comics into album form even if they had no thematic unity (thus perverting the meaning of 'graphic novel' into a marketing tool). [...] Moreover, the emphasis was now on adult material: it was believed that this was where the sales would be in the future" (Sabin 1996, 167).

Something similar happened on the other side of the Atlantic, if only in more diverse ways: the changing comics culture there depended at first on the small-scale or even secret distribution of the sex-and-drug-infused underground comics (created by Robert Crumb, Bill Griffith, Manuel Rodriguez, and others) through record or so-called head stores; in the 1980s and 90s, it depended on small alternative publishers, providing a forum for a number of *auteurs,* several of them women (Jessica Abel, Julie Doucet, or Mary Fleener). These alternative publications were generally satirical, political, or (auto)biographical, often serialized in magazines (such as *Zap, Raw, Acme Novelty Library*), and more episodic than their successors from after the turn of the millennium, which were often immediately published in book format (cf. Hatfield 2005: 26). Important American comics artists of the alternative period were Art Spiegelman, Harvey Pekar, Chris Ware, and Daniel Clowes. What Futuropolis and later L'Association was for French *auteurs,* Fantagraphics (1976–) was for Anglophone alternative comics; it was followed by alternative publishers like Pacific Comics, Top Shelf Productions, and Drawn & Quarterly in the 1980s and 90s. Besides, it should be added that a small but significant number of alternative comics were self-published and today are out of print. To sum up, on both sides of the Atlantic, from the 1970s on, a new *type* of comics began to emerge from the shadow of the big mainstream publishers.

As a rough overview of Francophone graphic narratives, let me propose the following (and certainly incomplete) list of long-form works from the 1990s until now, ordered according to subgenres, most of which may be categorized as graphic novels (Fig. 2.3):[31]

---

[31] A good part of the works in this chart are referenced and elaborated on, more or less extensively, in Miller 2008: 57–65, McKinney 2008, chs. 5–7, 10, and Rousseau/Gravé-Rousseau 2009: 103–110.

graphic journalism or travelogue	Guy Delisle, *Shenzhen* (2000), *Pyongyang* (2003), *Chroniques birmanes* (2007), *Chroniques de Jérusalem* (2011)
	Emmanuel Guibert, Didier Lefèvre, and Frédéric Lemercier, *Le photographe* (3 vols., 2003–2006)
	David B., *Journal d'Italie, vol. 1: Trieste Bologne* (2010)
graphic memoir/ (auto)biography	Lewis Trondheim, *Approximativement* (1995)
	Frederik Peeters, *Pillules bleues* (2001)
	Julie Doucet, *Ciboire de Criss!* (1996); *J comme Je* (2005)
	David B., *Ascension du haut mal* (6 vols., 1996–2004)
	Fabrice Neaud, *Journal* (4 vols., 1996–2003)
	Jean-Christophe Menu, *Livret de phamille* (2000)
	Marjane Satrapi, *Persepolis* (4 vols., 2002–2003)
	Étienne Davodeau, *Les mauvaises gens* (2005); *Les ignorants* (2011)
	Jung Sik Hun, *Couleur de peau miel* (3 vols., 2007–2013)
	Jacques Tardi, *Moi René Tardi, prisonnier de guerre au Stalag II B* (2 vols., 2012/14)
	Jean-Michel Dupont and Mezzo, *Love in Vain* (2014)
historical novel	Baru, Jean-Marc Thévenet and Daniel Ledran, *Le chemin de l'Amérique* (1990)
	Christian Lax and Frank Giroud, *Les Oubliés d'Annam* (3 vols., 1990/1, 2000)
	Jacques Tardi, *C'était la guerre des tranchées* (1993);
	Jean-Philippe Stassen, *Déogratias* (2000)
	David Prudhomme, *Rébétiko* (2009)
adventure/fantasy	Jacques Tardi, *Les aventures extraordinaires d'Adèle Blanc-Sec* (9 vols., 1976–2007)
	François Schuiten and Benoît Peeters, *Les cités obscures* (12 vols., 1983–2009)
	Manu Larcenet, *Blast* (4 vols., 2009–2014)
postcolonial identity	Manu Larcenet, *Le combat ordinaire* (4 vols, 2003–2008)
	Marguerite Abouet and Clément Oubrerie, *Aya de Yopougon* (6 vols., 2005–2010)
	Michel Rabagliati, *Paul* (7 vols., 1999–2011)
metafiction	Dupuy and Berberian, *Journal d'un album* (1994)
	Marc-Antoine Mathieu, *Julius Corentin Acquefaques, prisonnier des rêves* (6 vols., 1990–2013)

Fig. 2.3: Francophone long-form comics from 1990 until now

3 Graphic Novels and the Problem of Categorization

3.1 Academic Interest in Comics and Graphic Novels

Only relatively recently have comics and particularly graphic novels become subject to serious academic scrutiny. As opposed to didactic or pedagogical literature on comics,[1] serious academic studies on the history, semiotics, and aesthetics of comics did not exist in Anglo-America before the 1990s (cf. Lopes 2009: 164), and they were scarcely numbered. The lion's share of works in that line appeared in the last ten years, almost simultaneously with the second hype of the graphic novel, as it became visible in high street bookstores and the programs of the major publishers. Before,

> [s]ignificant innovations include the establishment of the International Comics Art Forum (ICAF) in 1995, the launching of the *International Journal of Comic Art* (IJOCA) in 1999, the founding of the Comic Art and Comics area of the Popular Culture Association in 1992, and the more recent emergence of online journals, including *Image and Narrative*, *ImageTexT*, and *Signs: Studies in Graphical* [sic] *Narratives*. (Heer/Worcester 2009: xiv)

A yearly event stirring academic interest is the Comic/s Art Conference (CAC), held within the San Diego Comic Con(vention), founded in 1970: a phalanx of panels and round tables aimed at professionals (creators, publishers, editors) and fans, existing since 1992.

The big bulk of monographs and essay collections, besides print-edited conversations with famous creators like Charles Schulz, Robert Crumb, Alan Moore, Harvey Pekar, Art Spiegelman, and others was published by the University Press of Mississippi (more than 65 titles),[2] which undoubtedly is the leading house in current comics research publication. Apart from the literature on comics in general, essay collections and monographs about graphic novels have started to

---

[1] In Germany, for example, this literature existed as early as in the 1970s, e.g. Alfred Clemens Baumgärtner, *Die Welt der Comics* (1971) or Paul Burgdorf, *Comics im Unterricht* (1976). A cultural study of *Asterix* was undertaken by André Stoll, *Asterix. Das Trivialepos Frankreichs. Bild- und Sprachästhetik eines Bestseller-Comics* (1974).

[2] Noteworthy monographs by the University of Mississippi Press are Robert C. Harvey, *The Art of the Comic Book: An Aesthetic History* (1996); ibid., *The Art of the Funnies: An Aesthetic History* (1994); Charles Hatfield, *Alternative Comics: An Emerging Literature* (2005); Thierry Groensteen, *The System of Comics* (1999/2007), to name but a few.

become more numerous.³ The big majority of papers on graphic novels are to be found either in periodicals or essay collections, including conference volumes. In 2006, Hillary Chute and Marianne DeKoven stated that

> [t]here does not yet exist an established critical apparatus for graphic narrative. In fact, from a literary perspective – as regards critical works by professional academics – there is little rigorous critical apparatus for any genre of comics, with the notable exception of a significant body of essays on *Maus* [...] (Chute/DeKoven 2006: 770)

I agree with this thesis as far as graphic novels are concerned (or "graphic narratives," as the authors have it); yet the second part of their thesis about comics in general should be modified, considering what has been and was published since 2006 and before. Considering a period of one and a half decades of intensive academic research until today, a "critical apparatus" on comics in general could easily be set up, including different theoretical approaches such as reader-response, structuralist, semiotic, cultural studies-oriented, etc.

In fact, the trailblazers of academic thought on comics were the "non-scholarly researchers – critics, practitioners, journalists, and avocational researchers" (Troutman 2010: 437, qtd. in Miodrag 2013: 4). Most representative of these Anglophone practitioner-critics undoubtedly is Scott McCloud, and his book *Understanding Comics* (1993) probably has been the most often quoted source book on comics as well as the number-one bestseller of its kind. As it was recently put, however, works like McCloud's have often been "theoretically unsophisticated" (Miodrag 2013: 4). Indeed, seen in the light of full-fledged theoretical approaches like Thierry Groensteen's *The System of Comics* (2007),⁴ McCloud's *Understanding Comics* seems rather unsystematic and lacking in terminological coherence. Generally, Anglophone comics criticism has broadly been considered less sophisticated than its Francophone counterpart (see Miodrag 2013: 109 for references), and the translation and publication of Groensteen's *Système de la bande dessinée* (1999) at the University Press of Mississippi in 2007 – and the rather prompt translation of his follow-up, *Bande dessinée et narration* (2011, the English translation *Comics and Narration* was published in 2013) – are significant of the weight recently attributed to French comics theory.

---

3 Cf. Jan Baetens, *The Graphic Novel* (2001), ibid./Hugo Frey, *The Graphic Novel: An Introduction* (2015), Hillary Chute, *Graphic Women: Life Narrative and Contemporary Comics* (2010), Stephen E. Tabachnick, *Teaching the Graphic Novel* (2009), Douglas Wolk, *Reading Comics: How Graphic Novels Work and What They Mean* (2007) and Daniel Stein/Jan-Noël Thon, *From Comic Strips to Graphic Novels* (2013).
4 Orig. *Système de la bande dessinée*, 1999, followed up by *Bande dessinée et narration: Système de la bande dessinée 2*, 2011, Engl. transl. *Comics and Narration*, 2013.

3.2 General Categorization Criteria for Graphic Novels

To date, experts have rather kept off from describing the graphic novel in terms of a (sub)genre or a typology. Instead, they called it a "format" (e.g. Freedman 2011: 42, Frahm 2014: 55), or they applied more or less imprecise criteria – often coming close to buzz words – such as lengthiness, thematic unity, seriousness or authenticity of the subject matter, autobiography, cartoonicity, adult orientation, and complexity. Considering the variety of what has been published (and sold) as graphic novels, the above criteria seem quite blurry and, as such, of little critical value.

3.2.1 Lengthiness and Serialization

Roger Sabin describes graphic novels as "'lengthy comics in book form with a thematic unity.' [...] They] opened up fresh story telling possibilities. Put simply, in a longer narrative there was more scope for building up tension, generating atmosphere, developing characters and so on" (Sabin 1996: 165). 'Lengthy' here implies a general comparison with the traditional American or Franco-Belgian comic book volumes of 32 or 48 pages, and "thematic unity" supposedly refers to unserialized publication formats (cf. Platthaus 2010). This, of course, is an objectifiable criterion even though it does not legitimize a thorough problematization of a genre category as here undertaken. In addition, many graphic novels, for example Alan Moore and Dave Gibbons' *Watchmen* (1986–1987), Art Spiegelman's *Maus*, or Charles Burns' *Black Hole* (1993–2004, see also his more recent trilogy *X'ed Out*, 2010, *The Hive*, 2012, *Sugar Skull*, 2014), defy the non-serialization argument since they started out in installments with similar numbers of pages before being lengthened, as *Maus*, or compiled in large volumes (cf. Freedman 2011: 38–39).

Looking at the publishing history, it interestingly appears that graphic novels have actually been around during two different periods. In Britain and the U.S. in the late 1980s, as the comics market started to crash,

> just about every new comics series was commissioned on the basis that it would eventually be collected into a graphic novel, while at the same time there was a rush to repackage runs of four, six or eight comics into album form even if they had no thematic unity (thus perverting the meaning of 'graphic novel' into a marketing tool).[...] Moreover, the emphasis was now on adult material: it was believed that this was where the sales would be in the future [...] (Sabin 1996: 167)

Since the Second Hype of the graphic novel from 2000 on, many of these works have not been repackaged or remarketed comic books but were immediately published in book format (cf. Hatfield 2005: 161), for example Craig Thompson's *Blankets* and *Habibi*, Alison Bechdel's *Fun Home*, Shaun Tan's *The Arrival*, David Mazzucchelli's *Asterios Polyp*, Reinhard Kleist's *Der Boxer*, Apostolos Doxiadis and Christos Papadimitriou's *Logicomix*, David Prudhomme's *Rébétiko*, Frank Miller's *Holy Terror*, and Mana Neyestani's *Une métamorphose iranienne* – to mention only a few.

3.2.2 Seriousness and Authenticity

The seriousness of the subject matter is another issue (cf. Tan 2001: 39), at least for a certain number of works sold as graphic novels from 1980 on. Seriousness implies a claim to truth that comics generally abdicate from (cf. Gardner 2008: 12). In the case of *Maus*, this would relate to the historical and biographical background, which is also the story material: the Holocaust and Art Spiegelman's father's ordeal during WWII. Other issues at stake are the graphic novels' intellectual challenge in terms of complexity (Becker 2009: 239, Sabin 1996: 165) as well as their mercantile value or status: today, graphic novels often come in large prestigious volumes or pricy single editions.[5] Then again, it is argued that this is a marketing strategy bringing the comics from the newspaper kiosk to the book store (cf. Sabin 1996: 167).

Although it is interesting to note, these attributes, meant to distinguish graphic novels from traditional or prototypical comic books, are vague and often seem overgeneralized. Therefore, I would principally side with Jakob Dittmar, who holds that "the dividing line between comic series and graphic novel or *bande dessinée* is fuzzy" (Dittmar 2008: 25). Yet this is an obstacle to categorization only if I cling to classical Aristotelian categories. I shall demonstrate below how *prototypical categories* offer escape from the fuzziness predicament (chapter 3.3).

Generally, Will Eisner's *A Contract with God* (1978) is seen as the first graphic novel,[6] "a novel in comic form," although it is not a lengthy narrative and repre-

---

[5] Cf. Sabin op. cit., Dittmar 2008: 24, and Hoppler et al. 2009: 63–64. Here it must be added that the current popular comic books are significantly more expensive than (reissued) paperbacks in general and sell for around 15 to 25 Euros a copy, on average. As for a comparison with graphic novels, the currently available trade paperback of Craig Thompson's *Blankets* (2003) sells for around 30 Euros, the hard back for around 40 Euros a copy.
[6] Cf. Tabachnick in Tabachnick 2009: 13, and many others; Merino holds that "Héctor Germán Oesterheld invented the graphic novel [...]. He preceded both Will Eisner and Art Spiegelman in labeling the genre, which arose with such literary force in Argentina. He called it 'the new comic' " (Merino in Tabachnick 2009: 272).

sents a collection of four short graphic narratives displaying a remarkable (auto)-biographical impetus. As Eisner wrote in the preface, the setting for "A Contract with God," a caricature of a street in the Bronx, is "the biography of the street itself [...]."[7] Similarly, the story's Jewish protagonist, Frimme Hersh, is Will Eisner's alter ego and so is "Willie," the young boy in the story "Cookalein,"[8] and the apartment house in "Super" is "the house where I [W.E.] lived as a young boy" (ibid.). Apart from "The Street Singer," which concerns, as Eisner wrote in the preface, a phenomenon of the Depression years, the volume *A Contract with God* is to a certain extent (auto)biographic, an attribute that links up with 'seriousness' (see above), implying that there is more to the story than sheer imagination. David Kunzle, by contrast, refers to another kind of seriousness: in his understanding, even the earliest graphic narrative strips tell "a story which is both moral and topical" (Kunzle 1973: 2, qtd. in Meskin 2007: 369, see also 371).

The graphic novel, it seems, is a kind of *comic d'auteur* since its origin is closely linked with the first tendencies of conventional comics to become autonomous from the mass market at the end of the 1960s (Becker 2009: 240). Such tendencies are seen from 1972 onward in the publication of the first underground comics, like in Robert Crumb's four-page story "The Confessions of R. Crumb" (1972) and Justin Green's surreal *Binky Brown Meets the Holy Virgin Mary* (1972, cf. Gardner 2008: 1, 7, 14 and Schikowski 2009: 97). From then on, "there has certainly been a steady progression of autobiographical memoirs within the comics form, to the extent that today one can identify sub-genres and historical movements within autobiographical comics" (Gardner 2008: 1, cf. Baetens/Frey 2015: 176–179, Hatfield 2005: 100–101). Similarly to Eisner's protagonists, Green's Binky clearly bears autobiographical traits (cf. Green 2009: 55–56) as he suffers from an obsessive compulsive disorder due to his strictly Catholic upbringing and a traumatic guilt experience (playing ball, he smashed a statue of the Virgin Mary). What is new, compared to Eisner, is the introduction of an author-character telling about and legitimizing Binky's/the author's alter ego's neurosis in a prefatory "Confession" (cf. Gardner 2008: 8–10, Hatfield 2005: 134). Yet this author-character, with the exception of one small panel (Green 2009: 19) does not figure in the actual narrative. In Crumb's "Confessions," there is an

---

7 "[...] through the physical evolution of the block, the rise and fall of the tenement building at No. 55 [Dropsie Avenue] and the ethnic and social changes of its stream of occupants" (Eisner 2006: x).

8 " 'Cookalein' is a combination of invention and recall. It is an honest account of my coming of age" (Eisner 2006: xiv).

author-character that, iconized and caricatured as he may be, is the subject and protagonist of the narrative throughout.

Green and Crumb seem to confirm what Alison Bechdel said decades later in a 2007 interview with regard to her own work *Fun Home*: "I always felt like there was something inherently autobiographical about cartooning [...] [I]t does feel like it almost demands people to write autobiographies" (cited in Gardner 2008: 1). Chris Ware's *Jimmy Corrigan* seems to confirm this statement: here, as in *Fun Home*, the extremely problematic relation of the father and the child is in the foreground.[9] Other more recent graphic novels like Lynda Barry's *One Hundred Demons* (2002), Marjane Satrapi's *Persepolis* (2000–2003), David B[eauchard].'s *Epileptic* (1996–2004),[10] and Craig Thompson's *Blankets* (2003) are also clearly autobiographical with a strong focus on problematic child-parent/s relationships (cf. Wolk 2007: 12, 208, 228).

To sum up, by looking at the development of the graphic novel through Eisner and *underground* and through the 1980s and the 2000s, I would associate the latter period of the graphic novel more closely with graphic autobiography, or graphic memoirs, although not all graphic novels from this period fall into this category. Further, a non-negligible number of graphic memoirs differ from the rest of the comics production by an increased concern about their authentic subject matter and author-narrator protagonists. Barry's *One Hundred Demons* is representative in that respect: opposite the table of contents, it says: "Please note: This is a work of autobifictionalography."[11] The pages of the "Intro" chapter elaborate on this playful label: they show the grown-up author-protagonist as she is drawing and thinking at her desk. The captions of the first two-panel spread read: "Is it autobiography if parts of it are not true?" and "Is it fiction if parts of it are?" (Barry 2002: 7).

According to Gardner, "the rise of graphic memoir responds to a more particular need of the present moment, seeking as it does to move autobiography [...] beyond the dead-end concerns over authenticity in which it has been cornered

---

9 In the "Corrigenda" (Ware 2000: np.), Ware writes that *Jimmy Corrigan* is "semi-autobiographical".
10 Originally published in Paris in six volumes under the heading *Ascension du haut-mal* by L'Association. Vols. I–III were published in English as *Epileptic* in one single volume by the same house in 2002.
11 Barry 2002: np., see vertical snippet on the left edge of the fourth page of the verbal-pictorial paratext. The label "autobifictionalography" is repeated in red handwriting underneath the table of contents.

and constrained for a generation" (Gardner 2008: 21). Gardner's statement seems even more cogent when looking at the ways *Epileptic* comes to terms with authenticity. Grown-up David, its narrating protagonist, tells his mother: "But it's all true what I'm writing. And I'm not telling the whole story" (B[eauchard]. 2005: 95). He emphasizes that what interests him is serious, that it "is the struggle against disease and death" (ibid. 96). Yet as a teen cartoonist, he had a representation problem:

> I want to tell the whole story. My brother's epilepsy, the physicians, macrobiotics, spiritualism, the gurus, the communes./But I don't know how to draw it./And I don't yet realize that it'll take me another 20 years to get there. (ibid. 291)

Growing to be an adult is the solution to David's drawing problem,[12] and this in turn is allegorical of a criterion to distinguish graphic novels from comic books – adult orientation – which, in another interesting way, accounts for the way Barry designed *One Hundred Demons*: the two square panels per page are literally crushed by the captions and speech balloons, which take up two thirds to three quarters of the panel space on average. This together with the "multilayered composition" (Chute 2010: 113) suggests that the target readers are rather not children or adolescents.

A serious questioning of the labels depth, seriousness, and authenticity is essential for the establishment of more tangible criteria to distinguish the graphic novel from traditional comic books on the one hand and graphic memoirs on the other, that is with respect to "the specific conjunctions of visual and verbal text in this genre of autobiography, and also to the subject positions that narrators negotiate in and through comics" (Whitlock 2006, qtd. in Watson 2008: 28). Looking at autobiography as a genre superordinate to graphic novels, however, will lead us into a categorial *cul de sac*: works like *One Hundred Demons* will then figure as a category subordinate to autobiography – which is nonsensical because a very large number of graphic novels are not autobiographical. The confusion about the genre affiliation of the graphic novel results, I would hold, from looking at autobiography as a superordinate category – and not as a way or mode of writing, which is a historical invariant (cf. Hempfer 1973: 27). If I consider autobiography as a way of writing and graphic memoirs as a historical text group, predicaments like the above can be avoided.

---

12 This reminds us of Art's similar drawing problems in *Maus II* (cf. Spiegelman 2003: 206).

3.2.3 Cartoonicity

Since graphic novels are "cross-discursive: composed in words and images, written and drawn" (Chute/DeKoven 2006: 768), analytical interest should be shifted to the different or more complex ways texts and images relate to each other, as it has been suggested.[13] In this sense, the cartoonicity (or iconicity) of the characters may be looked at to further narrow the definitional or descriptive focus on the graphic novel as compared to other types of graphic narratives.

Cartoonicity is said to lie in the reduction of the whole to single, disproportionally stylized details (Packard 2009: 41). Ed Tan even calls them "formulaic" (Tan 2001: 31). Specifically, comics, in contrast to graphic novels, seem to stylize emotions in the act of drawing: "comic strip characters look like personifications of the basic emotions [...]. [...] This exaggeration of feeling, together with a complete absence of awareness and control, also lends a quality of childishness to characters" (Tan 2001: 37–38, cf. Dittmar 2008: 94).

> It seems attractive, then, to set comics apart from the graphic novel by the degree to which they facilitate recognition by as many different people as possible. [...] the more complex graphic novel relies less, or not at all, on representing character emotion using universally recognisable facial expressions. (Tan 2001: 31, see also 32–34).

Tan cites Spiegelman's *Maus* as the paragon of the above hypothesis: the mice's/Jews' faces are virtually without expression, which contributes to the artistic achievement of this work. Bechdel's *Fun Home* can be brought up in the same context: her protagonist Alison's face is capable of expressions, yet they are not comparable in simplification and style to comic character expressions, the reason lying indubitably in the graphic realism of Bechdel's characters, which are distinctly more marked than Spiegelman's anthropomorphizations. However, looking at *Binky Brown, One Hundred Demons,* or *Persepolis,* I observe a striking reduction of the characters' faces to basic, comic character emotions, especially in *Persepolis*. Again, the case is different in *Jimmy Corrigan*, whose characters' looks do come across as childish (cf. Tan 2001: 38), yet with facial expressions that are mostly hard to classify, given the fact that the panel viewing range is often wide and the figures are consequently small. These points reconsidered, cartoonicity does rather not seem to be a reliable criterion to distinguish graphic novels from comic books.

---

[13] "There is a tendency for readers who come from literary backgrounds to read over design, as though the artwork existed only to render the plot visible and move protagonists from place to place" (Rosen in Tabachnick 2009: 58).

3.2.4 Complexity

The last of the above big issues is the graphic novel's intellectual challenge due to its complexity. Hatfield writes:

> In fact comic art is growing more complex all the time. The form is in flux, becoming more self-conscious in its explorations as creators increasingly recognize the knowledge and sophistication of readers. [...] authors have come to expect readers who are experienced, playful, and tolerant of discontinuity. This vision of a knowing readership has changed the art form [...] (Hatfield 2005: 66)

Unfortunately, there is no agreement about what complexity concretely means. Does it concern a more sophisticated text/image relation or plot or simply more text coming with the images as, for example, in *Fun Home*? Or is complexity, if I stick with this label, just a neutral word for erudition or adult-appropriateness?[14] In his general defense of comics as a politically subversive genre, Versaci posits that their sophistication "comes through 'multiplicity of perspectives and layering,' or 'smaller narratives within a larger one' [...]."[15] On the basis mainly of Versaci (2007), McCloud (1993), and Wolk (2007), Crutcher (2011) describes complexity in diverse Batman reruns from the 2000s with regard to multiple narrators and "layered voices", color, lettering, atmosphere, character psychology, and human condition. Whereas McCloud and Versaci generally speak of 'comics' or 'comic books,' Wolk and Crutcher (and others, of course) use the term 'graphic novel', yet they do not differentiate the two (see Crutcher's title: "Complexity in the Comic *and* Graphic Novel Medium [...]", my italics). It is therefore critically relevant now to distinguish the two in 'family' terms of semiotically related, multimedial texts or as types, superordinate (books of comics) and subordinate: the graphic novel being a specific type of books of comics which should be set apart from traditional comic books, quantitatively and qualitatively, according to a number of concrete parameters to be put forth (like in Versaci or Crutcher) which contribute to their complexity. Of all criteria here discussed (lengthiness/thematic unity, seriousness/authenticity, autobiographic narration, adult orientation, iconicity), complexity seems to me most potent and cogent, under the condition that its parameters be scalar on their own and differential when taken together (as opposed to clear-cut or absolute).

---

[14] "*Fun Home* is a tale full of references to literature and mythology. It assumes and constructs an erudite reader. (This is no comic book for youngsters)" (Pearl 2008: 287, cf. Versaci 2007: 28).
[15] Versaci 2007: 23, quoted in Crutcher 2011: 54, cf. 55.

3.3 From Prototypes to a Typology of Complexity

Before elaborating on a differentiated, schematic typology of complexity, let me first clarify a part of the terminology concerning graphic narratives in general.

3.3.1 Format, Medium, Mode, and Genre

The most frequent buzz terms occurring in practically all the publications on comics and graphic novels are *format, medium, mode* and *genre*. – If Will Eisner wrote in a general way that "[t]he format of comics presents a montage of both word and image," (Eisner 2008: 2), the question is legitimate if "format" here should not be substituted by 'medium.' There is an overlap, and even a considerable one, as long as these terms are used in no specific context. Then, however, they function as more or less blurry concepts barring us from insights about a specific type of multimodal text. In fact, *format* first originated in books and news printing before it was used in marketing and advertising, in the TV industry, and in computer or information technology (like the game show format, the tabloid as opposed to the broadsheet, or a computer data format, cf. Lacey 2000: 206) – that is in the larger context of distribution. In this sense, Gabilliet convincingly uses the term when he writes about the 1986 publication format of *Batman: the Dark Knight Returns* that it was "[p]rinted as a prestige format comic book on glossy paper with cardboard covers [...]" (Gabilliet 2010: 92, 96). Thus, graphic novels are related to in terms of format when the issues are quality paper, hard cover, number of pages per volume (length), target group (adults), or number of runs; and certainly, these aspects cannot be separated from the phenomenon in question. Yet they represent the particular context of marketing and distribution, whereas the focal issues here are *genre* (types of literature) and meaning production (the semiotics of the verbal and the pictorial). What is confusing in this context is that in popular language use, formats like the game show are sometimes called genres – legitimately, that is, when speakers express their likes or dislikes for a certain *type* of media. In this case, of course, the context is not marketing or distribution but the reception of media in a broader sense – the speakers might as well talk about their likes of novels or dramas. Accordingly, speakers of French idiomatically say *Ce n'est pas mon genre* for anything they do not like. It is noteworthy here that the terminological fuzziness arises not from the terms *format* or *genre* themselves but from their usage in different discourses, registers, or contexts.

Another buzz term frequently mixed up and in with genre is *medium*. Originating from communication theory, it actually means a communication channel[16]; in the meantime, however, *medium* has taken on many connotations not least because it has been used in both cultural and technical contexts, for example with reference to the internet and phenomena like blogs or to the social media like Facebook, Twitter, etc. (cf. Ryan/Thon 2014, I.1, np.) In academic publications about comics and graphic novels, it generally applies to

a) comics as a plurimedial communication channel in which the pictorial and the verbal influence the reception of the other or intertwine with respect to meaning production[17];
b) comics as an artistic, multimodal discourse with its codes and rules[18];
c) comics as a genre combining different *modes* of writing, usually the comic (in the original sense of the predicate), dramatic, and the epic or narrative mode.[19]

Some experts speak of the graphic novel as a medium in itself, overlapping to a certain extent with traditional comic books.[20] This, however, seems implausible when we consider that "the constraints and possibilities offered by media are dictated by their material substance and mode of encoding" (Ryan 2005: 20). Irina Rajewsky has pointed out that a medium poses material limitations which its users cannot ultimately circumvent with the specific means and tools proper to that medium (Rajewsky 2007: 37). Genre rules or conventions, in contrast, are cultural and conventional boundaries that can be played with or trespassed, as

---

16 Cf. Lacey 1998: 28; Ryan in Ryan 2004: 16; Rippl/Etter 2013: 192–193.
17 Cf. Balzer 2007: 127–128; Duncan/Smith 2009: 20–49; Hatfield 2005: 7; lacking the necessary media reading competence, Fredric Wertham asserted that the pictures hampered the reception of the text in his infamous 1954 pamphlet *Seduction of the Innocent*; for Hermann Josef Schnackerts (1980), the verbal renders meaning of the visual ambiguous; and for Ronald Schmitt, the "word text and the pictorial text are continually deconstructing each other" (1992, qtd. in Schüwer 2008: 317–319).
18 Cf. Ryan in Ryan 2004: 1–2, Chute/Dekoven 2006: 768, Groensteen 2007: 22, Meskin 2009: 239, Pantaleo 2011: 127, Ryan in Ryan 2014, I:1, np.: "Comics and illustrated stories [...] share the modes of language and image, but they certainly differ in their use of these modes [...]."
19 Cf. Dittmar 2008: 27–29; for Genette, who does not account for comics, genres can traverse modes and vice versa (cf. Genette 2004: 70). Alastair Fowler (1982) conceives of modes as essential features mixing, to a greater or lesser extent, in a genre. In this respect, he is not far from Gérard Genette, who holds that genres can traverse modes, and works can traverse genres.
20 Cf. Crutcher 2011, Eubanks 2011: 187, Pearl 2008: 290–291; Stephen Weiner writes that "in 1998 the University of Massachusetts sponsored 'The Graphic Novel: A Twentieth Anniversary Conference on an Emerging Literary and Artistic Medium,' a three-day symposium featuring cartoonist Will Eisner" (Weiner 2010: 11).

by a comic or graphic novel: thus Alan Moore and Eddie Campbell's *From Hell* (1999) reads as a crime novel as well as a historical novel; or Posy Simmonds' *Gemma Bovery* (1999) reads as postmodern metafiction or as a fictional (auto)-biography. Yet both specimens are made in the medium of comics with its proper information carriers: words and images in a sequence.

As can be seen, the usages of the term *medium* and *mode* are far from being consistent, which accounts for the categorization problems arising with particular phenomena in multimodal – or should I say multimedial? – texts. Then again, with the advent of the recent approaches like cognitive and transmedial narratology (Ryan 2004 and 2014, Wolf 2002 and 2011), which see narrative either as a cognitive macrostructure activated across media or as the center around which diverse media converge, genre has been losing ground to the overall dominance of the media paradigm, implying that media "have different capabilities for transmitting as well as shaping narratives" (Wolf 2011: 166).

I shall employ *medium,* as in b), for comics as discourse with its codes, obeying certain rules or functioning according to certain semiotic and linguistic principles. In short, my interest is in the meaning production from the verbal and pictorial fabric of the medium in general and the individual work in particular. If the verbal and pictorial components in that work are called medium or mode will be of little importance for the approach to be outlined on the following pages. Apart from that, it goes without saying that any individual work may also be looked at as a communication medium, but this – again – is another approach.[21]

Comic books as well as graphic novels are historical text groups or *genres* which change in quantity (or comprehensiveness) and quality through time and are characterized by a set of central and peripheral features (or attributes). Genres stand in opposition to the way of writing (*Schreibweise,* cf. Hempfer 1973/2010) or *mode* which characterizes them (usually the comic and/or narrative mode) among other features like the story or plot, character constellations, mise en scène, etc.

Unfortunately, the term *genre* is no less ambiguous than *format* or *medium.* As Gabriele Rippl and Lukas Etter have it, "it is very hard to decide where the medium ends and genre begins" (Rippl/Etter 2013: 194). When Anglo-Americans speak of genre, they usually mean genre conventions or ways in which films, comics, verbal narratives, etc. are put together and read as stories[22]: it is argued, for example, that

---

[21] Cf. Swales 1990, who focuses on discursive utterances in different text types and uses *genre* in the title of his book.
[22] Cf. Abell 2012: 77–79, Coogan 2012: 203–220, Duncan/Smith 2009: 196ff.; Thwaites et al. 2002: 107, Fishelov 1993: 82–83. Kannenberg remarks that in *Jimmy Corrigan* as well as in his *Acme*

> [t]he superhero genre is a kind of story, one with specific plots, characters, settings, themes, icons, and effects. [...] It] was a *kind* of story, one that could be imitated and reproduced over and over again with variation, but which held constant to certain elements. Imitation and repetition are necessary for a genre to come into existence. (Coogan 2012: 203–204, italics in the original)

Comics as a medium, on the other hand, may feature any genre like superheroes, science fiction, fantasy, or horror. This can be highly confusing, not least in the light of conventional genre theory; generally, a superhero story, for example, may be presented as a drama (or tragicomedy) or a verbal novel. Martin Schüwer, by contrast, links genre and medium quite differently when he asks why the superheroes constitute such a congenial genre for the comics medium (2008: 81). Comics, he says, basically condense temporal duration in single images: single panels show at least parts of if not whole movements, mostly. Human perception, in turn, is characterized by temporal duration condensation as well as by sensorimotor experience of the present.[23] Unlike any other genre, superhero stories are built on sensorimotor effects and, with every image, posit a sensorimotor present: a jump, an impact, or a stroke (ibid.).

All this considered, two questions beg to be asked:
1) What (exactly) is genre?
2) In what (kind of) genre category do comic books and graphic novels fit?

In the framework of this book, I cannot elaborate on the research on genre in general, yet it should be mentioned that the more recent writings on this subject present themselves as extremely heterogeneous, if not chaotic, with regard to definition, terminology, and systematicness.[24] One of the principal problems lies in the term *genre* itself: it possesses more than one meaning (see above) and, in addition, it is diachronic, referring to texts from historically different

---

Novelty Library, Chris Ware invokes genres which he then alters "in service to larger thematic issues" (2001: 190).

23 Schüwer here draws back on Henri Bergson's writings on matter and memory (1896): the present, experienced as indivisible, possesses duration in its own right. It is composed of perception referring to the past and action oriented toward the future: "We are dealing with 'a combined system of perception and movement'" (Schüwer 2008: 81, see also 62ff.).

24 In this context, Ansgar Nünning speaks of a terminological anarchy ("Begriffsanarchie", Nünning 2007: 73). Certain experts even hold that the majority of papers or approaches on this topic are based on terminological *ad hoc* creations or labels, which have scarcely been reflected on and are therefore of moderate critical value (cf. Neumann/Nünning 2007: 2). What is missing are comprehensive and systematic classifications or approaches like those by Klaus Hempfer (1973/2010) or Rüdiger Zymner (2003).

socio-cultural systems (cf. Hempfer 2010: 23). Genre has been defined in terms of numerous paradigms: cognitive schemas (Sinding 2002, who largely borrows from Lakoff's cognitive models), types of discursive utterances (Swales 1990), further in terms of historical constructs (Cohen 1986), socio-political use-values (Beebee 1994), deep metaphors structuring genre reflection (Fishelov 1993), relations to other genres (Todorov 1976/1990), or transtextual relations (Genette 1979/2004), to name but a few.

Trying to come to grips with the terminology, I find that I often cannot talk about one concept without talking about another at the same time. This is even more striking when I realize, as Genette has it, that genre and mode are two fundamentally different categories: genre is a literary category whereas mode is a linguistic category from the special area of pragmatics (i.e. in terms of utterance types, cf. Genette 2004: 64). Yet how does all this fit together? To put it simply, it does, and then it doesn't, which probably is the reason why genre theory has been a developing field until today – although with comprehensive and systematic approaches rather few in number.

To sum up: I reserve the term *format* for marketing/distribution contexts; *medium* for comics as an artistic, multimodal discourse with its codes and rules; and *genre* for historical text groups consisting of literary works like comic strips, books, or graphic novels (question #1). I shall now elaborate on question #2: Into what (kind of) genre category do comic books and the graphic novel fit?

3.3.2 From Classical Categories to Family Resemblances

The main reason why critics have stayed away from elaborate (and systematic) genre categorizations is that the boundaries between 'comics' and 'graphic novels' have been perceived as more or less fuzzy (cf. Dittmar 2008: 25). The confusion resulting from this lies above all in the fact that too much attention has been drawn to the category boundaries, which is due to a principal postulate of the classical category approach (stemming from Aristotle's *Metaphysics*): an object is or is not a member of a category; in our context: *Watchmen*, for example, is or is not a graphic novel. Or: *Watchmen* is a graphic novel and not a traditional comic book. The decision that an object belongs to category A and not B is made on the basis of so-called essential features or attributes contained in or defining a category. In our context, that could mean, for example, that *Watchmen* is self-referential. This attribute is absent in *The League of Extraordinary Gentlemen*. Therefore, the latter is not a graphic novel (this, of course, being an overly simplistic conclusion).

Attributes in classical categories are binary, that is they are either present or absent in an object. In my last example, there are no *degrees* of self-referentiality, and problems of this kind become even more striking when a category is defined by a number of attributes, and an object exhibits some of them but not all. Such objects would be excluded from the (classical) category, although they may be similar in one or even more than one respect.[25] This is so because "the Aristotelian model of categories assumed a perfect correlation between the defining attributes of a category. [... B]y knowing the category to which a thing belongs, one knows with complete certainty that certain attributes will co-occur" (Taylor 2003: 52). The fact that there is no middle position in the Aristotelian model, no in-between category, precludes the category membership of objects which are nevertheless similar, if only to a certain degree, and which should not be offhandedly dismissed.

In a classical category, all members possess an equal status (ibid. 21), which constitutes another predicament. There are only perfect examples of a category, no better nor moderately good examples. In other words, classical categories do not account for what cognitive psychologists and linguists call *prototype effects*. They "arise from incongruities between our cognitive models and our experience of the world" (Sinding 2002: 193). As a general consequence, "[w]ith only Aristotelian categories at our disposal, new data would often demand, for their categorization, the creation of new categories, or a redefinition of existing categories" (Taylor 2003: 58). To put it differently, classical categories cannot possibly provide the structural stability necessary to come to grips with many phenomena or objects to be assigned a place in our mind.

Prototype theory, although (of course) not free from weaknesses itself, offers escape from these predicaments. The basis of this theory prefigures in Ludwig Wittgenstein's aphoristic remarks about games (board, card, ball, children's games, etc.) in his *Philosophical Investigations* (1946–1953): games are not characterized by a single recurring feature but by a family resemblance, "a complicated network of similarities overlapping and criss-crossing: sometimes overall similarities, sometimes similarities of detail. I can think of no better expression [...] than 'family resemblances' [...]" (qtd. in Taylor 2003: 42–43 and Hempfer 2010: 18–20). This is easy to understand when I think of 'skill' as an essential feature or attribute of a game and the predicaments emerging with it: 'skill' is a graded concept to start with, and the skill needed in chess is obviously different from the skill needed in tennis (cf. Taylor 2003: 65–66). To sum up, there are different kinds of skill, not one of which would represent the smallest common denominator of all games.

---

[25] Cf. McCloud's exclusion of the cartoon from his essentialist definition of comics as "[j]uxtaposed pictorial and other images in deliberate sequence" (McCloud 1994: 9/20).

The use of Wittgenstein's family resemblance approach as a vantage point is nothing new in genre theory (indeed, it has been used since the 1960s, cf. Fowler 1982: 43); neither is it obsolete (cf. Fishelov 1993, Hempfer 2010, or Sinding 2002). However, it has been criticized for its weaknesses: "a family resemblance theory can make anything resemble anything" (Swales 1990: 50–51, cf. Sinding 2002: 183–184, and Chandler 2). John Swales gives the following example (Fig. 3.1):

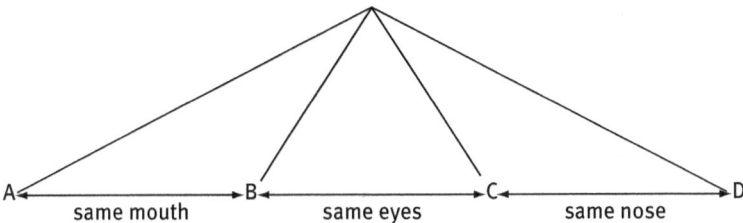

Fig. 3.1: Family resemblance according to Swales (1990: 51)

> Thus whilst B and C share a common feature, A and D have nothing in common themselves except that they share a different feature with B and C. So a knife is like a spoon because they are both eating instruments, and a spoon is like a teapot because they are both used to contain liquids, and a teapot is like a suitcase because they both have handles, so a knife is like a suitcase (Swales 1990: 51, cf. Fricke in Zymner 2010: 8–9).

Alastair Fowler holds against Wittgensteinian theory that in its primitive form, it would "sweep away not only traditional genre theory but all generalizing about literature and aesthetics" (Fowler 1982: 42). All this notwithstanding, Wittgenstein's insight that there generally is a scope of vagueness in every-day expressions as well as in technical, register-specific terms makes his language philosophy an important reference point when I look at similar past investigations in mathematics, philosophy, linguistics, and psychology.

3.3.3 Fuzzy Boundaries: From Family Resemblances to Prototypical Categories

Before Wittgenstein, Bertrand Russell discovered his famous paradox, which revealed the logical crux in set theory (as by Georg Cantor and Gottlob Frege). As it happens, this paradox is also a theme in the graphic novel *Logicomix* (Doxiadis/Papadimitriou 2009: 163/168). What is here given to the readers in the comics medium is basically a category issue: conceiving of a 'set of all sets which do not contain themselves' led Russell to the question whether such a set contains itself or not. The answer turned out to be paradoxical: if the set of all sets contains itself, it does not; and if it does not contain itself, it does. Russell's paradox "subverts the notion of 'set' as a collection defined by a common property... And with it, Logic!" (Doxiadis/Papadimitriou 2009: 168) There seems to be no "common property" that would define all sets, in other words, the set concept contains a scope of vagueness despite the fact that it is a technical term (in logical discourse). However, *set* is also a concept in ordinary language, in which aspect it is similar to many literary critical concepts.[26] Therefore, a certain scope of vagueness must be allowed for with register-specific as well as register-unspecific terms, and thus for any technical term related to literary genre.[27]

In the early 1970s, the linguist William Labov proved in his field research that many linguistic categories do not possess clear boundaries but a representational core, bundling the central characteristics of a category (cf. Labov 1973, quoted in Hempfer 2010: 21 and Taylor 2003: 43–44). At around the same time, Eleanor Rosch, a cognitive psychologist, developed the prototype concept and proved that not all members of a category are equally representative of that category. She gave a list with items of furniture to 200 American college students who had to judge "to what extent each of the sixty household items could be regarded as a good example of the category 'furniture' " (Taylor 2003: 46). The students had to grade each item on a 7-point scale ranging from 1 (= very good example) through 4 (= moderately good example) to 7 (= bad example). It was found that a chair, sofa, or a couch were better examples of furniture than, for example, a piano or a telephone (ibid.). In other words, Rosch studied the prototype effects of the students' category assignments. Apart from her often quoted furniture test, Rosch conducted nine more similar tests (about the categories fruit, vehicle, weapon, vegetable, tool, bird, sport, toy, and clothing) and showed that "degree of membership in a category [...] is in fact a psychologically very real notion" (ibid. 47). Yet she distinguishes between *natural kind categories* and *nominal kind categories*: 'bird' is a natural category since it corresponds to a

---

[26] It is known that Russell solved the antinomy (as the paradox was also called) by distinguishing different 'types' of sets, in stratified, hierarchical order, to exclude the problem of self-referentiality.
[27] Cf. Margolin 1981: 16–17: "Most literary critical concepts, however, are either taken over from ordinary language, *i.e.* presystematic cultural awareness, or at best occur in a number of loose pretheoretical systems ("approaches"). Some initial measure of intentional vagueness is hence inevitable for all such concepts. [...] The sense of the predicate in general is therefore neither unique nor closed. Within each theory, predicates such as 'gothic' or 'fantastique' possess a well-defined reference class and a fully specified, probably closed, sense. Such predicates are hence exact within the confines of each individual theory. On the other hand, the various theories of the gothic, for example, share reference classes, but only *part* of the sense of this predicate. The meaning of the concept as a whole is therefore partially vague."

real phenomenon in nature; nominal kinds like 'toy' or 'vehicle' are definable in analytic terms ('A toy is something children play with,' 'A vehicle is a means of locomotion'). Independently from natural or nominal kind, Rosch proved that there are no clear boundaries, nor is there either-or membership (ibid.). Thus, membership in a prototypical category is "a matter of gradience" (Taylor 1989: 54, qtd. in Hempfer 2010: 21). As Devitt writes: "Genre theorists need to see genre as both/and rather than either/or" (2000: 705).

How does all this apply to literature or, more specifically, to our problem of categorizing the graphic novel as (a) text group(s)? According to the empirical findings from linguistics and psychology, I propose the following category schema (Fig. 3.2):

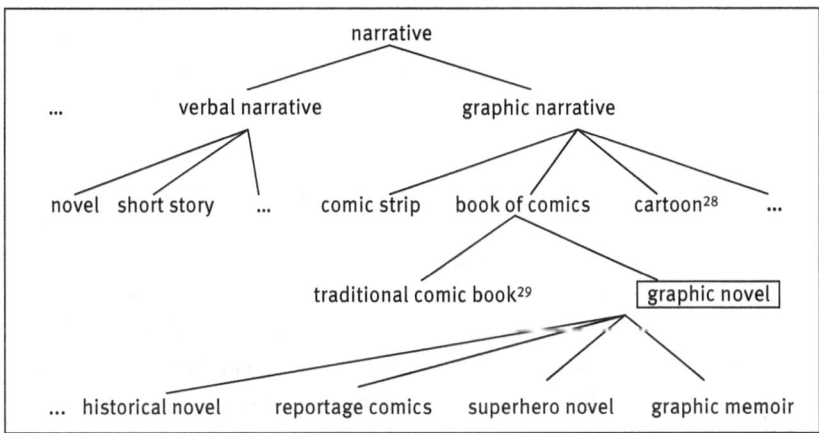

Fig. 3.2: Narrative, category tree including graphic novels

As the findings about prototypicality suggest, this schema works on two axes, the horizontal and the vertical. The vertical axis represents superordinate and subordinate categories. Here, the term graphic narrative[30] is used as a superordi-

---

28 Even a one-panel cartoon implies a narrative backdrop or substratum (cf. Harry Morgan, *Principes des littératures dessinées*, 2003, and Aron Kibedi Varga. *Discours, récit, image*, 1989: 98, qtd. in Groensteen 2013: ch. 2, np.). From a semiotic point of view, the single image cartoon may contain an indication of action (cf. Breithaupt 2002, qtd. in Fuchs 2006: 217).
29 American or Franco-Belgian format (*bande dessinée*) or longer, yet without the rhetorical/stylistic complexity, as in action, superhero, adventure, fantasy, or horror comics, essentially written for adolescents (see ch. 2.1).
30 Hillary Chute's "graphic narrative" is a rather offhanded definition which, after a few lines of explication, she does not further elaborate on (cf. Chute 2010: 3). Her main concern is the analysis of single specific long-form graphic works by women in terms of ethics, aesthetics, and politics.

nate category to cartoons, comic strips, and books of comics in general, the latter being superordinate to the traditional comic book and the graphic novel. Since graphic narratives are a combination of the pictorial and the textual medium, they are set apart from purely verbal narratives. The popular and frequently used category 'comics' as a text group has been deliberately abolished. It is, of course, debatable if graphic narratives count as a kind of literature,[31] the next (or second next) superordinate category in the above hierarchy (Fig. 3.2). The cardinal point in this schema is that graphic novels, like traditional comic books, are looked at as a (sub)genre to books of comics and graphic narratives in general.[32] Moving down the vertical axis,

> we would say that each category possesses exactly the features of the immediately dominating category, plus one (or more) additional distinguishing features. Items on the same level of categorization all share the features of the immediately dominating category, but each is distinguished from the other categories on the same level by the presence of a unique feature (or set of features). (Taylor 2003: 49)

To sum up, subcategories distinguish themselves from the superordinate category by at least one *distinguishing* feature, which, by definition, is *not* a core feature shared with the superordinate category. Therefore, works like Joe Sacco's *Palestine*, for example, are members of a subcategory to graphic novels (reportage comics): besides the fact that they uncompromisingly share the rhetorical devices of graphic novels – this being the reason to keep the 'novel' in the term – reportage comics possess the distinguishing feature of 'claim to factuality/authenticity.'

In graphic (auto)biographies or memoirs, we find the same distinguishing feature.[33] Generally speaking, in all graphic novels which make a more or less explicit claim to factuality/authenticity, the rhetorical devices of fiction – verbal

---

In her subsequent work-specific analyses, she can therefore easily dispense with a theory-based genre approach.

31 Cf. Wolk 2007: 14; Moore 2003: 3–4; John/McIver 2004: 43. Aaron Meskin, for example, conceives of comics as a hybrid art form whose preponderance of images precludes the notion of comics as literature. Comics are "autographic" (a term he borrows from Nelson Goodman) because layout is an essential feature: comics, unlike verbal narratives (novels or short stories) do not allow for forgery since they require "mechanical reproduction from a template or, perhaps, another authentic instance" (Meskin 2009: 231). Meskin admits, however, that all this depends on the definition of literature.

32 "[...] graphic narrative [is] a medium that is able to tell stories through the combination of word and image. However, graphic narrative can also be considered as a genre which encompasses several subgenres such as the comic strip, the comic book and the graphic novel" (Rippl/Etter 2013: 194).

33 "[...] the power of memory must always share the act of self-representation with the devices of fiction" (Gardner 2008: 6, cf. Pedri 2013: 133).

and pictorial – are so preponderant that these works are presented as fiction in the first place. By rhetorical devices of fiction I understand, for example, cartoony (as opposed to realistic) images, anthropomorphic beings,[34] narratorial script or possibly a full-fledged narrator (see ch. 4.5), cross-cutting or *montage* (see ch. 4.3.1.1), color-coded narrative levels or subplots, verbal and/or pictorial paratext (see ch. 4.4.1), structural performativity (see ch. 3.3.4.5), or metalepsis (cf. Hescher 2014b/2014c).

Factuality/authenticity therefore is *not* a core feature that graphic memoirs or reportage comics would share with their superordinate category ('graphic novels'). Consequently, 'narrative' has been posited above as the top category with both verbal and graphic narrative as subcategories, regardless of the distinguishing feature of 'factuality/authenticity.' In Fig. 3.2, the category of 'graphic novel' contains graphic superhero novels as well as graphic memoirs, reportage comics, and historical (graphic) novels, all of which possess different features distinguishing them from the superordinate category.

If, in an alternative schema, 'narrative' were posited as superordinate and 'fictional narrative' and 'nonfiction' as subordinate, graphic novels would occur twice: under 'fictional narrative' as well as under 'nonfiction' (Fig. 3.2a):

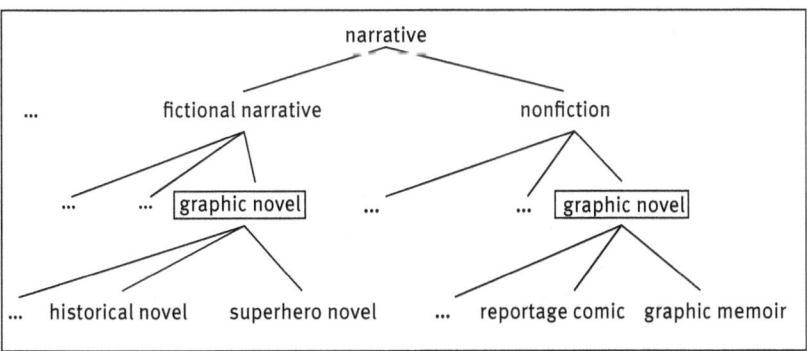

Fig. 3.2a: Alternative category tree with 'factuality/authenticity' as a core feature

In such a taxonomy, graphic memoirs and reportage comics would share 'factuality/authenticity' as a *core* feature with their superordinate category. This,

---

34 In the context of a transmedial narratology, which is not fixated on the factuality/fictionality paradigm, Werner Wolf defines that representations of story worlds "are centered around anthropomorphic beings who are capable of conscious choices, plans and activities, and experience emotions and desires" (Wolf 2011: 159).

however, contradicts my view explained above that all graphic novels, through the dominance of rhetorical devices of fiction, bear a fictional make-up in the first place and that 'factuality/authenticity' is a *distinguishing* feature, not shared with the next higher category. What additionally speaks against such a category tree as in Fig. 3.2a is that, in postmodernist fashion (see ch. 1), graphic memoirs, reportage comics, and travelogues generally question the status of the factuality/authenticity paradigm: they do so by explicitly and self-referentially thematizing it through their protagonists or artist-writers (for example, in the works of Guibert, Lefèvre, and Lemercier, Sacco, and Bechdel) or through the verbal-pictorial discourse, in their experiments with layout, coloring, or metaleptic devices (as in Talbot or Neyestani).

In Fig. 3.2, the graphic novel, which is on the same hierarchical level as the traditional comic book, by virtue of its prototypicality also admits works that are not traditional comic books but installments of a coherent series not yet published in book format, which, however, may be published in book format at a later point in time (which has been the case of many best-selling graphic novels, older or more recent, such as *Maus, Watchmen, Jimmy Corrigan, Persepolis, Palestine, Black Hole,* etc.). A current example of this could be the seven-issue series *Before Watchmen* (DC Comics, 2013– : a prequel to *Watchmen* from 1986–1987, featuring the main characters from this graphic bestseller and a number of renowned artists, above all Brian Azzarello, Michael Straczysnki, and Joe & Andy Kubert).

Since the above categories (Fig. 3.2) may look at first like classical categories, it is vital for the prototypical approach to emphasize that not all the category members on the horizontal axis have the same status. Despite their overlap with regard to attributes, graphic novels, comic strips, traditional comic books, for instance, differ on the grounds of their attributes and the number of attributes, that is they are not equal, as in classical categories. Taylor holds that "some attributes might be shared by only a few members of a category; there might even be categories with no attributes shared by all their members" (Taylor 2003: 53, the latter case is, of course, extreme and rather theoretical).

To sum up, what matters about prototypical categories is
- that the focus is on their cores or central features (cf. Fishelov 1993: 63), not their boundaries; categories typically have fuzzy boundaries and may overlap; because of the resulting flexibility (cf. Rosch/Lloyd 1978: 30), they offer the necessary structural stability for the category assignment in our minds and do not always have to be recreated or redefined;
- that members of one category do not necessarily share all the attributes bound up with that category: prototypical categories admit imperfect correlation among attributes;

- that there is no either/or membership in a category: members of one category are not equal, so that an object can be a better or moderately good example, more or less representative of that category (prototype effect).

Looking back at the vast number of graphic novels published in the last thirty years, differentiation is needed regarding the subcategories or -types of the genre. In Fig. 3.2, I subdivided the graphic novel, for purposes of illustration, into three subtypes; it goes without saying that this falls short of the number of subtypes or subgenres currently brought up in the critical literature. Let me therefore give a more detailed overview (Fig. 3.3):

Subgenres of the Graphic Novel	
superhero novel	Miller, *The Dark Knight*; Morrison/McKean, *Arkham Asylum*; Moore/Gibbons, *Watchmen*; …
graphic memoir	Spiegelman, *Maus*; Satrapi, *Persepolis*; Bechdel, *Fun Home*; Trondheim, *Approximativement*; …
graphic biography (including fictional biographies)	Kleist, *Der Boxer*; Simmonds, *Gemma Bovery*; Mezzo/Dupont, *Love in Vain*; …
graphic journalism, reportage or travel comics	Sacco, *Palestine* and other works; DeLisle, *Shenzhen* and others works; Guibert/Lefèvre/Lemercier, *Le photographe*; Kleist, *Havanna*; …
historical novels	Moore/Campbell, *From Hell*; Meter/Yelin, *Gift*; Vance/Burr, *On the Ropes*; Tardi, *C'était la guerre des tranchées*; Lutes, *Berlin*; …
fantasy	Gaiman, *The Sandman*; Burns, *Black Hole*; Carey/Gross, *The Unwritten*; …
steampunk	Moore/O'Neill, *The League of Extraordinary Gentlemen*; Ellis, *Aetheric Mechanics*; …
metafiction	Mathieu, *L'origine* and other works; Talbot, *Alice in Sunderland*; Neyestani, *Une métamorphose iranienne*; …
science comics	Doxiadis/Papadimitriou, *Logicomix*; Piccioni/Balbi, *Cosmicomic*; Goodwin, *Economix*; …

Fig. 3.3: Subgenres of the graphic novel

I mentioned earlier that it is essential for prototypical categories to overlap. The individual works here have been assigned for purposes of illustration although they often represent a mix of different (sub)genres, even the historically first graphic novel specimens: *Watchmen*, for example, can be read as a dystopian novel and a parody of the superhero genre with a particularly postmodern twist in that it playfully rewrites Cold War history; *Maus* can be read as metafiction, a comic book about Art Spiegelman's making of a comic book, as a historical novel about the holocaust, and as a biography of Vladek Spiegelman; *Palestine* and *Le photographe* can be read as self-referential metafiction and as educational comics in that they are not only made to entertain but with the intention to instruct (or to be educational, cf. Hangartner in Hangartner 2013: 14); *From Hell* and *Black Hole* read as a horror novels, and *On the Ropes* as a fictional biography and a historical novel; last but not least, *Logicomix* reads as self-referential metafiction and as a joint autobiography. This depends, of course, on the additional central attribute (or unique distinguishing feature, see above) I assign to the subtype: in graphic journalism, for example, this would be a narrating character who is or acts (as) a journalist or a comparable person (thus in *Shenzhen*, the narrator DeLisle is a private employee who acts like a journalist); at the same time, DeLisle is a factual author, for which reason *Shenzhen* can be read as an autobiography or travelogue, like David B.'s *Journal d'Italie*. The blending of genre features, of course, is nothing specific to graphic novels and has been happening since the origin of the novel genre. – Let me add that in Fig. 3.3, I deliberately left out the graphic adaptations of verbal narratives and plays. Departing from my personal reading experience, I find that of all the adaptations read, only *City of Glass* (2004) scores high enough on the complexity graph to be called a graphic novel; the rest I would subsume under illustrated novels, educational comics,[35] or simply under lengthy comic books.

3.3.4 From Prototypes to a Typology

Like every approach, the prototype approach also has its weaknesses. Taylor writes: "In order to keep our categories maximally distinct, and hence maximally informative, we need to focus on the basic level of categorization, more specifically, on the more central members of *basic level categories*" (Taylor 2003: 53, my italics). We assign objects, phenomena, or abstract concepts to categories in order to structure our sensory and cognitive data. The ultimate goal is to

---

[35] Leonard Rifas laconically claims that "[t]he quality of being 'educational' can be found to some degree in any comic book" (qtd. in Davidson 2008: 3). In his categorization, illustrated adaptations of novels and plays figure under educational comics not least because 'educational comics' itself is what has here been called an analytical category in that it "encompasses a large constellation of related (and somewhat overlapping) categories" (qtd. in Davidson 2008, note #1).

establish order among the mental representations of the world around and the cognitive processes and schemas inside us. One principle underlying this structuring or ordering is what Eleanor Rosch called *cognitive economy*: "maximum information with least cognitive effort is achieved if categories map the perceived world structure as closely as possible" (cf. Rosch/Lloyd 1978: 28). The other principle is that "the perceived world is not an unstructured total set of equiprobable co-occurring attributes" (ibid. 29). Rosch gives the example that we associate the attribute 'wings' with feathers rather than with 'fur' because the empirical world provides a large number of entities – birds – proving the correctness of this association (ibid.): everybody will admit that a robin or hawk is a better example of the co-occurrence of wings and feathers than, for instance, a penguin (although penguins also belong to the bird family). This is to say that attributes are not randomly associated, and our linguistic and cognitive preferences would prove that wrong.

This is where basic level categories step in. According to Rosch, they both "(a) maximize the number of attributes shared by members of the category; and (b) minimize the number of attributes shared with members of other categories" (not referenced, qtd. in Taylor 2003: 66). This is, of course, what we find in perfected form in classical categories. The basic level categories (or terms) reduce the prototype effect to a degree that maximum information combines with structural stability (see above). Thinking back to the origin of the word *prototype* (Greek: *prototypon*), meaning primitive form, a principle weakness of prototype theory becomes visible. To put it simply: you can make a (prototypical) pencil drawing of a chair or a bird; try to do so with a game or a graphic novel, and you will run into problems. This has to do with two things: firstly, the basic level terms work well with natural kind categories[36] (see above) and not well for nominal kind categories; secondly, games and graphic novels are abstract analytical terms. In fact, the attributes defining a category can be so cognitively complex as to become categories or prototypes themselves. René Dirven once called this phenomenon the recursiveness of prototypicality (not referenced, qtd. in Taylor 2003: 66). But this is actually not really a problem but a general characteristic of cognitive structures:

> Decomposing an attribute into its constituent attributes might go some way toward solving the second of these problems; it does not necessarily remove its prototype structure. [...] It is one of the myths of the classical theory that complex concepts are ultimately reducible

---

[36] The basic level "emerges from everyday human interaction in a physical environment and a culture. Factors defining the basic level include gestalt perception, motor interaction, mental images, and cultural importance" (Lakoff 1987: 112, qtd. in Sinding 2002: 186).

> to sets of binary primitives. [...] Cognitive structures often need to be understood more as holistic, gestalt configurations, than as attribute bundles. (ibid.)

What does constitute a problem is that Rosch's prototype findings on furniture and other natural kind categories as well as her equally famous findings about color prototypes[37] are first and foremost based on *visual* gestalt configurations and therefore hardly appropriate for abstract analytical objects or nominal kind categories.

As for these, if I consider games, it is a problem to speak of actual prototypes when there are only better or moderately good (or simply bad) examples of a category – would tennis or chess or maybe hopscotch be adequate prototypes? Would *Watchmen, Maus,* or *Palestine* serve as a prototype of the graphic novel? The answer would be neither or all of them. As a consequence, I should speak of *types* rather than prototypes, at least in the case of nominal kind categories. Rosch herself admits: "To speak of *a prototype* at all is simply a convenient grammatical fiction; what is really referred to are judgements of degrees of prototypicality" (cf. Rosch/Lloyd 1978: 40, qtd. in Hempfer 2010: 22, emphasis in the original). At least for nominal kind categories, which I would claim are more complex than natural kind categories, it takes types rather than prototypes to adequately describe a phenomenon; accordingly, I hold that it takes more than two or three types to analytically cope with a *complex* phenomenon like graphic novels. In fact, I would allow for a larger set of systemically related types to distinguish graphic novels from other graphic narratives and propose a *typology* to describe them as a kind of graphic narrative with one additional feature: *complexity*. Contrary to other potentially distinguishing features (adult orientation or the superhero story, for example), complexity itself behaves prototypically in that it is, like the graphic novel, a complex analytical concept to be defined in turn by a set of types, the exact number of which is left open at this point ($T_1, T_2, \ldots T_n$).[38] In order to do justice to Taylor's stipulation that membership in a prototypical category is a matter of gradience (see above), $T_1, T_2, \ldots T_n$ should resemble their superordinate category *complexity* in *gradience*, that is they should admit the assessment of a graphic work in terms of 'a high/medium/low degree of $T_1/T_2/\ldots T_n$' (Fig. 3.4):

---

[37] Cf. Heider [=Rosch], "Focal Color Areas and the Development of Color Names" (1971) and ibid., "Universals in Color Naming and Memory" (1972).

[38] When Hatfield, for example, writes that "comic art is growing more complex all the time" (Hatfield 2005: 66), he does not have prototypical categories in mind but uses complexity as a general label to describe what he (correctly) sees as a historical change.

3.3 From Prototypes to a Typology of Complexity

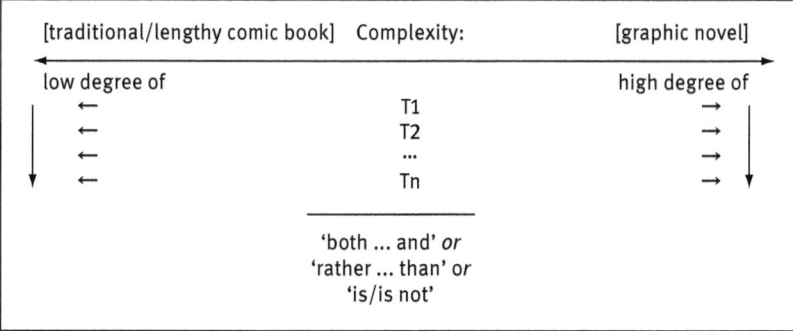

Fig. 3.4: Complexity gradient (general)

Such a typological conception of the graphic novel as distinguished from the superordinate graphic narratives through several scalar *types* of complexity implies the following assets:
- essentialism, based on a sole core feature and resulting exclusions of individual works being similar yet not identical with respect to the core feature, is averted;
- the types permit gradation in terms of 'a high/medium/low degree of T1, T2, ... Tn' (scalar horizontal level);
- in their sum, the types also allow for a differential assessment of a graphic work in terms of 'both ... and,' 'more/rather ... than,' as well as 'is/is not' (vertical level).

Graphic novels are a specific type of a book of comics that can be set apart from traditional comic books, quantitatively and qualitatively, according to a number of concrete parameters to be put forth which contribute to their complexity. Complexity behaves perfectly prototypically in that it is a complex analytical concept definable and defined by a set of types (T1, T2, ... Tn) which in turn are analytical and behave prototypically to the extent that they are graded (or gradable). It is generally arguable what concrete types stand in best for T1, T2, ... Tn. Considering the historical development of the graphic novel and the features brought up in comics criticism until now, I propose the following seven types in the schema below (Fig. 3.5):

```
[traditional/lengthy comic book]        COMPLEXITY:              [graphic novel]
  ←      (1) multilayered plot and narration                →
  ←      (2) multifunctional use of color                   →
  ←      (3) complex text/image relation                    →
  ←      (4) meaning-enhancing panel design/layout          →
  ←      (5) structural performativity                      →
  ←      (6) multiplicity of references to texts/media      →
  ←      (7) self-referential and metafictional devices     →

                          'both ... and' or
                          'rather ... than' or
                             'is/is not'
```

Fig. 3.5: Complexity gradient (specific)

To recall: the parameters in this cline are scalar on their own and differential when taken together (as opposed to clear-cut or absolute). Thus, they do justice to the fuzziness of the category borders, that is their prototypicality. The cline functions on a horizontal and a vertical axis. Horizontal: for an individual graphic novel, the score marks to the parameters one through seven can be moved from the extreme left to the extreme right on the continuum, according to the degree of complexity of the work (of course, a single parameter's place on the continuum is merely conceivable in terms of range and not of an exact spot). Vertical: the score marks are added up (approximately). For the majority of graphic works, not all the seven parameters will attain a high degree. For example: *Maus* scores very high on all the parameter scales except, of course, (2); on the other hand, *The League of Extraordinary Gentlemen, Vol. 1*, (Moore/O'Neill 2000) scores extremely high on (6) and high on (1) but quite low on the rest of the parameter scales; therefore, I would call it a lengthy or enhanced comic book rather than a graphic novel like *Maus*.[39]

Complexity, with its seven subcategories, is the core feature of graphic novels which distinguishes them from books of comics in the superordinate category and from traditional comic books on the same category level. In the framework of this approach, I shall not discuss in detail the core features of

---

[39] Sebastian Domsch (2012) elaborates on the work's many intertextual references of Victorian fiction. Paul D. Lopes, in contrast, calls it a crime pulp graphic novel (cf. Lopes 2009: 158). – The case is very different with the *Black Dossier* from the *Extraordinary Gentlemen* series (Moore/O'Neill 2000): in terms of complexity, this work will count as a full-fledged graphic novel after applying the above seven parameters.

graphic narratives or the comics medium in general. Besides complexity, to put it briefly, I take the coexistence of verbal text (which in the critical literature is often referred to as the verbal track) and sequential images (or the pictorial track) as a basic given in graphic novels. I have deliberately excluded factuality and fictionality from the above cline (Fig. 3.5). They are not plausible subcategories to complexity and therefore cannot function as distinguishing features. A graphic novel is not more or less complex because it is 'factual' or 'fictional,' labels often applied, for example, to graphic memoirs and journalism or to graphic superhero or fantasy novels, respectively).[40]

To sum up, graphic novels are complex graphic narratives, and complexity as a core feature defines them as a *genre* or historical text group, not as a medium; moreover, complexity accounts for the text group including its subgroups, which are liable to change in quantity (or comprehensiveness) and quality through time. Complexity in turn is an analytical category, consisting of a set of gradable typical subcategories, of which I have proposed seven (see Fig. 3.5), which I shall now set forth in greater detail.

3.3.4.1 Multilayered Plot and Narration

To anticipate: when I write "plot and narration," this is to say that not every graphic novel comes with narratorial captions transmitting a fleshed-out narratorial identity; often, the caption script is so minimalistic that it is limited to short local or temporal adverbial phrases with not even verbs or personal pronouns. Some of the complexity parameters used in Versaci and Crutcher (see above, chapter 3.3.4) may be looked at, with certain distinctions, in terms of plot and narration, such as the multiplicity of character psychology, points of view, and layered voices. As for plot, Charles Burns' *Black Hole* (2005) is said to display "a chronology complicated enough that it takes a few readings to work out – Black Hole is riddled with flashbacks, flash-forwards, and multiple perspectives" (Wolk 2007: 336–337). In David B.'s autobiographic *Epileptic*, to add one more example, David's and his parents' dealing with Jean-Christophe's epileptic seizures constitute the main action, the lengthy substrands of action

---

40 Here lies a weighty terminological and conceptual problem. If we hold on to classical narratology, there is no such thing as a fictional graphic novel because 'fictional' implies a mode of representation pertaining to verbal narrative fiction, in which the mediating and transmitting communication system – reified in the fictional narrator – generates the whole (verbal) discourse. However, there is not a narrator in graphic narratives who would be solely responsible for generating both the verbal and the pictorial track. I shall elaborate on this point and the implications for the narration in graphic narratives below (chapters 4.1 and 4.2).

being the grandparents' and their ancestors' lives as well as the lives of several artists and intellectuals (Loeb, Oshawa, Swedenborg, Steiner).

An extremely high level of sophistication of both plot and narration exists in Alan Moore and Dave Gibbons' *Watchmen* (1986–1987, cf. Wolk 2007: 241). I counted more than twenty strands of action, including the main plot (if there is just one), and about twenty-five major and minor characters, not counting the 'extras.' Also, the narrative is complicated by the *mise en abyme* comic "The Black Freighter," mirroring the main plot and diverse substrands; in addition, the first two chapters – and respectively, the whole novel – are framed by narratorial captions containing Rorschach's journal entries, the plot-related cause of which is revealed on the last two pages of the book (chapter XII, 31–32, cf. Hescher 2013: 192–193). Last but not least, at the end of each of the twelve chapters, we find fictitious paratextual documents of different genres, non-fictional and fictional in their makeup, obviously aiming at the readers' orientation and reception of both the individual chapters and the work as a whole. Verbal text dominates in these 'false documents,' and the few pictorial elements are limited to illustration; some but not all of these documents contain a speaker or a narrating voice.

How these subplots and their narrating voices connect to each other textually and pictorially is another remarkable feature of complexity. In *Maus* and *Watchmen*, the transition from one plot or story frame to the other is often realized through graphic matches and inserted captions with specific typefaces, framings, and background colors (Figs. 3.6 and 3.7).

Fig. 3.6: Spiegelman 2003: 14–15, graphic match

Fig. 3.7: Moore/Gibbons 2008: V, 9–10, inserted caption, graphic match

In the example from *Maus* (Fig. 3.6), Vladek Spiegelman is pedaling on his stationary training bike while telling about his life in Poland before the start of WWII. The pictorial link between the two splashes is the round framing of Vladek as a young man, who, as he has it, "looked just like Rudolph Valentino." The framing is repeated in the non-diegetic Valentino poster behind Vladek and in the shape of the wheel of his bike. The two panels from *Watchmen* (Fig. 3.7, the panel on the left is the final panel on its page; the one on the right is the first on the following page) represent the castaway from the mise en abyme comic and the ex-vigilante Daniel Dreiberg alias Nite Owl as they are chewing on a bite taken from a seagull/a chicken thigh. The chewing and the bite taken is verbally alluded to in the narratorial caption (Fig. 3.7, left panel, "Nothing would take it from me") and the speech balloon (Fig. 3.7, right panel, "chew on that"). Thus, in both examples, we are dealing with a verbal-pictorial match.

Probably the paragon of multilayered plot is Richard McGuire's graphic novel *Here* (2014), of which six black and white pages first appeared in the second volume of Art Spiegelman and Françoise Mouly's comics anthology *RAW* in 1989 (cf. Platthaus 2015). As in the example below (Fig. 3.8), up to six (and sometimes more) temporal layers are inserted on a double-page spread.

They show event-states from prehistoric times through the sixteenth and seventeenth century until the year 2314 from the vantage point of a corner in a living room of a house built in 1907; respectively, when an inserted panel shows a prehistoric scenery, it is from the spot where that house or the living room will be built. The splashes and the inserted panels often feature banal or repetitive events but also unusual incidents and even disasters (as a nuclear or environmental catastrophe seems to have occurred in 2314, toward the end of the novel). There is no narratorial script apart from the numbers of the years, and balloon speech is extremely sparse.

Fig. 3.8: McGuire 2014, np., temporary layers through inserted panels

3.3.4.2 Multireferential Use of Color

Color relates to the form and content of an image, and its use may be formulaic, thematic, and naturalistic (cf. Dittmar 2008: 162). Also, characters are recognized through color. "Most mainstream comic books have traditionally been ablaze with the bright primary colors (red, blue, and yellow) thought to appeal to adolescent males. Certainly the colorful costumes are part of the appeal of superheroes" (Duncan/Smith 2009: 142). This appeal, of course, is much related to the age of the target group, that is male children or adolescents, and color perception also depends on social and educational factors (cf. Dittmar 2008: 160). Yet most graphic novels are adult-oriented, and so is Lynda Barry's *One Hundred Demons*. It is mainly drawn in primary colors, which, taken together with the character design, seem to especially appeal to female children and teenagers. Yet the way the narrative is constructed suggests that it is clearly adult-oriented: geared toward those adults who remember their childhood and adolescence well – or too well, regarding the diverse traumas the book alludes to, including suicide and sexual abuse.

Not all graphic novels come in color. Among some which do, color is put to differentiated use. In David Mazzucchelli's *Asterios Polyp*, for instance, Asterios, the protagonist, is drawn in bright cyan whenever he behaves like a domineering chauvinist; in addition, the limbs of his body change into transparent, basic geometrical forms (mainly cylinders). His wife Hana, in contrast, is drawn in an aura of magenta cross-hatching whenever she is in a defensive position (Fig. 3.9).

Fig. 3.9: Mazzucchelli 2009, np., color-coded characters as pictorial allegories

The use of these two primary ink colors underscores the contrast between the two characters, their emotional state, and the way they perceive the story world (*perceive* here includes the cognitive perception).⁴¹ At the end of the book, and after a period of separation and insight, Asterios has turned into an amiable guy whose personality blends in with Hana's. The penultimate sequence depicting the resulting harmony between them is rendered in unsaturated complementary colors (red/green and yellow/purple; cf. Duncan 2012: 54). In *Asterios Polyp*, therefore, color creates contrast and harmony, and it "indicate[s] changes in perceptual focalization and distance [...] the various graphic styles and colors are *metaphorically* attributed to given characters, connoting their world view, experience, or emotional state" (Mikkonen 2013: 115).

Generally, color is used to "illustrate the expressive potential [...] in graphic narratives" (ibid. 113). Thus, in the first volume of Manu Larcenet's best-selling series *Blast* (2009), the protagonist Polza Mancini, an ex-writer and murder suspect, tells two police inspectors about his overwhelming epiphanic and somatic experience he calls "the Blast" (ibid. 43), which he describes as a kind of spiritual and physical rebirth. Around his head, the image sequence shows outbursts of color resembling early childhood drawings (Fig. 3.10), which read as the expression of a preternatural form of subjectivity.

Fig. 3.10: Larcenet 2009: 43, color outburst (expressive function)

---

41 Cf. Dittmar 2008: 161. Generally, "color can create or amplify emotion in the story" (Duncan/Smith 2009: 142). Compare Groensteen 2013, ch. 5.3.3, np., Mikkonen 2013: 115, and Miodrag 2013: 174–179, and Duncan 2012: 43–54, for a more detailed analysis of color-generated meanings.

Apart from that, color is used as a marker of diegetic planes: Ignazio, Asterios's imaginary twin (the narrator, who was still-born), and the Asterios of the metafictional episodes are rendered in a saturated yellow.[42] A comparable marking of diegetic planes through color is found in Doxiadis and Papadimitriou's *Logicomix* as well as in Mary and Bryan Talbot's *Dotter of Her Father's Eyes* (2012, extradiegetic and intradiegetic plane) and in Moore and Gibbons' *Watchmen* (the analeptic red-blooded murder sequence, occurring three times in the novel, see ch. 4.3.1, Fig. 4.7).

Brownish, blackish, and reddish colors underscore horror (cf. Dittmar 2008: 164). The 1989 Batman rewriting *Arkham Asylum* by Grant Morrison and Dave McKean is an outstanding example of this. Its collage-like relief look (which resembles pictorial art of the 1980s and 90s), often used as background to a double page, bears highly saturated kinds of brown, black, grey, red, and blue, the last of which connotes cold and particularly fear – which, of course, caters to the story's themes: childhood memories, cold-blooded murder, and repressed fears.[43]

It is a typical feature of Chris Ware's work to pictorially mark the diverse strands of action in the long works of fiction. Thus, in *Jimmy Corrigan*, different gradations and varieties of tint are used on the scenery of the settings and in the graphic schemas representing the chronological links between the subplots (Fig. 3.11). Colors here serve as indexes of time and place and as a visual-pictorial aid for readers to (re)construct the diverse story lines; the change of tints in the scenery of the images may remind them of one metaphor Ware extemporizes on in the paratextual "[Mock] Introduction," printed on the left inside hard cover on a light yellow background: in *Jimmy Corrigan*, readers watch the stories unfold in the manner of a "pictographic theater," on a kind of 'revolving stage' with a frequently changing setting.

Last but not least, color can serve as an illusion-disturbing device: in Bryan Talbot's *Alice in Sunderland* (2007), screamingly artificial colors combined with pixelating bring about a defamiliarization effect that underscores both the constructedness of the stories about Lewis Carroll and the town of Sunderland, and the metafictionality of the novel as a whole (see above, Fig. 3.5, type 7).

---

42 Besides, yellow also connotes extinction (the fire destroying Asterios' house and the asteroid that eventually destroys Asterios and Hana), ideality (Ursula Major, the "goddess," or Steven "Spotty" Drizzle, the seer), and (stereo)type (Mañana, the Mexican bar tender and Geronimo Pinque's girlfriend, and their Ford Mustang).

43 Cf. Dittmar 2008: 163, Morrison/McKean 1989/2004, n. p.: see the first 13 double pages after the imprint *et passim*.

Fig. 3.11: Ware 2000, np., colors as indexes of time and place

3.3.4.3 Complex Text/Image Relation

This concerns general quantitative and specific qualitative aspects. Graphic novels like *Maus, Watchmen, One Hundred Demons,* and *Fun Home* generally work with large amounts of text; others like *Arkham Asylum, Jimmy Corrigan, Black Hole, Blankets, Asterios Polyp* do not. Certainly, the sheer quantity of text or the text/image ratio in a graphic novel is in no way a quality criterion nor a genre characteristic.[44] Yet it is legitimate to speak of text-oriented and image-oriented graphic novels; and it is probable that the text-oriented specimens are, in general, more readily identified as representative of the graphic novel genre – for no plausible reason, however, given that the complexity of signification increases by diversifying the use and design of images and panels.[45]

---

[44] "Generally, it is established that even an extremely text-oriented comic can be convincing as a comic. There is no supremacy of the images over the text" (Dittmar 2008: 99).
[45] Interestingly enough, many critics refused to recognize *Maus* as a comic book because it was obviously good (Duncan/Smith 2009: 1, 16, and Gordon 2010: 186). This was certainly also fostered by the large amount of text *Maus* comes with.

Asterios Polyp is a good example of text/image complexity since it experiments with different typefaces and framing. Unframed captions in small to large capital letters signify the imaginary (dead) twin Ignazio, who narrates the story, as long as he remains invisible. When he appears together with his brother in the metadiegetic episodes, the letters occur in speech balloons, and besides, the character shapes are filled with a bright yellow (see above, chapter 3.3.4.2). Apart from that, every character has his/her own typeface and speech balloon shape (e.g. Hana's are roundish, Asterios' are rectangular, Ursula's resemble clouds). It is interesting in this context that *Asterios Polyp* contains many episodes in which there is no text at all (except, at times, sound lettering, see the tree house sequence or Asterios' dream descent into the underworld, which, in addition, is colored in a dark purple). It would be naïve to conclude that, because of the absence of text, the meaning generation is less complex. According to Scott McCloud, the text/image complexity generally increases with additive or parallel combinations, with montage, and with interdependent combinations (cf. McCloud 1994: 154–155). Also, pictures add something when they take up cues from a speech balloon from the same image (Fig. 3.7) or from the one before. In *Watchmen,* this often occurs when one subplot segues into the next (Fig. 3.12).

Fig. 3.12: Moore/Gibbons 2008: V, 12–13, text/image relation 'cuff/link'

Here, the image in the second panel displays Adrian Veidt alias Ozymandias putting on a cuff link, which cross-refers to the word *link* in the speech balloon from the opposite panel, which again is placed at the same height as the cuff link. This, of course, is different from graphic matches in which an image refers to another image through similar pictorial shapes.

Fun Home certainly is one of the most text-oriented graphic novels, perhaps verging on textual overkill. In addition to the speech balloons and captions, which Bechdel uses inside the panels and the gutters, she often tags her images, which draws extra attention to specific details in them and adds to the whole narrative construct building up in the readers' mind. In this sense, the tags may be seen as textual-pictorial connectors, constituting narrative threads in their own right (see chapter 4.4.6 for more details on tags).

3.3.4.4 Meaning-Enhancing Panel Design/Layout

Graphic novel artists seem to be more prone to experimenting with panels or frames. Elisabeth Rosen, who uses these terms synonymously, writes that panels "convey mood, indicate character, signal movement and reveal theme." Moreover, they "reinforce the emotional state of its narrator" (Rosen 2009: 59). This seems to be particularly true for graphic memoirs such as David B.'s *Epileptic* and Craig Thompson's *Blankets*. Rosen analyzes how Thompson controls time "by depicting a single moment over the course of several panels" (Rosen 2009: 63; cf. Thompson 2003: 171–173). The artist uses disappearing panel borders combined with faded backgrounds "to depict the solipsism of a first love" or intense moments (see bleed in Thompson 2003: 172). Besides, Thompson varies the thickness of certain panel borders to connote emotions like fear, guilt, and oppression as well as convex and concave shapes to indicate dynamic or dramatic action (Fig. 3.13).[46] In the example below, observing the first five panels together leaves the impression that the two brothers are in rough sea although they are just playing. Benoît Peeters calls this type of layout, in which the panel form serves the action, rhetorical (cf. Peeters 1993: 23–25).

---

[46] See the sequence when Raina's father comes back home and discovers his daughter sleeping in her bed with Craig (Thompson 2003: 441). The thickness of the border increases with each panel and denotes the exercise of oppression, embodied in the father, who is approaching Raina's room until he opens the door and looks in: here, the border of the fifth and last panel is at its thickest – and the oppression at its peak.

Fig. 3.13: Thompson 2003: 409, panel borders/shapes (expressive function)

In *Fun Home*, Bechdel once makes specific use of 24 "traditional" square-box-style panels over a full double page for the scene in which Alison and Bruce drive to see a movie (Fig. 3.14).[47] This is their last confrontation shortly before Bruce dies, and embarrassing stretches of silence betray that it is not the kind of

---

[47] Cf. Watson 2008: 43, *Fun Home* 220–221; Watson holds that the "two-page sequence is the only time that Bechdel uses the square-box-style of the traditional comic book."

heart-to-heart talk that Alison hoped for. The 24 same-sized moment-to-moment frames (showing the characters in profile as they are sitting in Bruce's car, basically unchanging in posture) amplify the passing time of the drive and the embarrassment involved in it for both characters, caused by the stretches of silence and the minimalist confession that Bruce makes. Of course, the lengthiness of the graphic novel fosters such space-consuming panel uses, whereas panel designs as found in *Blankets* could be employed in traditional comic books, also. However, it seems as if graphic novel artists are particularly daring with regard to panels: thus in *Fun Home*, Bechdel employs captions like panels, often boxed up inside other panels, and she tags characters or things displayed therein.[48]

Fig. 3.14: Bechdel 2006: 222–223, moment-to-moment frames (expressive function)

David Mazzucchelli may be counted among the exceedingly creative artists concerning panel design. In *Asterios Polyp*, he frequently uses empty pages on which he disorderedly strews framed or open (sub)panels; or he employs round and at times overlapping panels (ambivalent in connotation), splashes and splash panels, and other more fanciful forms.

---

48 Cf. Bechdel 2006: 63, 104–105, 179 et passim; for tags, cf. ibid. 146, 199, 212 *et passim*.

A very original use of panel design and layout is to be found in *Arkham Asylum*, by Grant Morrison and Dave McKean (Fig. 3.15). Practically all the panels, even those arranged in traditional order, look like horizontally oriented pieces of glass, as if from a mirror, reflecting memories or glimpses of visions and memories, potentiating the unreality and horror of the things reported. McKean's originality lies in the fact that he often uses oblong, upright, and slim panels on a single or double splash over a background itself teeming with signs and motifs that must be read against the panels and vice versa.

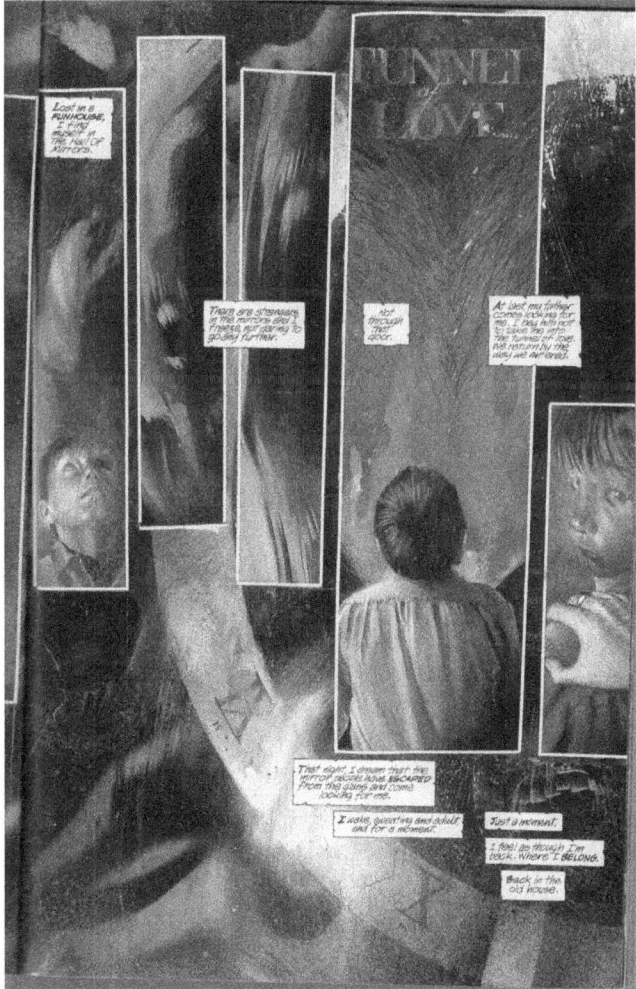

Fig. 3.15: Morrison/McKean 2004, np., inserted oblong verticals

This makes the reading demanding – and confirms the thesis that graphic novels are more complex than traditional or merely lengthy comic books – like the reading of a dream, "woven tightly around a small number of symbolic elements, which combine and recombine throughout."[49]

In Bryan Talbot's playfully postmodern graphic novel *Alice in Sunderland*, we find a mind-boggling use of panel design and layout (Fig. 3.16). To foreground the metafictionality of this work, Talbot uses combinations of mise en abyme, the recursive appearance of a story within a story, and metalepsis, a kind of narrative "short circuit" (Genette 2004a: 14) or intrusive change of the narrative plane. On this double page spread, there are numerous inserted 'panels,' with mostly unusual framings such as an iris mask, part-framing or no framing at all. The third panel on the left, for example, is a mise en abyme mirroring the full double page spread *ad infinitum*. The character in the foreground, who we see from the back in a high-angle view, reappears in a masked insert on the bottom right of the left half of the spread; it is a metaleptic device, like the butterfly, which figures several times on this spread. The background to the panels is a blur of images from other pages or spreads in the work (for a detailed analysis of this spread, see Hescher 2014c). Here, the metaleptic and mise en abyme saturated layout derives from the work's artistic creed that stories are more or (rather) less reliable constructions and the impetus of postmodern playfulness.

After *Jimmy Corrigan* (2000) and *Quimby the Mouse* (2003), Chris Ware's most daring experiment in panel design and layout is *Building Stories* (2012). Gene Kannenberg has it that "[i]n Ware's work, layout and design govern visual and thematic complexities, wherein the words and the images are conjoined in such a way that it is not possible to discuss one without considering the other" (Kannenberg 2001: np.). *Building Stories* consists of a cardboard cover box containing fourteen different types of print: small strip booklets, broadsheets of different sizes, thin hardbacks, and a large board that, once unfolded, is reminiscent in its own way of the façade of a playhouse. *Building Stories* is a complex experiment in panel design and layout and print format that challenges reading habits more than Ware's older works. For example, there neither is a beginning nor an ending to 'one' story, only little episodic stories held together by the binding of their format. And despite the roundup of the cardboard box,

---

[49] Cf. annex to the 2004 re-edition of *Arkham Asylum*, author's comment to script p. 2, bottom red print. The oblong panels are metaphorical and call up a network of references to other media, e.g. the two chimneys refer to Batman's ears, the asylum chimneys, the chimneys of the March Hare in *Alice's Adventures in Wonderland* (1865, ch. VI).

3.3 From Prototypes to a Typology of Complexity — 71

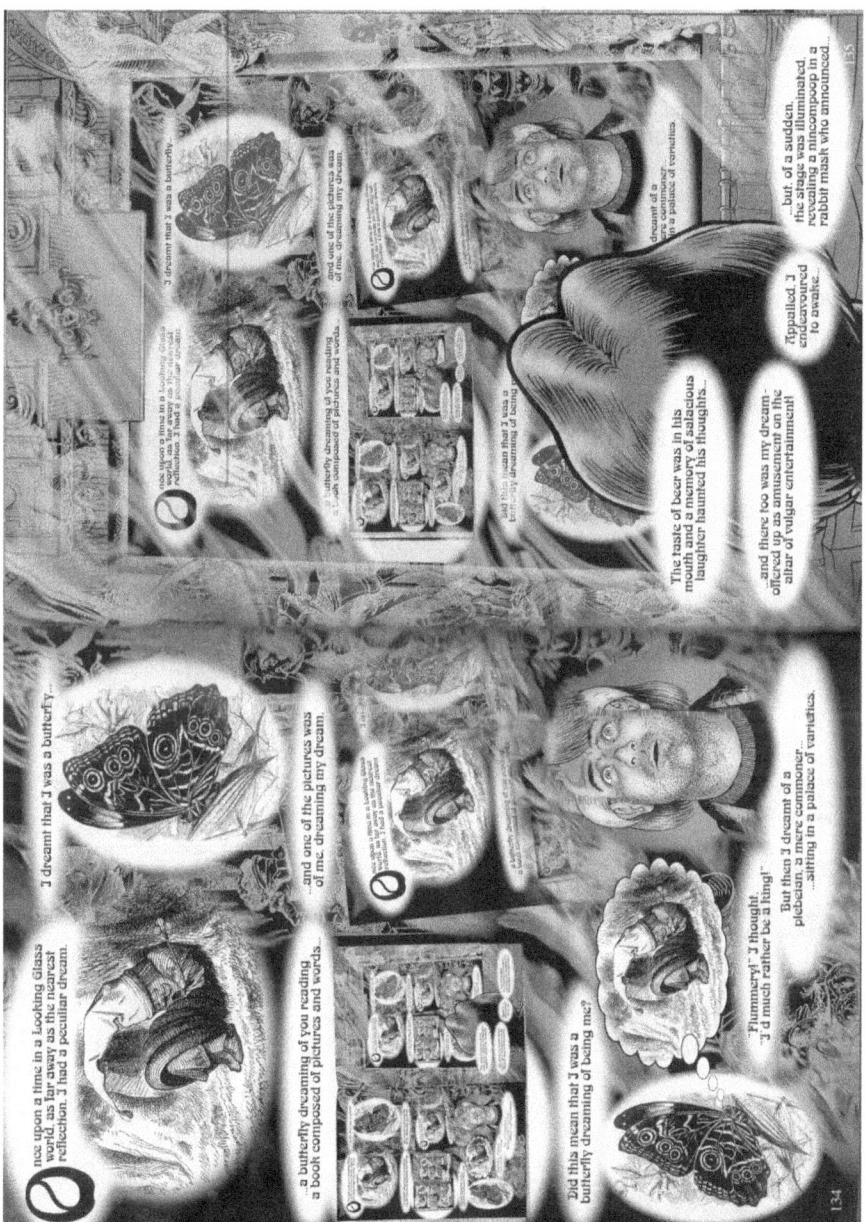

Fig. 3.16: Talbot 2007: 134–135, metafictional panel design and layout

all "conventional assurances of a stable text" are undermined: the until then interlinearly-correlatively conceived panels are now versatile. Respectively, the diverse types of print may be freely combined or even evoke rampant cursory readings. Stable, in the sense of a memory storage, is only the house, which is some 100 years old and takes itself stock of its history. (Serles 2014: 92, quoting Kuhlmann/Ball 2010)

The stories in *Building Stories* are connected to each other through (the architecture of) the house: each print item is located in an outline of one of its floors, which serves as a grid or metalayout to the whole collection of stories. The metalayout is displayed on the bottom of the cover box, showing miniatures of the 14 print items and from each miniature, a dashed line runs either to the spot in the house where that print item has been deposited or to images of a young black-haired woman, the former tenant of the top floor and focal character in the majority of the stories (Fig. 3.17). Thus, the story bundles in their various formats are laid out on a metaplane on the bottom of the cover box, where, as metonymies of themselves, they figure as the verbal-pictorial paratext to the stories they contain.

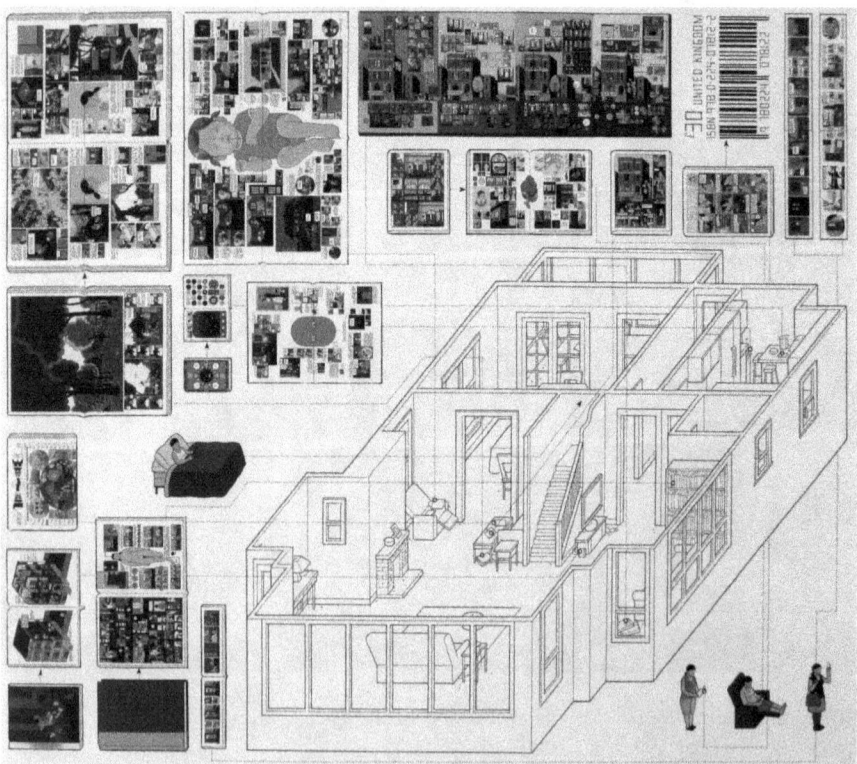

Fig. 3.17: Ware 2012, metareferential bottom of cover box

3.3.4.5 Structural Performativity

Text and image may appeal directly or indirectly to readers, thus adding to the complexity of comic books. They create an awareness on the part of the readers that they are reading and observing images in a graphic novel, and they remind them that there is an "author or narrator who reflects on her/his act of writing and, in so doing, constitutes (or deconstructs) himself as an author" (Häsner et al. 2011: 83–84). In this sense, text-image-reader appeal is a type of *structural performativity* (cf. ibid.), particular to self-reflexive and metafictional graphic novels; at the same time, self-reflexiveness and metafictionality form a subcategory to complexity. Therefore, text-image-reader appeal bears conceptual overlap with type 7 of the above complexity cline (see chapter 3.3.4, Fig. 3.5). Before I elaborate on structural performativity, let me give examples of text-image-reader appeal from diverse graphic novels.

Appeal to readers can be found in both *Maus* and *Fun Home*: in Spiegelman, the readers look at a double page close-up of an almost life-sized left hand holding a previously published Spiegelman comic book page (Spiegelman 2003: 102–105); in Bechdel, it is a similar spread showing a photograph of the family's ex-babysitter Roy (Fig. 3.18, similarly designed panels on pp. 120 and 205).

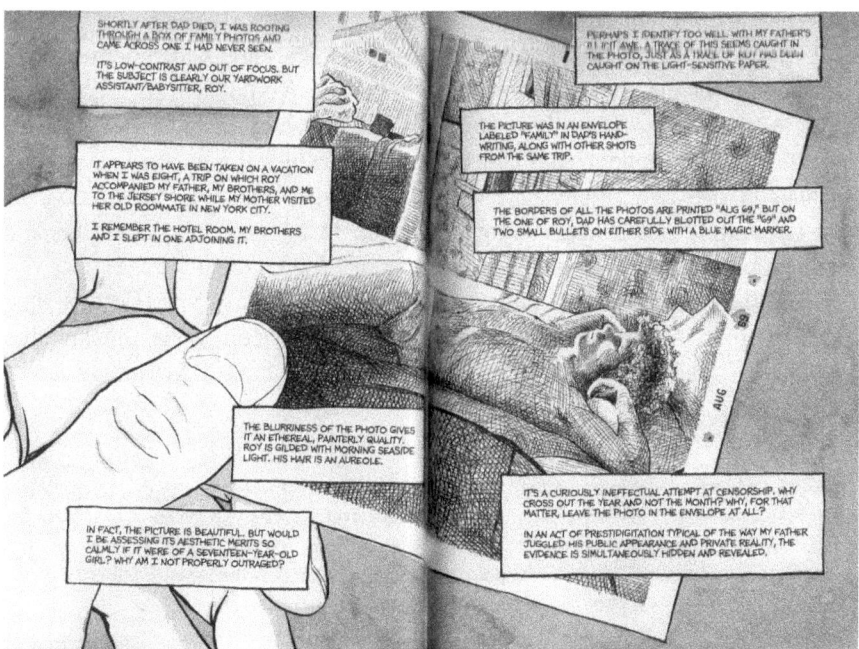

Fig. 3.18: Bechdel 2006: 100–101, text-image-reader appeal

The part of the hand holding the photograph is where the readers' hands hold the book; the hand is drawn in life-size. Here, the readers involuntarily seem to take Alison's position in an act of "autobiographical identification" (Watson 2008: 33) – which holds equally true for the Spiegelman example. Obviously, this act may also be seen as complicit or voyeuristic (ibid., 46), and the awareness thereof as an effect of the construction of the page. It literally draws the readers into the act of looking, which is again subject to display. What is to be looked at, here, is not so much the photograph but an exemplary act of *looking*. Moreover, these pages in *Maus* and *Fun Home* qualify as self-referential or metafictional. On the whole, *Fun Home* is designed like a photo book: on the title page to every chapter, we find a drawn photograph 'fixed' with photo album stickers.

The zoetrope cut-out with instructions from an early passage in Ware's *Jimmy Corrigan* is a differently original variant of structural performativity (Fig. 3.19).[50] Cut out and put together, the zoetrope is supposed to render a moving image of the tinman walking, Jimmy's oneiric alter ego from the preceding sequence on a crutch. The tinman is also an intertextual/intermedial[51] reference to Frank L. Baum's bestselling children's novel *The Wonderful Wizard of Oz* (1900) and an allegory of Jimmy's loneliness and inability to connect to other people. The zoetrope cut-out interrupts the sequence of panels and is to be understood as a "project or toy that Jimmy himself attempts to construct while traveling on the plane to meet the father he has never known" (Bredehoft 2006: 869). Thomas A. Bredehoft here speaks of "a literalization of reader-character identification: the reader who cuts out and assembles the zoetrope is literally engaged in the same activity as Jimmy" (ibid. 870). On the other hand, it is clear that the cutting out of the zoetrope is meant to happen only in the readers' imagination[52]: nobody would destroy the book s/he is reading (cf. Serles 2014: 93), and the instructions on the verso to the cut-out make the "project" a sheer mockery of Jimmy, the author – considering that *Jimmy Corrigan* is "semiautobiographical" – and the readers.[53] The ploy of the instruction text is that it does not

---

50 There are two more cut-outs in *Jimmy Corrigan*: one on the inside fold of the book jacket, representing the protagonist, and another some 200 pages into the novel, representing the home of William Corrigan, "the glazier of 1708 Peachwood [...], complete with horse, coach, coffin, trees and shrubs, and – perhaps most surprising of all – 'imaginary giant grasshoppers' " (Bredehoft 2006: 879).
51 For the problem inherent in the terminology, see the following chapter 3.3.4.6.
52 Significantly enough, the heading to the instructions read: "Memorize all instructions before waking up [sic] the pieces on the other side" (Ware 2000: np.); the subordinate clause is rendered in a smaller, black, typeface than the main clause, which comes in upper case light blue italics.
53 Cf. "Corrigenda," Ware 2000: np., inside back cover; they are signed by the author.

mention Jimmy's name, for it is consistently written in imperatives. It seems to address Jimmy, who is on the plane, and among the graphic enhancements to the instructions, we even find a small image of him in a round framing. Then again, through its avoidance of proper names and addresses, the text-image prompts the readers to empathize with Jimmy and to look at the zoetrope through Jimmy's eyes. Like him, they must feel coerced and alter-determined when they read: "Don't touch the person next to you, or yourself, or mom. *No!* Pay close attention to the woman's instructioning – back to business. Class passengers – cut out – cut out of paper like before. *Come on!* [...]" (Ware 2000, "Memorize all instructions," np.).

Last but not least, readers may be asked to physically take part in the perception of the characters' story world. On their quest for a new vanishing point in *La 2,333e dimension* (2004), Marc-Antoine Mathieu's *Prisoner of Dreams*, Julius Corentin Acquefacques, and his roommate Hilarion Ozéclat make the

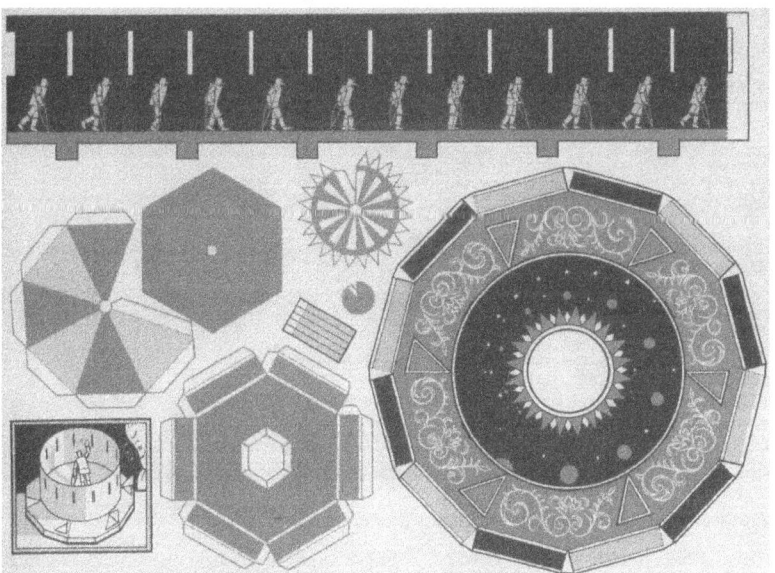

Fig. 3.19: Ware 2000: np., zoetrope cut-out (text-image-reader appeal)

acquaintance of Dédé alias Dilbert Dugommier, the "director for the distribution of diverse *décors*" (sceneries figuring in comics panels). Dugommier is shown in a POV image as he advises the protagonists to put on 3-D frames in order to avoid a "headache" in his strangely other-dimensional world (Fig. 3.20). Glued inside the panel in which the director's hand is shown to reach out, we find a physical set of 3-D frames to be donned to look at the anaglyph 3-D images of this episode without a headache and to perceive the story world as three-dimensional.⁵⁴ The image is composed in such a way that readers have the impression that Dugommier hands them the glasses in person.

All of the examples given in this section display the authors' deliberate use of metalepsis, a transgression of ontological levels from within the narrative. Generally, metalepses are part of *structural performativity*, that is textual strategies and structures serving the simulation of corporeality, sensory presence, or event-like enactment (*ereignishaftem Vollzug*, Häsner et al. 2011: 83). "Metalepses are a highly artificial tool for the simulation or suggestion of presence; they display the narrating and narrated world as a continuum in which immediate interaction between author, character, and reader is possible." "[T]he text," or as in this case the image-text, "underscores its own mediality and enacts what it is talking about; thus, it 'does' what is not subsumable under its explicit propositional content by going beyond and counteracting it" (ibid. 83–84). Through the offer of the physical 3-D glasses, the author simulates the physical presence of his readers in the story world since they literally see the action through the same (3-D) 'eyes' as Julius and Hilarion.

Fig. 3.20: Mathieu 2004: 47, physical 3-D frames (metalepsis)

With the cut-out pattern/instructions, the author of *Jimmy Corrigan* interrupts the preceding image sequence in favor of an image whose ontological status is different from the status of a narrative panel. Although the text-image of the cut-out is a representation and not a physical object like the 3-D frames in *La 2,333e*

---

54 Alan Moore and Kevin O'Neill employ the same device in the ending of *The League of Extraordinary Gentlemen: Black Dossier* (2007).

dimension, its salient pictorial status simulates the readers' presence in Jimmy's (story)world by giving them the (temporary) feeling that they literally *are* Jimmy, as he is looking at the cut-out pattern or as he is reading the instructions. Likewise, the life-sized hands in *Maus* and *Fun Home*, holding the pages of the graphic novel or the photograph, simulate the physical presence of the reader-observers and their joining of gazes with the authors'.

To conclude, let me come back to the 3-D episode in Mathieu's *La 2,333e dimension*. The previous story to this episode consists in Julius's 'dreaming' – as in all of the Julius Corentin Acquefacques stories, it is always uncertain if the protagonist is actually waking or dreaming – that he is guilty of losing the vanishing point, which provides the third dimension to his comics universe (cf. Mathieu 2004: 11–16). Respectively, in the following episodes, the characters and sceneries are drawn as two-dimensionally flat. When Julius and Hilarion encounter "Dédé" Dilbert Dugommier, the administrator of comics image sceneries, the latter explains to them that his surname "Dédé" also is "2D" or "2 dés" ("two dice" – Dugommier is a kind of mock demiurge of the comics universe, rolling the dice). "2D" again is a pun on two-dimensionality, which, at first glance, seems to jar with the three-dimensionality of Dugommier's universe, seen through 3-D frames. In his highly self-referential Acquefacques series, and in *La 2,333e dimension* in particular, Mathieu seems to point out that comics images are actually two-dimensional and that readers add the third dimension subconsciously, in their imagination. By seeing the world from the demiurge's (here: Julius and Hilarion's) vantage point, readers using the 3-D frames suddenly become aware of the actual two-dimensionality of comics images. Thus, the physical perception experience of three-dimensionality conjures up the third dimension as "presence and, respectively, co-presence" to two-dimensionality (Häsner et al. 2011: 83).

3.3.4.6 Multiplicity of References to Texts/Media

As for multimedial texts in general, the differentiation between intra- and intermedial references in such works collapses. Also, it depends, first and foremost, on the status I assign them: graphic novels, as in this case, can be looked at as 'texts' (in a conventional, restricted sense),[55] as media, or as iconotexts.[56] The manifold refer-

---

[55] I reject the broader definition of the term 'text' since this would render the concept of intermediality useless (cf. Rajewsky 2002: 52–53).
[56] "[I]conotext refers to an artifact in which the verbal and the visual signs mingle to produce rhetoric that depends on the co-presence of words and images" (Wagner 1996: 16).

ences to Batman in Frank Miller's *The Dark Knight Returns* (Miller 1986: 1–4), for example, or Moore and Gibbons' parody of the superhero/vigilante tradition in *Watchmen* are intramedial references. Yet when *Watchmen* quotes from St. John's Revelation, from Job and Isaiah, Nietzsche, from Shelley's Ozymandias poem, and from song lyrics by Dylan and John Cale, it is difficult to decide whether these references are intramedial (here: intertextual) or intermedial.[57]

Fun Home, as a particular case, is saturated with references to single works of high modernist and other twentieth-century verbal literature, particularly to Joyce's *Ulysses* and Proust's *Recherche*, but also to children's literature, Camus, Wilde, Fitzgerald, etc., as well as to literature as a communicative system (cf. Rajewsky 2002: 65). Watson calls *Fun Home* "an autobiographical Künstlerroman, [which] glossed Joyce's Portrait of the Artist, with Stephen Dedalus as one alter ego for Alison" (Watson 2008; 30; cf. Freedman 2009: 130). *Fun Home*'s specificity lies in that its multiple references (not just the ones to modernist fiction or poetry) involve the panel design, the speech balloons, and the narratorial captions, that is the graphic novel as a complex whole. In many instances, the literary works are shown as concrete objects: books, print excerpts, or single pages are *images drawn* and not only verbally referred to. Apart from literature, *Fun Home* refers to handwritten and typed letters, newspaper pages, diaries, notes, advertisements, maps, and, above all, photographs, which are more realistically drawn than the characters and the setting.[58] Critics like Jan Baetens and Hugo Frey hold that "[i]n the graphic novel, there is a discrete but irrefutable tendency to include photographic material next to drawn images [as in *Maus* or *Le photographe*]" (Baetens/Frey 2015: 140). The representations of these media alter the reception of the novel as a multimedial text: in the reception process, the literary and non-literary texts or media gain in complexity and semiotic dynamics: they become text-images involving the gutters, captions,

---

57 Freedman, who uses 'comics' as an "umbrella term" and calls 'graphic novel' a comic book format, speaks of a "paucity of vocabulary for discussing hybrid languages of text and image" (Freedman 2011: 42).

58 This does not suggest that the drawn photographs were reproduced from historical originals nor that they should be considered more authentic than print or handwriting: see Watson for the way Bechdel herself staged the poses of all the characters in the photographs before drawing them (cf. Watson 2008: 36–37, Chute 2010: 200–203). Against an alleged dominance of the photograph in terms of realism speaks the fact that Bechdel often inserts framed captions in the respective panels which cover up parts of the photographs (cf. Bechdel 2006: 100–101 and 120). A similar strategy is used for literary print excerpts (ibid., 222, 226 and 228).

speech balloons, and the panel images.⁵⁹ What is clearly modernist about *Fun Home* is that its text-images require to be looked at and read, construed, like some surrealist paintings by René Magritte – particularly *La trahison des images* (1929), in the sense of 'This is not a text/photo/letter...' (but an image thereof).⁶⁰ Looking at a drawn photograph of Alison or Bruce, for example, urges the observer to recall that it is not Alison nor Bruce but a representation of them in a specific medium. Bechdel uses text-images to foreground representation as if she wanted to say that the media – photographs and literature above all – and not her childhood memories are what is most real to her in the process of (re)constructing Bruce's and her own identity: in one instance, she says that her parents "are most real to [her] in fictional terms" (Bechdel 2006: 67). In this respect, Bechdel's text-

---

59 W.J.T. Mitchell uses the term "imagetext," based on the very general and deconstructivist premises that the textual is in the visual and vice versa (Mitchell 2009: 116–123). – Manfred Pfister divides works in which text is embedded in the image into three categories: a) works in which text functions as index, like tags or captions; b) in which text is part of the pictorial fiction, e.g. still-lives with books whose titles can be read; c) in which text is "no longer motivated in terms of a pictorial fiction – either because there is no fiction which would or could sustain them, or because they problematize or subvert the fiction. Thus unsustained by representational conventions, letters, words, texts or even books turn into elements of the pictorial medium and become one with its other elements [...]" (Pfister 1993: 323). Pfister calls this third category 'word-image' (ibid., 322). – *Fun Home* fits in all three categories: in a) because every comic book uses captions or indices like tags; in b) because the visual representation of literature and other printed text is part of the 'fiction' and relevant for the plot; and c) when looking at the panel, for example, showing a half-page of *Ulysses* (Bechdel 2006: 226), we are not supposed to read the text as if it were the plot of *Fun Home*. Instead, through the inserted caption, Bruce's hand-written annotation in the margin, and Alison's comments in the gutter we are brought to read it as a biographic *text-image* of Bruce and of Alison, the latter of whom is struggling with this text like she struggles with her father and his sexual orientation. We experience a similar struggle in our act of reading, which is slowed down because of the conflicting aesthetic (cf. *aisthesis*, perception) and discursive modalities of writing. The print of the *Ulysses* page does not function as discourse but as an image, as a "writing-image [Schrift/Bild]," as Daniela Dröscher calls it (Dröscher 2007: 216). – In 1990, Wilhelm Föckersperger created a drawing that shows Roland Barthes' book *L'empire des signes* (1970) standing up and half open, showing on the left a splash image of a hand drawing a Japanese sign and on the right a page of print (cf. Föckersperger 1993: 317). The drawing is so realistic that we might mistake it for a photograph. Föckersperger writes that both the image and the printed text of Barthes' book have changed their semiotic status through the drawing (ibid., 318). As in Föckersperger's drawing, literary texts and images of literature in *Fun Home* gain in semiotic dynamics and become text-images: texts to be read like and through images – and images to be read like and through texts.
60 "René Magritte stated in his programmatic picture essay 'Les mots et les images' (1929) that 'in a painting, words are of the same substance as images;' and Joan Miró refused to make any distinction whatsoever between painting and poetry" (Pfister 1993: 323).

images may also qualify as biographic, and the whole novel as self-referential or metafictional.[61]

In *Arkham Asylum*, Morrison and McKean use multiple references differently from Bechdel: besides the epigraphic quote from chapter VI in Lewis Carroll's *Alice's Adventures in Wonderland* (1865), in which Alice discusses madness with the Cheshire Cat, the authors use an alias of the (mad) Hatter, Jervis Tetch, as a character in the main plot, who Batman sees or hallucinates when he arrives at Arkham Asylum (Fig. 3.21).

Fig. 3.21: Morrison/McKean 2004: np., intertextual/intermedial reference

By the words Tetch says to Batman, by the design of the splash containing the epigraph, and by the design and behavior of the characters, numerous cross-references to Carroll's *magnum opus* are installed, often with playfully parodic twists.[62] In *Arkham Asylum*, therefore, like in *Fun Home*, textual and pictorial

---

[61] Cf. Wolf's broader definition of metafiction (Wolf 1993: 228). Watson calls *Fun Home* an "autobiographical meta-story" (Watson 2008: 36).
[62] For example, when Alice is referred to as a 'mad blond bitch,' Tetch's resemblance with the hookah-smoking caterpillar from ch. V in *Alice's Adventures in Wonderland*, the two Arkham chimneys from the epigraph referring to the chimneys of the March Hare's house and to Batman's ears when he confronts Tetch (cf. Morrison/McKean 1989: np.).

elements cross-refer to each other and increase the complexity of the respective work, which has also been referred to as a 'media mix.'[63] However, since in *Arkham Asylum* the image clearly dominates the text, I would call this reference network *image-texts* (rather than text-images, as in Bechdel).

3.3.4.7 Self-Referential Narration and Metafictional Devices

"Adult comics and graphic novels are a form that are especially capable of making meta-commentary and reflexive references to existing titles, creators, and even whole genres" (Baetens/Frey 2015: 99). *Maus*, the historical paragon of metafictionality among graphic novels, is at least as much a book about Art's anxiety of making "a comic strip" about this monstrous subject[64] as it is about Vladek Spiegelman's WWII ordeal. Besides having been among the first graphic novels, *avant la lettre*, it has been the first specimen of a genre that today is called graphic memoir or (auto)biography. Herein, it resembles *Slaughterhouse Five* (1969), in which the author-narrator Kurt Vonnegut struggles with his writing of an autobiographic anti-war book. Also, and not least because of their play with genres, *Maus* and *Slaughterhouse Five* are to be counted among the experimentally postmodern works of literature at the time of their publication.

If I decided to treat in this section "self-referential narration" next to "metafictional devices," this is because self-referentiality implies either a framed narrative structure (including a narrator) or a narrating character thematizing
a) statements made and images drawn as linguistic and pictorial expressions,
b) the medium of comics, or
c) issues relating to the graphic novel (or its making) we are reading.

I do not agree with the claim that narrators are more present in graphic novels than in traditional comic books (cf. Baetens/Frey 2015: 10). This may be true for

---

63 Brooker (2000) writes: "McKean's paintings [...] mix media – pencil sketches, photographs, collages of lace, hessian and nails" (qtd. in Crutcher 2011: 63). Karen Berger remarks that it was McKean's "expert mix of media – painting, photography, sculpture, assemblage of odd objects – that created such a resonant and powerful look to this haunting and horrific tale" ("Changing the Face of Comics." Morrison/McKean 2004, afterword, np.).
64 "I feel so inadequate trying to reconstruct a reality that was worse than my darkest dreams. [...] There's so much I'll never be able to understand or visualize. I mean, reality is too *complex* for comics... So much has to be left out or distorted" (Spiegelman 2003: 176; emphasis in original). In book II, Art says to his "shrink": "No matter what I accomplish, it doesn't seem like much compared to surviving Auschwitz," ibid., 204); Art blames himself for being the real survivor, see 'shrink episode,' ibid., 199–206, and Art's confession to Françoise: "[...] but I somehow wish I had been in Auschwitz with my parents so I could really know what they lived through! ... I guess it's *some* kind of guilt about having had an easier life than they did" (ibid. 176; emphasis in the original).

some graphic memoirs but certainly not for all. – Verbal-narratorial script, by contrast, is often minimalistic if not completely absent. Apart from that, the mere existence of narratorial script is not sufficient to postulate a narrator. As I shall explain below, unless a narrator is marked as such, unless it possesses a proper spatio-temporal identity apart from the intradiegetic story, we are dealing with a narrating character rather than a narrator (see chapters 4.1, 4.2, and 4.5). In this sense, it is legitimate to postulate a narrator in *Maus*, whose frame narrative, in which Art makes his father retell his war experiences, contains many self-referential episodes thematizing Art's book in the making or cartooning in general (cf. Spiegelman 2003: 14, 25, 134–135, 171–172, 176 and 205–207). Apart from that, *Maus I* features an explicit intramedial reference to Spiegelman's previously published comic "Prisoner on the Hell Planet. A Case History."[65] This comic in the comic or mise en abyme (re)tells Art's mother's suicide and its aftermath. In this piece of graphic short fiction, Art wears concentration camp clothes, which represent the multifaceted guilt he feels towards his mother.[66] At the end of the episode, Art is put into prison where he bothers his fellow inmates with his nightly soliloquies addressed to his dead mother, for whose suicide he feels responsible.

Moore and Gibbons' *Watchmen* features a gothic pirate mise en abyme which parabolically mirrors the Cold War scare and the chain of events of the main plot.[67] In one of the many subplots, Bernie, a young black male, reads the comic book "Tales of the Black Freighter," given to him by the news vendor Bernhard, at whose stand Bernie hangs out. In the mise en abyme, a marooned castaway tries to return to his family to warn them of the coming of the "Black Freighter," a phantom pirate ship and an allegory of the acutely feared nuclear WWIII. The Black Freighter panels are marked by cross-hatching and by captions framed in the form of old parchments and figure simultaneously with the panels of the main plot and the subplots into which they segue at times in the form of graphic matches. The Black Freighter comic mirrors the main plot once more in that it was written by the fictional character Max Shea, who figures in one of the subplots and who is staying on an unknown island with the artist Hira Manish. Both of them design the alien monster, which will destroy New

---

[65] Originally published under the same heading in *Short Order Comix* #1, 1973, see Spiegelman 2003: 102–105.
[66] Also, Art feels guilty of being the "real survivor," of exposing Vladek to ridicule in the comic book, and of proving his father wrong through his own success (Spiegelman 2003: 204).
[67] Also see Douglas Wolk's account of the plot, text, and image complexity of *Watchmen* (Wolk 2007: 237–245).

York City near the end of *Watchmen*. Like his mise en abyme character, the castaway, Moore and Gibbons' author-character Shea is to die on board a black ship (cf. Moore/Gibbons 2008, ch. X, 17–18). Thus, plots and mise en abyme function like a fun house, in which mirrors mirror each other and capture the observer in their maze of reflections.

If the term 'graphic novel' is neither a mere salability label created for marketing purposes nor simply a portmanteau term for unclassifiable works of verbal and pictorial storytelling, it may be understood as a prototype category in the sense of what John Taylor called 'prototype-as-subcategory' (Taylor 2003: 64, qtd. in Hempfer 2010: 22). The main or superordinate category here would be books of comics (as opposed to strips or cartoons, see Fig. 3.2), of which one core feature can be defined as "'a sequence of discrete, juxtaposed pictures that comprise a narrative, either in their own right or when combined with text'" (Hayman/Pratt 2005: 423), the other core category being complexity.

The seven complexity scales above (Fig. 3.5) represent distinctive features (or specifications) and allow not only the assignment of a graphic work to an exclusive category ('graphic novel and not comic book' or vice versa) but also an assessment by degree of graphic works in terms of affiliation or resemblance ('rather/not a traditional comic book/graphic novel'). The gradation works on two levels: horizontally, on the level of the single parameter (in terms of 'more or less,' e.g. multireferential use of color), as well as vertically, in the sum of all the parameters. For example, in the case of David Prudhomme's *Rébétiko* (2009), there would be no parameter score mark at the right end of the scale. Thus, in the sum, *Rébétiko* lacks the complexity of a graphic novel and rather seems to be a lengthy traditional comic book. Shaun Tan's *The Arrival* (2006), in contrast, despite its objective absence of text, scores several times on the right end of the scale because of its multilayered plot, meaning-enhancing panel designs, multireferential use of color, and its multiplicity of references to other texts or media (e.g. to feature films and photographs). It bears closer resemblance to a graphic novel than to a traditional comic book (or picture book, for that matter) and could therefore be called a specific type of or a *silent* graphic novel.

3.3.5 A Short Parenthesis on Autobiography

Before closing this chapter, let me open a parenthesis on autobiographic writing in the context of classical vs. prototypical categories. I hold that a prototypical approach would solve major problems in the controversial debate about autobiography as a genre. In his paper "Autobiography as Authenticity," the Canadian comics expert, scholar, and translator of seminal works on comics, Bart Beaty, comments on Philippe Lejeune's definition of 'autobiography',[68] saying that

> the policing of the boundaries of autobiography in relation to other literary forms has become a major undertaking. Indeed, it is fair to say that the study of autobiography is dominated by inquiries into the particular traits of autobiography and comparisons between autobiography and other literary forms. (Beaty 2009: 227)

A few lines later, Beaty quotes Paul de Man, who commented on this kind of predicament in 1979, saying that one problem in this struggle is "the attempt to define and to treat autobiography as if it were a literary genre among others."[69] Of course, de Man did not have prototypical categories in mind – his target was the supposedly authentic self (which turns out to be an allegory of reading). The general struggle concerning "particular traits of autobiography" is an obvious result of the fact that autobiography has been conceived as a historical text group (one literary genre among others) instead of as a way of writing or mode (and a historical invariant, see above). In this respect, another statement of de Man's from the same 1979 paper reads as a mirror of a typical confusion in more than just the field of comics:

> By making autobiography into a genre, one elevates it above the literary status of mere reportage, chronicle, or memoir and gives it a place, albeit a modest one, among the canonical hierarchies of the major literary genres. This does not go without some embarrassment, since compared to tragedy, or epic, or lyric poetry, autobiography always looks slightly disreputable and self-indulgent in a way that may be symptomatic of its incompatibility with the monumental dignity of aesthetic values.... Empirically as well as theoretically, autobiography lends itself poorly to generic definition; each specific instance seems to be an exception to the norm [...] (de Man 1979: 919–920)

Reportage, chronicle, or memoir should be treated as historical text groups to be assigned to more than just one (prototypical) category, for example as a type of graphic novel or of fictional or non-fictional narrative texts (see chapter 3.3.3, Fig. 3.2). The fact that (not only) for de Man, "autobiography lends itself poorly to generic definition [because] each specific instance seems to be an exception to the norm" is a diagnosis of the problems to be had with classical categories, in which

---

[68] "Retrospective prose narrative written by a real person concerning his own existence, where the focus is his individual life, in particular the story of his personality" (Philippe Lejeune, *On Autobiography*, 1989: 4, qtd. in Beaty 2009: 227).

[69] Beaty indirectly quotes de Man from William C. Spengemann, *The Forms of Autobiography* (1980: 207).

boundaries are clear and the features or attributes perfectly correlated. In order to account for the numerous exceptions to the norm – considering besides that in many fields, norms now have become generally questionable – flexible categories are needed that allow for overlap and non-correlation of attributes. In the context of graphic narratives, I observe two hypes of (autobio)graphic writing: the first starting in the 1990s and the second starting in 2000 (cf. Beaty 2009: 227). In the 1990s, those were usually graphic (short) stories or episodes from the life of an author-protagonist (with Harvey Pekar's stories as a role model); from 2000 on, autobiographic writing has adopted a distinctly long – call it novel – form, published not only by the so-called indies (or what has survived of them) but by major publishing houses, often unserialized and in book format.

As can be seen from this highly specific context, autobiographic writing comes in historical groups or forms, the attributes of which will overlap and vary at the same time, according to the respective group. Some comics experts have called the latter group of autobiographic writing graphic memoirs – and respectively, I call the specimens from the 1990s graphic short fiction (Pekar and others).

Beaty, from whose diagnosis of the genre problem I started out, clearly states the inherent predicament of conceiving 'autobiography' in classical categories, yet he does not propose a convincing solution or approach to cope with it. Instead, he brings up examples of autobiographic comics, among others Marjane Satrapi's *Persepolis*, to state that

> her work is by no means normative. The visual aspects of autobiographical approaches within contemporary European comics are remarkably heterogenous and plural despite evidence of considerable overlap within the thematics of the movement. Moreover, because the narrative content of so many autobiographical comics is roughly analogous, it is primarily through the process of rendering and visualization that these works differ from each other. (Beaty 2009: 232)

Viewed from the angle of prototypical categories, the above statement of fact is hardly surprising. Yet Beaty underscores the importance of the different means of visualization, which are of cardinal importance. It has already been mentioned that the pictorial elements, and particularly the way words relate to images, are a phenomenon that critics of single works have been paying closer attention to. Therefore, most of my typology parameters concern the ways words and images cross-refer to each other – in similar, yet different (prototypical) ways.

3.4 Critical Approaches to Comics and Graphic Novels

The preceding section has been about the classification of the graphic novel as a particular (proto)type of books of comics and, on the next superordinate level, of graphic narratives. Now the focus will be on how graphic novels (or, put simply, complex comics) produce meaning on both the verbal *and* the pictorial plane. That comics is a mixed or 'hybrid' medium deploying verbal and pictorial signs is a truism; and as I do not intend to reinvent the wheel, I shall not rehash comics theory. Besides, a lot of what has been written in terms of comics theory is rather heterogeneous in nature. Thus, Neil Cohn's *The Visual Language of Comics: Introduction to the Structure and Cognition of Sequential Images* (2013), strictly speaking, is not even a book on comics but an investigation of the processing of silent narrative images, inspired by linguistics (morphology) and cognitive science. Cohn, it must be noted, deliberately excludes the verbal track from a medial configuration the specificity of which, after all, lies in its use of both text *and* sequential images.[70] That cognitive aspects have been touched upon in diverse approaches, especially the perception or reception process, is neither unusual nor dubious in principle. How problematic this approach may be will become evident in the following chapters.

I intend to assess, as roughly as possible and as precisely as necessary, major critical approaches
- that look at comics and graphic novels primarily as aesthetic, not scientific, objects (as does Cohn)
- and their potential to account for *complex* forms or ways of meaning production. This paradigm is, of course, closely tied to reading competence, or the degree of comics literacy; for as with verbal narratives, untrained readers are likely to overlook a lot in graphic novels.

Since "comics criticism is still a burgeoning rather than an established field for scholarship" (Miodrag 2013: 250), I shall start with the 'godfathers' of comics theory, the most cited and broadly accepted practitioners of the medium before dealing with more recent approaches of comics theory.

---

[70] In fact, Cohn (2013) could adapt his approach to cave drawings as well as to sign language, as he himself explains in the introductory chapter. He probably chose 'comics' because it has been a very popular subject of study in the last ten years. The comics images or image sequences he refers to, in addition to their being wordless, have been taken mainly from adventure and fantasy comics and appear as obviously simplistic. The manipulation of some single sequences, on the example of which Cohn demonstrates diverse aspects of image processing, would prove pointless, if not impossible, with sequences from complex graphic novels like Chris Ware's *Jimmy Corrigan* or *Building Stories* (in addition to the fact that his approach would not be able to account for the word-image connections).

3.4.1 Will Eisner's Practical Sequentiality

Will Eisner (1917–2005) is famous for his 'novel' *A Contract with God* (1978) – which is broadly viewed as the first graphic novel (see ch. 2.2) – and his urban crime-fighter series *The Spirit* (1940–1952). According to the title of his standard work of comics theory, *Comics and Sequential Art* (1985, re-edited and updated posthumously in 2008), Eisner conceives of graphic narratives as a sequence of framed images: "Critical to the success of a visual narrative is the ability to convey time" (Eisner 2008: 24). His understanding that in comics, time "is an essential structural element" (ibid.), is essentialist and relies on classical categories. However, his concept of time, which is so central in his approach, remains rather vague; nowhere does he expound on it, be it in terms of story (or fictive) time, discourse (or reading) time, or time as a concept or additive construct in the meaning building process, as it happens in the mind of the readers (cf. Cohn 2010: 136).

Above all, Eisner gives overt priority to the image: comics are first and foremost visual. This can be seen in the importance he attributes to lettering "as an extension of the imagery" (ibid. 2) and letters as "devised out of images" (ibid. 8) – two highly contentious statements anticipating Scott McCloud's equation of the visual and verbal sign. Basically everything in Eisner is geared toward visuality: "the viewer's response to a given scene is influenced by his position as a spectator" (ibid. 92), and at the end of *Comics and Sequential Art*'s second chapter ("Imagery"), I read, in big red capitals: "It is possible to tell a story through imagery alone without the help of words" (ibid. 10). Although there are silent works of genius among graphic novels and their forerunners, there is simply no accounting for verbal text in Eisner's book, everything is seen in terms of image/imagery: words, letters, lettering, speech balloons, frames, characters, mise en scène, etc. (cf. Miodrag 2013: 61). *Comics and Sequential Art* reads like a mindful, instructional and thoroughly illustrated handbook for future comics artists or students of comics, providing most of the basic terms of the 'comics lexicon' – a feature characteristic as well of McCloud's *Understanding Comics* (1993), which by now has been the most read and quoted comics manual.

3.4.2 Scott McCloud's (Mis)Understanding of Comics

Like Eisner, McCloud (*1960) is a practitioner and essentialist, influenced, on the surface, by the semiotic theories from the 1960s to the 1980s. The essentialist basis of *Understanding Comics* (1993, reissued in 1994) is Eisner's notion of comics as sequential art (1994: 5). McCloud's "comprehensive theory of the creative process and its implications for comics and for art in general" (ibid., "Introduction") and, more concretely, his definition of comics as "[j]uxtaposed pictorial and other images in deliberate sequence, intended to convey information and/or to produce an aesthetic response in the viewer," obviously excludes one type of comic art: the single-panel cartoon, as he admits (ibid. 20). This exclusion could easily be avoided, as shown above, with prototypical categories (see ch. 3.3.3). Although cartoons come in single panels, they imply a narrative substrate[71] and may be read as abridged strips.[72] According to the prototypical categories elaborated on above (Fig. 3.2), they fall under the graphic narratives (so there is no contradiction or aporia). The exclusion problem in McCloud emerges because of an essentialist definition relying on one core feature (sequential images) instead of a number of graded core and peripheral features, through which cartoons would fall into the same category as comic strips or books – although they would not have an equal status (see above, chapter 3.3.4). The solution McCloud proposes is typical of classical category use: for single-panel cartoons, he creates a new category, 'comic art' (ibid. 20), which is superfluous and must in turn remain rather empty – for what else would fall under comic art if comics are not art in the first place?

For McCloud, meaning is built from sequential images through transition, the way readers connect one panel to the following (or rather the preceding, as will be shown). There are, in sum, six kinds of transition according to his taxonomy, the most pertinent being the moment-to-moment and aspect-to-aspect

---

[71] "[...] an isolated image can be intrinsically narrative" (Groensteen 2007: 106). Recently, Groensteen modified this statement: "No longer: *Can a single image [...] contain a story*, but instead: *how does the single image produce meaning*" (2013: ch. 2, np.) Harry Morgan writes that he "recognize[s] the narrative potential in an isolated image where events before or after (the cause or the effect) can be deduced from the scene that is shown" (Morgan 2003: 41, qtd. in Groensteen 2013: ch. 2, np.). In his somewhat polemic critique of McCloud, John Holbo states that a single-panel cartoon is essentially narrative in style: single panels can depict more than one single moment – as in what Hatfield calls a "synchronistic panel" (Hatfield 2005: 53–56). According to Holbo, McCloud contradicts himself by using a synchronistic panel as an example of "time frames" (McCloud 1994: 94 and 95, panel #1). Holbo demonstrates that a single panel may imply gutters or, generally, a sequential order of things (Holbo 2012: 6–11). Similarly, Pascal Lefèvre holds that a single panel may consist "of several panels or frames" and that it may "contain a representation of a cause and an effect" (Lefèvre 2000: np.). Thomas E. Wartenberg writes that "an adequate definition of comics will have to include both single- and multiple-panel comics within a single framework" (Wartenberg 2012: 88).

[72] Cf. Morgan 2003: 41, qtd. in Groensteen 2013: ch. 2, np.

transitions.[73] To make transition happen, McCloud invokes 'closure' (ibid. 64–69), "the phenomenon of observing the parts but perceiving the whole" (ibid. 63). In other words: the 'filling of the gap between the single (sequential) images with meaning' is actively brought about by the readers (or "audience," as he calls them, ibid. 65) in the reading process. McCloud's vocabulary, as a matter of fact, is highly metaphorical and geared toward visuality, similarly to Eisner's (see above). McCloud also gives priority to the visual when he invokes the "visual iconography," which he calls "the vocabulary of comics, [and] closure its grammar" (ibid. 67).

In *Reinventing Comics* (2000), the follow-up to *Understanding Comics*, he couches his sequentiality argument in the conceptual metaphor – or metaphorical concept – of the "temporal map," which he understands as the "essence of comics" (McCloud 2000: 206–207). Neil Cohn, who broadly criticizes McCloud's concepts and terminology, points out that temporal mapping, a more radical version of transitions, implies that "temporality overarch[es] across all meaning" and is therefore unable to account for "temporally ambiguous panel relationships" as they are found, for example, in subject-to-subject and aspect-to-aspect transitions (Cohn 2010: 130). With this too laconically defined concept, implying that all transitions signal shifts in time, McCloud thus contradicts his own theorem of panel transition (cf. Miodrag 2013: 117).

There is another basic aporia inherent in temporal mapping: analyzing McCloud's theory through the lenses of semiotics and cognitive psychology, Cohn argues that in panels, there are no representations of time, objects, people, surroundings, etc. but *concepts* of these: "[...] meaning is entirely conceptual" (ibid. 133).

> Panels as units do not stand for moments or durations in fictive time, but direct attention to depictions of 'event states' [...] *from which* a sense of time is derived. Images are just significations made meaningful through cognitively based concepts [...] that each panel represents a moment or duration in time is merely an illusion, cast by the unconscious understanding of events and their parts. (ibid. 134, italics in the original)

Purporting to explicate a process of meaning making, McCloud falls into the trap of essentialism with his definitions and descriptions of what comics *are*, that is panels or sequential images – instead of focusing, for example, on what the readers' minds do when they connect them. After all, I agree with Hannah

---

[73] Cf. McCloud 1994: 70–72. In fact, the four remaining types of transition are not convincingly presented and may be subsumed under these two: thus, the action-to-action type may fall under moment-to-moment transitions, and the subject-to-subject, scene-to-scene, and the non-sequitur may be counted among aspect-to-aspect transitions. Cohn also criticized various aspects of these transition types (Cohn 2010: 129–130).

Miodrag that McCloud's temporal mapping falls short of defining the whole medium of comics (2013: 140), if it is not erroneous at the very basis.

In addition, there is an inherent misconception in the sequentiality theorem[74]: closure, for McCloud, is the essential feature in the reception process ("comics *is* closure," ibid. 67); the reader, he goes on to say, is the comics artist's "partner in crime" (ibid. 68): "Reader's deliberate, voluntary closure is comics' primary means of simulating time and motion" (ibid. 69). From today's standpoint, however, this seems rather simplistic. Cohn shows that "sequential image comprehension must be thought of as the union of conceptual information that is grouped via unconscious hierarchic structures in the mind. [...] the processes guiding sequential image comprehension remain inaccessible to conscious awareness" (Cohn 2010: 128).[75] From Cohn's vantage point, McCloud's "partner in crime" is an inappropriate metaphor and his closure theory erroneous at the basis:

> If closure occurs "in the gaps between the panels" then how does it work if a reader cannot make such a connection until the second panel is reached? That is, the gap cannot be filled unless it has already been passed over, making closure an additive inference that occurs at panels, not between them. (2010: 135)

Closure, says Cohn, is mostly achieved through indexicality in the panels, and he adds that "the gutter does not provide any meaning – the content of the panels and their union does" (ibid. 136). So, nothing actually 'happens' in the gutter. – Cohn's approach to the comprehension of sequential images may be very specific, yet it is thoroughly grounded in theory and thus allows us to reevaluate a broadly accepted work like McCloud's and to reveal its basic weaknesses – stemming, not least, from a clearly essentialist approach, classical categories, and a rather unreflected use of otherwise theoretically loaded terms.

With its claim to be a "comprehensive theory," *Understanding Comics* appears as structurally deficient and functionally obsolete. It cannot account for the complexity of graphic narratives, last but not least because of its notion of icons/iconi-

---

[74] That McCloud's essentialist view on sequentiality is rather problematic – not only with respect to complex graphic narratives – has been brought up, directly or indirectly, by Groensteen 2007/2013, Hatfield 2005, Miodrag 2013 (all discussed below).

[75] Cohn demonstrates the mental 'chunking' of panels by the aid of minimal sequences. This chunking may result in different meaning constructions (or interpretations) because panel sequences may be read as spatial or temporal chunks (cf. 2010: 141). For McCloud, in contrast, all chunks are temporal, as he says, reading comics is "moving through time" (McCloud 2000: 206). Arguing from cognitive psychology, Cohn deals the final blow to McCloud's sequentiality 'theory': "the meaning garnered for that 'chunking' emerges from the conceptual content of the representation itself – not from some overarching default principle like 'space = time', 'panels = moments', [or] 'closure' " (ibid. 142).

city. McCloud uses 'icon' as a "catch-all, interchangeably used to describe words and images" (Miodrag 2013: 149), and symbols, which he considers "one category of icon" (McCloud 1994: 27). Umberto Eco wrote as early as in 1975 that it would be better to get rid of iconic signs altogether: "It is a collection of phenomena bundled together under an all-purpose label [...]."[76] However, McCloud reintroduces a distinction between pictorial and non-pictorial icons with respect to meaning making: The meaning of the former is "fluid and variable," the meaning of words is "fixed and absolute" (ibid. 28). I would object that although commonly used symbols may be relatively fixed (yet not absolute), to assert a general fixedness and absoluteness with respect to words and text, however, is untenable because it simply ignores much of what has been written in the history of philosophy about writing and the instability of meaning.

McCloud postulates that through sheer abstraction from a realistic image, we eventually arrive at the verbal sign (Fig. 3.22):

Fig. 3.22: McCloud 1994: 48, image-word continuum

In McCloud's continuum, words are "the ultimate abstraction" (ibid. 47) and the verbal sign 'ultimately' is an icon. It is said, in other words, that the difference between writing and drawing, text and image, is just a matter of degree and that words basically function like images ("But just how 'different' are they?", McCloud 1994: 47). This is why McCloud's "theory" cannot account for complex and specific meaning production in comics, which is induced by exactly the different ways these codes signify. In fact: when words and images collapse, where would be the specificity of the medium? Would it have to be read like conventional verbal text or like a silent picture book? The distinction McCloud makes that "[p]ictures are **received**" and "writing is **perceived**" does not change the

---

[76] Eco 1976: 216, qtd. in Mitchell 1986: 57. Engl. transl. from *Trattato di semiotica generale*. Milano: Bompiani, 1975.

basic problem involved (McCloud 1994: 49, boldface in original). Eco, in contrast, refers 'perception' to pictorial icons (or images, cf. Eco 1976: 216, qtd. in Mitchell 1986: 58). Hatfield simply argues that the reception/perception distinction does simply not hold since pictures "must be decoded" (Hatfield 2005: 37). Seen from another angle, "McCloud's definition of comics wipes out the importance or need for words from its essence. [...] Perhaps McClouds's definition is a response to the dominance of the verbal sign that saturates large portions of narrative theory" (Lewis 2010: 72).

By asserting that "[w]ords, pictures and other icons are the **vocabulary** of the language called comics" (1994: 47, boldface in original), McCloud pursues an old, mostly semiotic tradition reaching back to the 1950s (Gombrich), 60s, and 70s (Barthes, Goodman, Eco). W.J.T. Mitchell writes that "[t]he commonplace of modern studies of images [...] is that they must be understood as a kind of language [...] images are now regarded as the sort of sign that presents a deceptive appearance of naturalness and transparency" (Mitchell 1986: 8, cf. Groensteen 2007: 9–10). Like the notion of sequentiality, McCloud's language metaphor is doubly misleading: firstly, verbal signifiers do not work by abstraction but by referring to other signifiers and concepts (or ideas); secondly, it is not the language *of* comics that matters for an understanding of meaning production but language *in* comics, in other words: different kinds of text (speech in balloons, captions, sound lettering, etc.), cross-referring not only to other verbal signs but also to images, contributing with the other parameters of comics to a network of signification – I shall expound on this in greater detail below. To really 'understand' the complexity of comics (and not some metaphor of it), I must recognize those cross-references, untangle that web of signification woven among the different types of signifiers.

To conclude: McCloud's *Understanding Comics* as well as its sequel is inadequate to address questions of complex meaning production in graphic narratives. Today, beginner students of comics should preferably use Eisner's *Comics and Sequential Art,* although it is older, to get acquainted with the basics of the comics lexicon (or comics 'shorthand'). In any way, neither Eisner nor McCloud go beyond the technical and the practical – which is not a liability to start with, unless I look at graphic narratives from a systematic or theory-oriented point of view.

3.4.3 Charles Hatfield's Alternatives to Sequentiality

Once the students are familiar with the comics lexicon, they should tackle the next stage of comics expertise by reading Charles Hatfield's seminal *Alternative Comics* (2005), a mixed work of illustrated comics historiography, theory, and case studies. Steeped in solid theoretical groundwork and reflected in its termi-

3.4 Critical Approaches to Comics and Graphic Novels — 93

nology, the most lucid pages about meaning production and reading strategies in comics are found in the second chapter, "An Art of Tensions: The Otherness of Comics Reading" (Hatfield 2005: 32–67).

In contrast to McCloud, who as an essentialist is interested in what comics are at the core, Hatfield (*1965) uses a reader-response approach. His main concern is outlined already at the beginning of chapter two, "What kind of experience is reading comics?" (ibid. 32). From the outset, he wants to account for the complexity of comics in general, and his choice examples are, as the title of his book suggests, either from underground, alternative comics (the forerunners of graphic novels from the 1980s and 90s), and graphic novels 'proper,' not from traditional comic books. In this sense, he says that "we must add several new complexities […] Comic art is composed of several kinds of *tension*,[77] in which various ways of reading […] must be played against each other […] comics readers must call upon different reading strategies […] than they would use in their reading of conventional written text" (ibid. 36). Like several experts (Miodrag, Groensteen, and McCloud, to name but a few), Hatfield sets graphic narratives apart from verbal narratives and with this denies them the (often unreflected) literature label.[78] Whereas McCloud collapses the word/image dichotomy, Hatfield continues to distinguish the functions of words and images because they "still exert a strong centripetal pull on the reading experience. […] The tension between codes is fundamental" (ibid. 37).

In his case studies, he analyzes, for example, multiple layers (as in Chris Ware's experimental graphic short fiction "I Guess") or diegetic and non-diegetic symbols (as in Eric Cartier's *Flip in Paradise*, 1990) – parameters that McCloud's "theory" cannot account for.[79] In addition, Hatfield underscores another fundamental weakness in McCloud's notion of closure and the various types of panel transition connected to it: "Verbal/visual interplay often muddies the pristine categories of transition that McCloud tries to establish […] (moment-to-moment, action to action […])" (ibid. 44). He further writes that "the process of transition-

---

[77] Hatfield distinguishes a total of four types of tension: 1. code vs. code, 2. single image vs. image in series, 3. sequence vs. surface, and 4. text as experience vs. text as object (2005: 36–64).
[78] Aaron Meskin writes that the preponderance of the image precludes the notion of comics as literature. Comics are "autographic" (a term he borrows from Nelson Goodman) because layout is an essential feature: Comics, unlike verbal narratives (novels or short stories) do not allow for forgery since they require "mechanical reproduction from a template or, perhaps, another authentic instance" (Meskin 2009: 231).
[79] I pointed out above that McCloud's collapsing of the word-image dichotomy (including the erroneous issue of abstraction in meaning production) results in the impossibility to account for the complex meaning production and the multiple readings that a work suggests.

ing, or closure, depends not only on the interplay between successive images but also on the interplay of different codes of signification: the verbal as well as the visual" (ibid.).

One central paradigm in this chapter of *Alternative Comics* is the notion of linear and tabular readings of the panels on the page (which is part of the tension between "sequence vs. surface").[80] For Hatfield, a single image is generally embedded in a cluster of images and it functions twofold: as a moment in a sequence of events on the one hand and as a graphic element in an atemporal design on the other (ibid. 48–52). Here, layout comes into play, or the page as "the total design unit" (ibid. 48, not as a physical object). As opposed to the conventional linear reading – or 'z-path/way' (from the last panel of the top tier to the first panel of the following tier and so forth) – the tabular reading may proceed vertically, diagonally, or in completely irregular or fragmentary ways across the page.[81] "Broadly, we may say that comics exploit *format* as a signifier in itself" (ibid. 52). By format, Hatfield understands the way the panels are distributed over the page.

Like Groensteen and Miodrag, for example, Hatfield views comics images not so much from their sequential side but more holistically, as a meaning-generating design element. As another aspect of the "sequence vs. surface" tension, he elaborates on synchronism in comics in the form of the polyptych or split panel and the synchronistic panel (cf. ibid. 52–58). The split and synchronistic panels perfectly exemplify that "time not only elapses between panels but also *within* them" (ibid.).[82] This is one more argument against McCloud's sequentiality concept: from the specific examples of synchronism, "we can see that the image-series alone does not determine timing in comics, for it is possible to have a series of panels in which no time seems to pass, as well as a single panel into which moments, hours, even days, are compressed" (ibid. 58).

Finally, Hatfield expounds on other parameters of meaning production, in which time or seriality is not involved, including different material kinds of text (typeface, size, etc.), drawing styles (like the clear or ratty line), or self-referential devices (ibid. 58–65). In this context, he also points to the growing complexity of comic art and the "long-form comics" in particular, in which such

---

80 The terms linear and tabular are borrowed from Pierre Fresnault-Deruelle (1976).
81 Miodrag describes these ways of reading as "scanning, retracing, and hopping around" (2013: 143).
82 In a split panel or polyptych, one or more figures move over a single continuous background, which in turn may be divided into smaller units by panel borders; at times, they may parse simultaneous actions into a number of frames. The synchronistic panel compares to the split panel, yet there are no panel borders (cf. Hatfield 2005: 52–58).

devices can be put to use to invoke more active reader participation (which is not seldom labeled 'sophistication').

3.4.4 Thierry Groensteen's Visual Arthrology

With the translation and publication of *Système de la bande dessinée* at the University Press of Mississippi (1999, engl. transl. *The System of Comics*, 2007), the work of Thierry Groensteen (*1957) has recently come into a wider focus; not least, this was also due to the limitations (and deficiencies) of Eisner's and McCloud's approaches, of which comics critics have increasingly become aware. The follow-up to this work, *Comics and Narration* (2013), has come out at the same publisher's.[83] Besides Martin Schüwer's *Wie Comics erzählen* (2008), it has been one of the few *recent* academic-systematic monographs in book length. In his follow-up, Groensteen picks up and revises some of his tenets and adds the focalization paradigm, which were not at issue in *System* (see below).

Groensteen conceives of comics as language and calls his approach "semiological" or "semiotic" (2007: 2), whereby he refutes the linguistic/semiotic notion of minimal signifying units (like morphemes or syllables) and concentrates on the comics codes: "the most important codes concern larger units, which are already highly elaborated. In this case, these codes govern the articulation, in time and space, of the units that we call 'panels'" (ibid. 4). In this sense, Groensteen considers the panel the "base unit" (ibid. 5).

Like Eisner and McCloud, he gives primacy to the image: comics is "*a predominantly visual narrative form*" (ibid. 12) – not simply a mix of text and images (ibid. 3). Contrary to the more recent, that is more specific and therefore less comprehensive, approaches, he does not view comics as 'hybrid.' His argument: the multiplicity of narrative forms or "*species*" (a metaphor borrowed from Ricœur) containing no text makes an equal status for text and image "obsolete" (ibid. 8). The logic behind this blanket argument is hard to see, given the gamut of genres and media compared: "novel, film, stage play, but also comics, the photo novel, and – why not? – also ballet and opera" (ibid.). This, I would hold, is making matters a bit too simple. Looking at text as subordinate to the "visual" (or pictorial) codes must reveal itself as deficient with regard to analytic pertinence and efficacy – and Hannah Miodrag's and Martin Schüwer's case studies provide a great amount of evidence to back up this hypothesis.

---

[83] Originally *Bande dessinée et narration: Système de la bande dessinée, tome 2*, 2011.

As opposed to Eisner and McCloud, Groensteen considers essentialist approaches "no doubt doomed to failure" (ibid. 12). Then again, passages like the following read almost as if they were taken out of *Understanding Comics*, the paragon of essentialist approaches:

> What is put on view is always a space that has been divided up, compartmentalized, a collection of juxtaposed frames [...] It demands to be traversed, crossed, glanced at, and analytically deciphered. This moment-to-moment reading does not take a lesser account of the totality of the panoptic field that constitutes the page [...] (ibid. 19)

To start with, Groensteen, like McCloud, holds on to the essentialist notion of sequentiality: "the relational play of a plurality of interdependent images as the unique ontological foundation of comics" (ibid. 17). The principle governing this foundation is "iconic solidarity," which he defines as "interdependent images that, participating in a series, present the double characteristic of being separated [...] and which are plastically and semantically over-determined by the fact of their coexistence *in praesentia*" (ibid. 18). What Groensteen adds to McCloud's sequentiality concept is the over-determination of the images and that they stand in what Hatfield/Fresnault-Deruelle would call tabular (as opposed to linear) relations. Iconic solidarity is an admittedly appealing metaphor but not an analytical concept.

The essentialist basis of Groensteen's system is all the more obvious in his assessment of the single-image cartoon: as opposed to an image sequence, Groensteen holds that "a single image can *evoke* a story, but that does not mean that it *tells* one. It is the juxtaposition of images [that] generates narratives" (2013: ch. 2, np.). The reference here made is to an even older work of theory than *Understanding Comics* (Aron Kibedi Varga, *Discours, récit, image*, 1989: 98), but it could have been, in fact, imputed to its author (cf. McCloud 1994: 8–9). That a cartoon or single image may be regarded as a (virtual or abridged) narrative is controversial, and Groensteen dedicates a whole sub-chapter to it in *Comics and Narration* (2013: ch. 2, 2.1, np.).[84] – Apart from prototypical categories (see ch. 3.3), a way out of this predicament could be a more radical cognitive turn toward the readers' minds: Neil Cohn, for example, writes that the closing of the gutter between two images cannot be attributed to the gutter but to the "*indexical quality*" of the panel content, which readers retain and process in the act of reading or interpreting (Cohn 2010: 136); and what Cohn found out about two images also holds for one, the cartoon: the 'evocation' (Groensteen) of a narrative,

---

[84] Harry Morgan, for example, holds that a daily panel, or cartoon, can be described as "a daily strip reduced to one panel" (qtd. in Groensteen 2013: ch. 2, np.).

3.4 Critical Approaches to Comics and Graphic Novels — 97

inferred from the single image, happens on the basis of the content of the single panel and its indexes. In both the image sequence and the cartoon, the narrative is cognitively inferred, gutter or no gutter.[85]

In Groensteen, essentialism exists and works just inside the system which he claims precludes essentialism. On the one hand, he defines comics as "a collection of codes" (2007: 6); on the other, he views "interdependent images as the unique ontological foundation of comics" (ibid. 17). These two definitions do not necessarily contradict each other in a system with classical categories in which comics are defined through one essential feature: sequential, interdependent images.[86] Apart from the one essential feature, Groensteen claims that in a system, "the problem posed to the analyst is not which code to privilege" (ibid. 6), yet he clearly privileges the pictorial and underprivileges the verbal track (see above). The large majority of comics consist of text as well as of images, and therefore Groensteen's system here has a problem spot. – In *Comics and Narration*, although half-heartedly, Groensteen takes back the privilege of the image, not least because in his follow-up, he increasingly includes long-form comics and graphic novels. Thus, in updating his *System of Comics*, he almost incidentally remarks: "both [text and image] play a full part in the narrative process. There is not, on the one hand, a text that tells [...] and on the other, images that show" (2013: ch. 5.1.1, np.).[87]

Groensteen's two key concepts in *System* are 'arthrology' and 'braiding.' By arthrology, he means the different sorts of relations among images in comics (2007: 21). He further distinguishes a *restricted* from a *general* arthrology (ibid. 22). The former accounts for the elementary, linear relations in terms of layout, breakdown, mise en scène; the latter for the translinear and distant relations, which Groensteen labels *braiding*: "They represent a more elaborated level of integration between the narrative flux [...] and the spatio-topical operation"

---

[85] Cohn takes his argument one step further away from essentialist sequentiality when he elaborates on the conceptuality of comics space: rather than representing time-space, as in McCloud, "panels seem to functionally divide up a *conceptual space* – that is additively built throughout the sequence – into units of attention" (ibid. 142, my emphasis). Only because pictorial information is conceptual can narratives be constructed "beyond the linear analysis" (2010: 135ff.).

[86] Groensteen backs up his argument with a reference to Yves Lacroix, who "summed up the specificity of the medium very ably in speaking of the '*soul* of comics [...] known as the serial status'" (2007: 7, my emphasis).

[87] Nonetheless, Groensteen further writes: "All my efforts in *The System of Comics* were directed towards demonstrating that a substantial part of the narration is carried by the images [...] To put it another way, there is undoubtedly a dissociation between the *told* (with words) and the *shown* (by drawings) [...] I had, moreover, defined comic art as a *predominantly visual narrative form*" (2013: ch. 5.1., np., italics in the original).

(ibid.). An example of braiding would be a visual or pictorial element connecting to (an)other visual or pictorial element(s) across panels, independently from the usual reading order (Z-path). – In the definition of braiding, another central term is brought up: spatio-topia, or the spatial distribution of the panels on the page, including the speech balloons (ibid. 21).

As a matter of course, it is simply impossible to supply a comprehensive graphic schema of Groensteen's system – as I would have liked to – because too many (sub)categories or parameters are related on multiple levels. To start with, I shall supply only a rough schematic representation (Fig. 3.23):

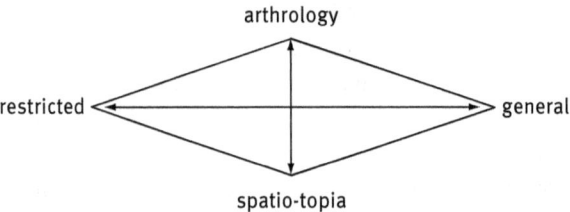

Fig. 3.23: Arthrology including spatio-topia, roughly visualized according to Groensteen 2007

Spatio-topia, "an arbitrarily detached subgroup" of arthrology (ibid. 22), comprizes the panel and its frame, the speech balloon, the strip, and the page (ibid. 21). Here, *System* imposes limits to an exact schematic representation of its categories: Groensteen holds that the relation between arthrology and spatio-topia is "dialogic" and "recursive." What sounds at first a bit nebulous[88] is quite plausible at second glance: the spatio-topical parameters may be isolated from the whole work for analysis' sake; in practice, however, they are always and already related, linearly and translinearly, across and beyond the single page, in the whole book of comics. Simultaneously, the spatio-topical parameters are related to the arthrological parameters, that is to layout, breakdown, the mise en scène (restricted arthrology), and braiding (general arthrology). To represent this graphically, I shall use a more complex schema than the above (Fig. 3.24):

---

[88] Spatio-topia as arthrology's subgroup has "no other autonomy than that which it recognizes for itself, at a given moment, to the heuristic ends. [...] one can define the mode of interaction between the authority of the spatio-topia and the arthrology as 'dialogic' and 'recursive'" (Groensteen 2007: 23). The latter two concepts, Groensteen borrows from Edgar Morin, *La méthode 3: La connaissance de la connaissance*, 1986: 98–101.

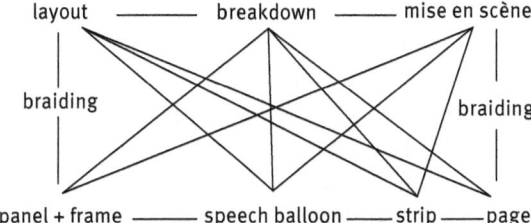

Fig. 3.24: Relations of all arthrological parameters, according to Groensteen 2007

Through visual or pictorial elements connecting across panels, for example, through an "iconic motif" (ibid. 151, see also 156–158), "the panels of a comic constitute a network, and even a system. [...] images that the breakdown holds at a distance, physically and contextually independent, are suddenly revealed as communicating closely" (ibid. 158).

Arthrology and braiding have often been referred to, yet only recently have they been critically scrutinized.[89] Despite their usefulness as a theoretical basis, they are not without problems. Since Groensteen (2007) privileges the visual/pictorial over the verbal, the arthrology as well as braiding cannot account for

---

[89] Cf. Cohn 2010 and Miodrag 2013. Cohn's critique is somewhat unfair or, as Miodrag has it, "custom-made to illustrate his [own] point" (2013: 128): Cohn generally reproaches Groensteen's arthrology for being "ultimately unable to describe how meaning is created in sequential images" (Cohn 2010: 128). Looking at comics from a cognitive angle, Cohn holds that information in comics is largely conceptual and meaning is built via unconscious hierarchic structures in the mind. He criticizes Groensteen's arthrology to imply merely "loosely defined connections [...] between sequential images [which] are inadequate to account for their understanding" (ibid.). Concretely, he avers that "if braiding serves as a model of comprehension, such unrestrained transitions (semantic relations between individual panels) between every possible panel in a document would overload the working memory of the human mind" (ibid. 137, cf. Cohn 2013: ch. 4.2). – I would hold that the mathematical calculation of possible transitions per total number of panels, which Cohn expounds on in his book *The Visual Language of Comics: Introduction to the Structure and Cognition of Sequential Images* (2013), is inappropriate because transitions across panels and across pages depend not least on the individual reader competence (cf. Cohn 2013: ch. 6), attention, the number and distinctness of cues, and the number of rereadings. Precisely because of limited working memory, readers will never exhaust all the mathematically possible transitions. To give an example: in Charles Burns' *Black Hole* (2005), on the first reading, it is maybe not obvious that the oblong vertical panel in which Chris is leaning on a tree trunk, drinking from a cup and musing over past events (some 38 pages into the narrative, which is non-paginated) serves as an opening frame to a flashback which is closed with a complementary panel some 14 pages later. I would agree, however, that Groensteen's cross-panel connections are rather loosely conceived.

complex text/image relations (see chapter 3.3.4.3) or, more generally, verbal-pictorial *cross-reference*. Any word on a comics page, be it in a caption, speech balloon, or just inside a panel, no matter if I look at it as a drawn or a plainly verbal signifier whose semantic information links up with visual elements on the page – any instance of text interacts, I would hold, directly or indirectly with the images (even in extreme cases such as Chris Ware's experimental short graphic narrative "I Guess," from *Quimby the Mouse*, 2003). That does not mean, of course, that the verbal and the pictorial blend or become one. Thus, instead of using 'arthrology' or 'braiding,' I prefer *cross-reference* as a concept to account for the verbal-pictorial linkings in graphic novels, panel-to-panel and across panels or pages, and propose the subcategories "text-image" and "image-texts" for the latter, depending on the medium that carries the dominant type of information (see chapter 3.3.4.6).

3.4.5 Martin Schüwer's Comprehensive Intermedial Approach

Wie Comics erzählen: Grundriss einer intermedialen Erzähltheorie der grafischen Literatur [How Comics Narrate: Outline of an Intermedial Narrative Theory of Graphic Literature] (2008), by Martin Schüwer (1970–2013), departs from two approaches: Werner Wolf's cognitive schema theory (2002) and Gilles Deleuze's cinematic theory (1983/1985), which Schüwer transposes onto comics. Wolf extends the concept of narration from classical narratology and postulates that – besides verbal narrative fiction – comics, films, and dramas also narrate (or tell a story). Within the context of frame theory, narrativity is conceived as a culturally acquired cognitive schema which allows the connection of different medial transmissions (Wolf 2002: 29, qtd. in Schüwer 2008: 24).

Deleuze's *L'image-mouvement* (1983) and *L'image-temps* (1985) represent both a philosophical and a cognitive approach to the perception and construction of single images and their reception in the conscious mind, which is backed up by Henri Bergson's philosophy on memory and film in *Matière et mémoire* (1896) and *L'Evolution créatrice* (1907). Schüwer's application of Deleuze's concepts of the movement and the time image is to serve as the springboard of an inquiry into meaning building from images in terms of both the image sequence and the layout of the comics page (*tableau*), which terminological distinction is owed to Benoît Peeters (1991/1993). Further, Schüwer discusses the interrelation of writing and images and last but not least, he seeks to overcome the shortcomings and predicaments of conventional narratology (as put forth by Genette, Chatman, and others) when applied to comics with regard to (verbal) narration and focalization (see chapter 4 for details). Considering its sheer length (570 pages) as well as the many case studies together with the countless illustrations, *Wie Comics erzählen* is obviously meant to be a reference work on comics theory and its application. It is, to my knowledge, the most comprehensive and systematic approach to comics existing.

The cardinal achievement of this book is how it uses Deleuze's work on cinema to elaborate on the construction of single images and the recipients' stringing them together as a narrative sequence. A key concept of this paradigm is the *sensorimotor* schema, according to which recipients can assemble disjunct pictorial elements of an action into a consistent narrative.[90] Comics, Schüwer holds, can activate this sensorimotor schema, which governs our daily experiences. Many images in natural perception and in comics reception are sensorimotor or *movement images*, geared toward situational change (action) and linear development (Schüwer 2008: 236).[91] The *time image* comes into play when the layout of the total page increases in salience by withdrawing attention from the action sequence and by producing meaning in its own right (ibid. 210, 237–238). To put it differently, movement images underscore the event-states in the narrated world; time images seem to comment or reflect on things disconnected from the narrated event-states (ibid. 30–37); they emerge indirectly through montage or directly through cross-panel references (e.g. graphic matches) –

---

90 According to Deleuze, living organisms perceive the spatially unformed images of their surroundings and refer them to what he calls 'image,' the conscious mind, or *perception image*. In this process, the perception image is indiscernibly transformed into a spatially formed *action* or *sensorimotor image*. This transformation happens through *affect* or *instinct*: the interval between pictorial stimulus and reaction (opened up by affect/instinct), is, at first, indeterminate; therefore, the reaction (the transformation into an action image) is a genuine action. – Apart from the sensorimotor images, there exist affect and/or instinct images, which are situated in between the perception and action image. Sensorimotor images represent a homogenous space in which the bodies find their place and act according to a goal. Affect and instinct images, by contrast, represent an arbitrary space consisting of fragments that can be no longer assembled and which is purely body-oriented. As opposed to space in sensorimotor images, goal-oriented action in arbitrary space is no longer possible (cf. Schüwer 2008: 201–207). Yet this does not principally hamper recipients from assembling the diverse images into a coherent narrative.
91 Schüwer's use of the Deleuzean pose, appearance (*Gestalt*), and the freeze frame in the representation of the movement of bodies (ch. 2) as well as those on central and multiple-point perspective and space (ch. 3) are prerequisite to understanding the Deleuzean images – and perhaps the most productive for future comics research. Movement and perspective serve to recognize space and vice versa (2008: 82). The crucial insight on these pages is that the superhero genre is particularly appropriate to the comics medium: the superheroes' assets (jumps, strokes, and impacts) are best accounted for in a medium whose essential features are the condensation of duration in single images and the representation of sensorimotor experience (ibid. 78–81).

both of which Schüwer subsumes under "textual memory."[92] Within the image sequence, however, the sensorimotor (or movement-)image generally dominates the time-image (ibid. 273–301).

With the transposal of Deleuze's movement and time image and Peeters's tableau paradigm onto comics, Schüwer presents a systematically coherent, non-semiotic, version of the sequentiality vs. simultaneity paradigm for comics with an appropriate backup from contemporary comics theory and philosophy: thus, the time image presupposes a meaning building potential within *and* beyond the image sequence, in the tabulary space of the comics page: "The tableau and sequence do not contain each other, they represent two complementary views of one and the same material comics page, two simultaneously existing structuralizations of the same elements" (ibid. 198–199). Similarly to Groensteen's *System*, yet in a significantly more elaborated and systematic fashion, *Wie Comics erzählen* confirms the tendency to look at comics from the angle of film rather than verbal literature and questions the controversial tenet of 'comics as literature.'

One weakness in Schüwer's approach is that it often stays too attached to McCloud's dated and erroneous concepts. For example, he holds on to the view that the comics panels represent minimal units (rendered obsolete by Groensteen, see above, and Miodrag, see below) and that the image sequence remains the essential feature in comics analysis (ibid. 37). This essentialism, relying on classical categories, precludes his approach from distinguishing, for example, the graphic novel from other books of comics (see ch. 3.3). In addition, Schüwer sticks to McCloud's problematic notion that the difference between writing and drawing, text and image, is just a matter of degree and that words basically function like images (Schüwer 2008: 343–352).

3.4.6 Hannah Miodrag's *Langue* vs. *Parole* in the "Web" of Comics

Hannah Miodrag's *Comics and Language: Reimagining Critical Discourse on Form* (UP of Mississippi, 2013) has emerged from readings of the existing critical literature on comics – its strengths and shortcomings – as well as on her own critical

---

[92] Borrowing from Sergej Eisenstein, Schüwer understands montage in a broader sense: firstly, as the linking of two shots or panels; secondly, as the arranging or assembling of all images into a whole. Unfortunately, he starts out to develop this paradigm from McCloud's six types of panel transitions – which has recently been heavily criticized as rather inefficient (Cohn 2010, Groensteen 2007, Hatfield 2005, Miodrag 2013). The cross-panel references (which Schüwer attributes partly to montage, partly to what he calls "textual memory"), revealing the time-image, account directly for the pictorial, yet merely indirectly for verbal references (Schüwer 2008: 273–276, cf. ch. 5, 303–478).

3.4 Critical Approaches to Comics and Graphic Novels — 103

practice and the dissatisfaction with the up to now widely accepted concepts in the field. Apart from the critique of the established concepts, her formalist-structuralist approach conceives of pictorial representation as *parole* (as opposed to *langue*): comics panels may be discrete but not minimal units of comics discourse. Moreover, she gives force to the importance of verbal-narratorial representation in the production of meaning.

Despite considerable employment of word mincing, it is quite clear that Miodrag reproaches particularly Anglophone critics (meaning the 'founding fathers' of comics theory) for " 'never reading, considering, interpreting what someone else has thought as a point of departure for what they think. It's all *ex nihilo*' " (ibid. 5). In other words: a non-negligible part of the so-called comics theory is non-chalantly uninformed, McCloud's *Understanding Comics* being the paragon of "*ex nihilo* text[s]," often elevated, however, " 'to the status of holy writ.' McCloud himself defends his uncontextualized speculations" (ibid. 6). It is from within this dissatisfaction that Miodrag challenges, among other things, the tenet that the visual dominates the verbal track in graphic narratives as in Kunzle, Eisner, McCloud, and even the quite systematic Groensteen (ibid. 11). Instead, she holds that comics "frequently incorporate highly literary writing" and "deploy words in [their] own specific ways" (ibid.). Further, Miodrag refutes the suggestion that "the visual and verbal interact [and] become an inextricable blend that can therefore be framed as a unified language in itself" (ibid.). Instead, she insists that "distinctions between the two modes and their operations persist" (ibid. 12). Indeed, in order to analyze the complexity of graphic novels, it seems inevitable for an approach to equally account for the verbal and pictorial modes of signification – without blending them into one.

Miodrag questions McCloud's privileging of sequentiality as well as his concept of the gap and gap filling and foregrounds the "simultaneity of narrative segments on the two-dimensional page ...." (ibid. 12, cf. "simultaneity of multiple panels," 114); she proves McCloud wrong with the example of Posy Simmonds' graphic novel *Gemma Bovery* (2001), in which she finds that the "kinds of 'gaps' that inform her work are not merely spaces between momentary panels in sequential strips" (ibid. 66). Miodrag's point here is that in practice, "the spaces in comics over which readers must make imaginative links are far more diverse" than the concepts of the gutter or gap have it in McCloud and others. "Simmonds' untraditional [collage-like] layouts segment text in ways that create pauses, turns, subversions, and punch lines. She directs the reading of her text through its spatial arrangement [...]" (2013: 66/78).

According to Miodrag, comics critics generally neglect the textual aspect of comics (ibid. 59). In order to "restore some [...] balance," she sets out to analyze George Herriman's Krazy Kat strips and finds that they are "intensely poetic, aesthetically rich, and inventively comical. [...] Words proliferate, not in service of conveying more meaning, but for their own aesthetic sake" (ibid. 19). More concretely, she shows that Herriman makes punning use of alliteration, synonyms, homonyms, homophones, that he mixes registers (ibid. 20/33), and that he plays with the minimal units of language by ungrammatically jumbling morphemes together (ibid. 21/23): "Comics critics' efforts to argue that pictures can communicate 'as well as words' fall flat in the face of a cartoonist like Herriman" (ibid. 29). – Similarly, Lynda Barry's cartoons are held to "undermine assertions about the primary role of images in conveying narrative information" (ibid. 41). Barry's juvenile characters are shown to use language totally idiosyncratically, against grammatical rules or social gender conventions. Miodrag's analysis of Barry culminates in the claim that none of the cartoons "could convey much of a narrative without their outlandish and engaging textual content [...] in Barry's work, words are primary. The literary value of her strips lies in their canny use of language and not the narrative content" (ibid. 57–58) – a similar statement is made about Herriman's use of words.

What might seem problematic in Miodrag's deliberately one-sided approach is totally legitimate under the condition that I look at it from the angle of prototypical categories, which she seems to tacitly presuppose: speaking of comics as a "web, [...] a connective tissue that enmeshes a multitude of textual fragments that can never be summarized by a single or even taxonomic set of 'core' feature(s)" (ibid. 67), she writes against the essentialism found in McCloud's, Eisner's, and Groensteen's sequentiality theorems and their underlying primacy of the pictorial. What constitutes a certain problem is that by scrutinizing Herriman's and Barry's strips in the first place, she is dealing with a genre that lacks the complexity of long-form graphic narratives. The most characteristic feature of Herriman's and Barry's strips, besides their individual drawing style (which is recognized in the works of every famous comics artist) and the minimal plot, is the characters' language use. Yet what other features would there be, given the low degree of complexity? As soon as Miodrag turns to complex works (the great majority being graphic novels),[93] the whole layout with its diverse elements or distinguishing features come into focus, from which she shows how verbal and visual signs are connected and how they encroach upon each other with regard to meaning production.

---

93 Posy Simmonds' *Gemma Bovery* (2001), Paul Auster, Paul Karasik, and David Mazzucchelli, *City of Glass* (2004), Chris Ware, *Jimmy Corrigan* (2000), Moore/Gibbons, *Watchmen* (1986–1987), Veronika Tanaka [= Bryan Talbot], *Metronome* (2008), David Mazzucchelli, *Asterios Polyp* (2009), Charles Burns, *Black Hole* (2005), and Frank Miller, *The Dark Knight Returns* (1986).

3.4 Critical Approaches to Comics and Graphic Novels — 105

Miodrag's major point is her rejection of the comics-as-language notion (for which she and several others from the same camp have been massively attacked by Neil Cohn [2014]). Instead, she reconceives the signifiers in comics by drawing back on structural linguistics in terms of *langue* and *parole*. Unlike the signifier/signified relation of arbitrary words, pictorial signs do not necessarily require to have been learnt in order to know what they represent: "visual signification is less constrained than language by a preexistent *langue*" (ibid. 9). Consequently, Miodrag refuses the concept of minimal units of visual signifiers: "In language, speakers are always reusing preexistent signs, whereas visual signification affords scope for creating new ones. [...] Visual *parole* can create new signs, and while repetition is possible it is not inevitable as it is with inherited language" (ibid. 43/131). Panels, Miodrag holds, are not the minimal units of the comics discourse, a tenet she shares with Groensteen (see above): panels "are plastically and semantically over-determined by the fact of their coexistence *in praesentia*" (Groensteen 2007: 18). But not only by their coexistence, it should be added: at least as much by the fact that they are (un)framed, come in different shapes, and differ in content. It might sound banal, but although examples are occasionally found (as in Chris Ware's *Jimmy Corrigan*), no two or more exactly identical panels normally occur in a graphic narrative (as opposed to a verbal text, which, by definition, is informed by redundancy in its use of morphemes, words, and phrases). In principle, every panel differs from its verbal pictorial co-text, although sometimes only minimally. Thus, how could any panel be a minimal unit? In this context, the graphic materiality of text ('drawn letters,' e.g. the words in the speech balloon, typeface, capital or lowercase letters, letter size, color, position in the image, etc.) constitutes the *parole* aspect of the abstract signifier, which depends on the multilayered verbal *and* pictorial co-text of the panel or page on which it is found. It is not identical with the *langue* aspect, that is endlessly repeatable signs referring to their purely verbal co-text. Narratorial captions, to bring up only one example, do not represent a purely verbal context since they are also framed and positioned on the page. This is why Miodrag's langue/parole distinction is preferable over the rather nebulous buzz phrase 'language of comics.'

In the end, Miodrag approves of and extends the concept of tabular readings[94] (2013: 115) to account for the verbal-pictorial "web" of the comics discourse. Only tabular readings can bring out the multilayered meanings and

---

[94] Originally created by Fresnault-Deruelle (1976), borrowed and carried further by Peeters (1993: 22), Hatfield (2005: 53 et passim), and Schüwer (2008: 160 et passim). Groensteen develops a similar reading strategy under the heading of braiding (cf. 2007: 144 et passim).

multiple references, verbal and pictorial, in the sequence and across sequences and pages. Without explicitly attaching a label, she demonstrates the efficacy and necessity of such 'holistic' readings with a number of graphic narratives by authors like Posy Simmonds, David Mazzucchelli, or Chris Ware, in regard to which linear readings would simply fail to grasp the main story as well as the multiple narrative layers embedded on one and the same page (including, for example, time shifts, see Miodrag 2013: 142). Thus, she underscores the importance of the simultaneity of the segmental pictorial and textual units ("lexias," a term from Roland Barthes' *S/Z*, 1970, borrowed through Kannenberg 2001) on the page in the meaning building process.

3.4.7 Conclusion

Looking at the older and more recent publications of critical writing on sequentiality vs. simultaneity in comics, I find that
- from the mid-2000s on, there is an increasing tendency away from essentialist definitions in terms of comics as sequential images. Some works, however, still cleave to this paradigm (Groensteen and, to a certain extent, Schüwer) although they ultimately go beyond it through the specificity of their approaches;
- panels are increasingly conceived as discrete and not as minimal units of the comics discourse (Groensteen, Hatfield, Miodrag);
- the metaphor 'language of comics' has been revealed as more misleading than helpful (Cohn, Miodrag);
- recent critics underscore the tabular or cross-panel relations of the images and the verbal/textual signification as distinct from pictorial signification (Hatfield, Schüwer, Miodrag);
- the notion of a "web" or "network" of signification across images in a sequence (Groensteen) and between the verbal and the pictorial (Miodrag) has gained in preponderance.

The last point in this list deserves elaboration. Shortly after McCloud, Robert C. Harvey expounded on word-image relations in *The Art of the Comic Book: An Aesthetic History* (1996). The serious drawback to his concepts of 'juxtaposition,' 'blending,' and 'balance' of words and images is that they exclusively concern the representation of action (cf. Harvey 1996: 53, 103). A similar limitation occurs in McCloud: apart from montage, what he calls 'parallel,' 'interdependent,' 'additive,' 'picture-, word-, and duo-specific combinations' is also exclusively oriented toward action (cf. McCloud 1994: 153–155). This is because of his essentialist definition of comics as sequential *movement* images, as Schüwer would have called them according to Deleuze, which is incapable of accounting for "temporally ambiguous panel relationships" (Cohn 2010: 130, see ch. 3.4.2) or *time* images. Only in montage, "where words are treated as integral *parts* of the picture" (McCloud 1994: 154, italics in the original) does McCloud potentially allow for meaning production beyond the representation of action, albeit without further commenting thereon.

What Groensteen and Miodrag understand by the "web" or "network" of signification goes firstly beyond the single panel, secondly across frames and spaces (empty or filled), and thirdly beyond the single page: the interesting issue about the comics discourse is how the verbal and the pictorial cross-refer to each other, how they intersect on different planes and generate meaning on a larger, more complex scale: in short, the verbal-pictorial *mise en scène* (see ch. 4.3.2.1). A good example of this are images or whole pages from Joe Sacco's graphic novel *Palestine*, where blocks of text like narrative captions, headings, or tags are strewn across pages, often in semantically loaded patterns, underlining, for example, the chaotic situation and auditory setting in the Gaza strip. On the side of the pictorial mise en scène, what adds meaning to the semantics of the words and images is the often extreme point of view of Sacco's images: the very low, high or super-wide angles from which the 'shots' seem to be taken (cf. Sacco 2001: 1, 37, 119 et passim). Point of view in panels and other parameters of the mise en scène (see ch. 4.3.1) and how they cross-refer to the verbal text certainly are paradigms that deserve more systematic attention in comics criticism.

4 Verbal and Pictorial Narration in Graphic Novels

4.1 Preliminary Reflections: Why Graphic Narratives Have no Transmitting Communication System and not Necessarily a Narrator

Besides plot, narration is one of seven subcategories of complexity, the core feature of graphic novels (see ch. 3.3.4.1). Crucial questions concerning the narration in basically all books of comics are, firstly, whether certain categories from classical, that is Genettean, narratology can be used on them at all and secondly, whether those categories can be used on both the verbal-narratorial and the pictorial track. To start with, and according to a widely accepted communicative approach, I would distinguish between what is internal and external to a text or another medial configuration (cf. Fieguth 1973 and Pfister 1988, qtd. in Rajewsky 2007: 38). Regarding a verbal fictional narrative, for example, the external communication system includes the empirical author and the readers (cf. Pfister 1988: 21); as for a feature film, it is the director and his/her team (screenwriter, producer, actors, cameramen, technicians, etc.) and the viewers; as for a theater performance, it implies the theater company (director, actors, lighting and sound technicians, etc.) and the theater audience. As far as a book of comics is concerned, the external communication system consists of the author (or the team of creators such as the script writer, the artist, who is responsible for the drawing, and possibly the letterer and/or the colorist) and the readers or reader-observers. The internal communication system pertaining to all these medial configurations consists of the fictional characters communicating on the plane of action. The specificity of the verbal fictional narrative resides in that its internal communication system is embedded in a mediating, or better, transmitting, system,[1] reified in the fictional narrator that is *solely* responsible for the production of the whole narration. This also is one cardinal point in

---

[1] Manfred Pfister calls this a "vermittelnde[s] Kommunikationssystem" (Pfister 1988: 21). I prefer *transmitting* to 'mediating' system in order to avoid a misconception that Irina Rajewsky revealed in a seminal article on Pfister's drama theory: although the "vermittelnde[...] Kommunikationssystem" is based on Genette's definition of the *récit*, which implies the speech criterion according to Plato, in Pfister's comparison of the narrative and the dramatic mode it eventually turns out to 'mediate' between the external and internal communication system (Rajewsky 2007: 48) – which in turn contradicts Genette's definition of the *récit* ["un récit de fiction est fictivement produit par son narrateur, et effectivement par son auteur (réel)"] as well as its implications (Genette 1983: 96).

Genette's narratology. In a wider narratological context, it is noteworthy that the transmitting system does not 'mediate' (see note 1) between the external and internal communication system but that it *transmits* the verbal 'report'[2] that constitutes the narration.

This is quite different in graphic narratives. If there is a verbal narrating voice speaking through caption script – which is by far not always the case – it cannot possibly be involved in bringing forth the pictorial components. Most graphic novels come with narratorial caption script, which, however, is often minimalistic, limited to short local and/or temporal adverbial phrases with no verbs or personal pronouns (cf. Mikkonen 2008: 308). Therefore, it is arguable whether it makes sense to generally posit a verbal narrator; also, despite the possibility of extensive caption script – as it can be found in a number of graphic memoirs – the question is whether there is a narrator or a character that happens to narrate (I shall elaborate on these points in greater detail in chapter 4.5).

As early as 2002 (albeit in the framework of an intermedial/cognitive approach), Werner Wolf posited that narrativity should not be limited to *narrator-transmitted* narration, that is to narratives in a narrower, epic, sense (cf. Wolf 2002: 31, see also Wolf 2011: 146). Although I am not concerned with an extension of the term 'narrativity,' I hold that, contrary to verbal narratives, graphic narratives are in principle not narrator-transmitted, for they lack a mediating or transmitting communication system specific of their kind. – Let me explain. Graphic narratives have often been likened to theater performances or films, and not seldom to both. Thierry Groensteen, for example, classifies theater, cinema, and comics "as mimetic, or dramatic, arts insofar as they present characters in action" (Groensteen 2013: 5.1.2, np.), borrowing André Gaudreault's monstration concept. For Gaudreault, who departs from verbal narrative fiction in the first place, monstration consists in "showing characters who act rather than *report* the events they *undergo* [*dire* les péripéties qu'ils *subissent*]" (Gaudreault 1988: 91, italics in the original). In drama – I shall elaborate on the similarities of comics and film below – *telling* is principally part of the internal communication system, to the extent that characters communicate with each other in the form of dialogues, including messenger reports or teichoscopy (viewing from a wall). According to Manfred Pfister's generally accepted communication-oriented approach, there is no mediating/transmitting system (see note 1), no fictional narrator, in drama.[3] Therefore, what happens on stage is primarily *shown*,

---

2 'Report' refers to the speech criterion in Plato and Aristotle (*diegesis/apaggelia*, cf. Platon 1990, vol. 4, 392c–394c, and Aristoteles 1982: 1448a, 19–20).
3 As for the 'narrating' or commenting devices in epic theater, Manfred Pfister has been proven wrong by Irina Rajewsky, who showed that stage managers, commentators, 'authors,' or

brought forth by the actors and those indirectly involved in the performance, as (visual) monstration.

Showing[4] therefore is the dominant mode in drama – as it is in comics. And despite the possible presence of narratorial caption script,[5] graphic novels also primarily show (see chapter 4.3.1 for details). 'Silent' graphic novels like Shaun Tan's *The Arrival*, Peter Kuper's *The System*, and, to a large extent, Richard McGuire's *Here* even completely dispense with words; although they do narrate, they do not tell (as a fictional narrator does). Thus, comics, like drama, lack the mediating/transmitting communication system and fictional narrator to bring forth the whole verbal-pictorial discourse. One might argue that in comics, mediacy is found in the sequential images, which, similarly to cinematic frames, occur as constructed and edited. Yet that mediacy[6] is factual, bound up with the external communication system – not fictional, like (the construct of) a narrator in a verbal fictional narrative (cf. Rajewsky 2007: 41). Comics images are finished givens (cf. Schüwer 2008: 390 and Thon 2013: 69) and not 'fiction,' contrary to a narrator. They may be drawn, designed, and edited, yet that is done by the comics artist, possibly in collaboration with the writer of the comics script and with additional members accomplishing different tasks in a team. Strictly speaking, there is always mediacy, or mediation, since all medial configurations – verbal narrative fiction, feature films, comics, dramas, etc. – use one or more codes (or modes). However, a particular form of mediacy is not necessarily constructed as fictional.

It is the specificity of graphic narratives that the verbal and the pictorial track combine in the production of meaning. This is why they should be considered as one, and the bringing forth of the two tracks should be attributed to one instance. But what exactly does, for example, the pictorial track include? Besides the images themselves, are (not) speech balloons also pictorial (cf. Miodrag 2013: 99–102)? Or sound lettering? And what about tags?[7] Several

---

commentating characters in a stage performance are not narrators, i.e. transmitters of a verbal discourse that constitutes a fictional narrative: the verbal comments of these epic devices notwithstanding, the happenings on stage are still to be brought forth by the actors and technicians (cf. Rajewsky 2007: 46–51).

4 Showing in comics, otherwise called monstration, must be strictly distinguished from the showing vs. telling paradigm applied to verbal narrative fiction, in which both modes are produced by a narrator.

5 Speech balloons may exist despite the absence of narratorial caption script; together with the caption script, they are subsumed under the verbal track.

6 Franz K. Stanzel speaks of *gestaltete Mittelbarkeit* (constructed mediacy) in the case of verbal narrative fiction (Stanzel 1995: 19).

7 Tags may be looked at as textual-pictorial connectors, see below, chapter 4.4.6.

critics have underscored the duality of writing and that "text reads as an image" (Eisner 2008: 10). Even narrative captions have a pictorial streak and can be used to enhance the production of meaning, for example, by the way they are framed, distributed over the page, or placed in a single panel. In Joe Sacco's graphic novel *Palestine*, the speech balloons and narrative captions often overlap the images and form a pattern in themselves and thus underscore the chaos of languages and conflicts in which the author finds himself (cf. Hillenbach 2013: 141–142). "This visualization of words precludes the easy dissection of visual and verbal that is possible where captions and pictures are concerned [...]. It is this graphic rendering of language [...] that presents the most efficacious challenge to the distinction between visual and verbal" (Miodrag 2013: 101). In graphic narratives, every word is connected to a pictorial entity (like speech balloons or the frames of captions, panels, or tags), if it is not itself verbal and pictorial to begin with (as sound lettering, which is more or less iconic). – John Holbo has verbal and graphic novels on one "continuum," implying a provocatively prototypical approach: "Typography *is* graphic design. Novels, being typed, are *graphic* novels. [...] Letterforms *are* images. They just aren't *pictures*" (Holbo 2012: 15, 17, italics in the original). Indeed, for Holbo, there is no actual boundary between the verbal and the graphic, the difference existing only quantitatively, in degrees – depending on the implied (core) features or categories. As a consequence, verbal and graphic novels would be together in one category. However, it is questionable if such a large category (containing verbal narrative fiction, illustrated narrative fiction, graphic narratives, children's and picture books, etc.) has critical pertinence. I separated graphic from verbal narratives because of two core features constituting one category each: the dominance of the verbal in verbal narratives and the dominance of the pictorial in graphic narratives (see ch. 3.3.3, Fig. 3.2).

From the beginnings of narratology up to now, diverse approaches (Genettean and post-Genettean, that is transmedial, cognitive, or communicative) have come to the fore, proposing ways to come to grips with the terms voice, perspective, point of view, and above all focalization, the concept most written on lately with regard to graphic narratives.[8] Some or parts of these approaches have been inspired by (not so recent) film theory. In this sense, comics panels have not seldom been likened to cinematic shots, although this comparison is not without problems. Indeed, it is not at all clear if a comics panel is similar to the cinematic frame or to the single image on the celluloid. With the increasing digitalization of films, the concept of the frame as a section of a reel has become more or less

---

8 See for example Herman 2009, Jesch/Stein 2009, cf. Lewis 2010, Horstkotte/Petri 2011, Kukkonen 2011, Mikkonen 2013, or Thon 2013.

obsolete, imposing a different definition of the shot. This considered, I take a shot to be the image(s) between two cuts (or instances of editing) – which definition is, in fact, rather different from the core features of a single panel: a cinematic shot presents one image in which there usually is movement; the comics panel, in every case, presents a still image.

The idea of images perceived or read in a sequence may be intriguing: in comics, the perception is accomplished by the reader, in the cinema, it is controlled by the projector (cf. Eisner 2008: 39/41, Groensteen 2007: 45). Yet with the advent of the VCR/DVD player, or more recently, the smartphone and the tablet computer, readers have been put in a position to control what they are viewing by being able to stop or 'browse' through the film. This achievement is being done away with in the gradual vanishing of the DVD/Blue Ray from the market and the increasing offers of providers and, respectively, the tendency of viewers (particularly the younger ones) to stream films, with which the possibilities of browsing or jumping backwards and forwards is lost. Yet one of the fundamental differences is that a cinematic shot admits movement within that shot, whereas a comics panel does not: movement here is constructed mentally in passing over to the subsequent images.[9] Apart from that, in a film projection, we see one image spread over one framed space (the screen), which it covers entirely; on a comics page, we find a number of images laid out in a specific order over the space of one page on which each image has its proper position (cf. Cook 2012: 169). Also, in contrast to the viewing of a film sequence, the reading of comics images is "intermittent, elliptical, jerky" (Groensteen 2007: 45) since readers pause and go back and forth at will. Another equally intriguing connection between film and comics can be seen in story boards – a pictorial metaphor employed in the graphic novels *Logicomix* (Doxiadis/Papadimitriou 2009) and *Palestine*. Originally, they were used by film directors, hiring more or less renowned artists to draw specific scenes or sets.[10] Let me sum up these

---

9 Also, "a single shot may include both a preparatory and completed action" and "a camera can be left recording, an entire action or even a full scene could be captured in one continuous shot [...]. [N]ot only do the elements within a film shot move [...], but the camera itself can move. Panning and zooming create alterations to a graphic scene that is continuous rather than discrete" (Cohn 2013, ch. 4).

10 Neil Cohn (2014), who transposes a cognitive "narrative grammar for visual language analogous to syntax" from comics onto film, writes: "the filming and editing process often begins with 'storyboarding,' where shots are drawn out in a form similar to the visual language used in comics. [... F]ilm uses the same narrative grammar except the units are not static panels, but moving segments of film" (ibid., ch. 4). Also see the catalogue to the exhibition *Zwischen Film und Kunst – Storyboards von Hitchcock bis Spielberg* (Museum für Film und Fernsehen, Berlin, [...]

and some more characteristics of feature films and graphic narratives in the following chart (Fig. 4.1):

NARRATIVE FILM	GRAPHIC NARRATIVE
consists of shots which usually show movement	consists of still images
the (one) projected image and the screen form one single unit (except split screens and similarly specific devices)	several images, possibly of different shapes and sizes, are placed on the space of a page in a particular order and in particular positions; the images/panels form discrete and "multiple units" (cf. Cook 2012: 171)
dictates 'realistic' images (cf. Chatman 1990: 40)	dictates iconic images
controls its reception through projection	received through individual reader habits
offers an unspecific plenitude of visual information[11]	offers (at least partly) a verbally specified / modified and iconically reduced amount of visual information
visually and verbally represents thought or mind states, e.g. through fade-out/blur or voice-over	presents verbal thought and mind states through verbal-iconic thought balloons or other verbal-pictorial or purely pictorial devices like perspective or color
may be rough-drafted or scripted in the form of a comics storyboard	represents a detailed and 'finished story board' in itself

Fig. 4.1: Narrative film vs. graphic narrative

Surely, not all these points are equally important for narration in graphic narratives, yet they represent basic media-specific givens from which reflections about verbal and pictorial narration should depart.

Considering the diverse approaches to narration in graphic narratives in the last five years alone – a period in which comics scholars have increasingly set out to work on this issue – there is a significant heterogeneity in terminology (especially in what concerns focalization or point of view), stemming, of course, from the narratological fields from which these approaches derive: from post-classical,

---

August 10–November 27, 2011). Ed. Katharina Henkel, Kristina Jaspers, and Peter Mänz. Bielefeld: Kerber Verlag, 2012.

11 "[... film] cannot *help* describing, though usually it does so only tacitly. Its evocation of details is incessantly rich" (Chatman 1990: 40). Chatman makes this statement in the context of description; yet I would extend it to the detailed pictorial information in general. Thus, François Jost speaks of an unspecified quantity of information that film offers (cf. Jost 1987: 15).

i.e. transmedial (Jan Christoph Meister, Marie-Laure Ryan, Werner Wolf) and cognitive narratology (David Herman, Monika Fludernik, Manfred Jahn) as well as from cinematic theory/narratology (David Bordwell, André Gaudreault, François Jost). At the same time, however, some of those having recently published on comics narration continue to struggle with classical, that is Genettean narratology, renewedly elaborating on its advantages and drawbacks and the criticism found in Seymour Chatman, Mieke Bal and others (cf. Horstkotte/Pedri 2011).

If I admit the radical difference between verbal narrative fiction and graphic narratives, then to what extent can any narratological concept matter that is geared toward verbal narrative fiction, in which, obviously, nothing is actually *shown* or *seen*? In Genette, of course, seeing has perceptual as well as cognitive connotations. In my approach, however, *showing* first and foremost relates to the image, its composition and the pictorial (point of) view presented in that image; only secondarily does *showing* relate to balloon speech or narratorial caption script (see chapters 4.4.2 and 4.4.3). It is incompatible with the (partly quite heterogeneous) concepts behind the showing vs. telling dichotomy, which has been applied to verbal narrative fiction, in which showing and telling presuppose a narrator or a narrating voice.[12] In graphic narratives, showing is primarily independent from a narrator or narratorial caption script.

Seeing here relates to the visual perception of the characters and readers. Readers see what a comics image shows them. However, what the readers see is not necessarily what the characters see who figure in the image, either metonymically or in full. Unless we are dealing with a genuine point of view image (henceforth POV image, which shows nothing of the viewing character and which is the exception rather than the rule in the sum total of a work's images), what characters 'see' is often different from what readers observe. For example, characters may look out of the frame or they may look at something beyond the axis leading through the projection center and the perspective center. Except for the POV image, character vision is often not subject to pictorial representation. It mostly cannot be visually perceived and has to be constructed by the readers. Whether they notice this at all or to what extent this matters for their construction

---

12 With reference to Plato's speech criterion and Wayne Booth's criticism of the naïve use of the concepts *showing* and *telling* by Anglo-Saxon critics of the late nineteenth and early twentieth century, Genette himself points out that there is no authentic (i.e. visual-pictorial) showing in verbal literature. As early as in *Figures III* ("Discours du récit"), he writes: "[...] the notion of *showing* itself, like those of imitation and narrative representation, [...] is perfectly illusionary: contrary to dramatic representation, no narrative [*récit*] can 'show' or 'imitate' the story it tells" (Genette 1972: 185).

4.1 Preliminary Reflections

of the plot is another question that I shall deal with below (see chapter 4.2). Apart from what characters 'see,' do not 'see,' or 'see' differently from the readers, in many images, it is totally unclear who sees what an image shows, as in an extreme-angle or panoramic shot, although there may be a narrator or narrating character (as I said above, in graphic narratives, showing is independent from a verbal narrator or narratorial caption script). To sum up: showing, as opposed to telling (which, if we use this term at all, would apply only to the narratorial script) is visual-pictorial. What characters see, however, is frequently not subject to pictorial representation and has to be constructed by the readers.

This is why showing and seeing have to be redefined when it comes to dealing with graphic narratives. Showing here is pictorial and relates to parameters like composition, perspective construction, vectorization, etc. Seeing, or character vision, is an authentic pictorial representation in the case of a POV image and a purely cognitive construction when it has to be inferred by the readers. As opposed to seeing (or perceiving) in Genette, it does not connote thinking or knowing, which primarily are subject to verbal-pictorial representation in thought balloons.

As a narratological term, showing is a metaphor of a certain way event-states are reported or presented by a fictional narrator[13] (hence Chatman's preference of "presenter" over narrator, cf. Chatman 1990: 113), and by constructing the narrative from the narrator's 'presentation,' readers imagine the story world and its event-states, including what the characters and narrators perceive, perceptually and cognitively. Hence in narratological discourse, seeing and perceiving are perceptual and cognitive terms.

Critics seem to agree upon necessary modifications to the classical narratological concepts regarding graphic narratives and have given them either a cognitive (Herman 2009, Horstkotte/Pedri 2011, Mikkonen 2013), transmedial (Rippl/Etter 2013), or a cinematic twist (Groensteen 2013). As mentioned above, scholars have just recently set out to publish on narration in graphic narratives so that, for the time being, only a limited body of research can be drawn upon.

If it can be agreed upon *showing* as the primary mode of representation in graphic narratives, reader reception should also be taken into view (cf. Grünewald 2014: 474–475). Readers cannot deny that they are seeing the drawn images on the page: images are 'dictated' to them (see Fig. 4.1, point 2). Of course, they imagine the space beyond the panel borders, including the margins and gutters, according to their mental images of the empirical environment. Martin Schüwer

---

[13] For more detailed information about showing as part of the showing vs. telling paradigm, see Klauk/Köppe 2013.

writes that readers will always interpret a panel as only a section (*Ausschnitt*) of the whole, for example, when a panel implies an *off* without actually showing it (cf. Schüwer 2008: 198). Therefore, reader imagination is not completely suspended in graphic narratives. The point of departure of my approach then is that
- in graphic narratives, the verbal and pictorial track inseparably work together, which makes for the specificity of the medium (cf. Groensteen 2013, ch. 5.1.1); together, the verbal and pictorial track generate text/image relations catering to meaning production on all levels. This does not imply, however, that the boundary between the verbal and the pictorial has 'broken down,' or that the two modes have become indistinguishable.

To grasp this complexity of meaning production is to grasp the core feature of graphic novels (as opposed to, for example, lengthy comic books, see ch. 3.2).[14] – My second point is that,
- generally, the terminology as defined in classical narratology, with the focalization concept at the forefront, is questionable with regard to graphic narratives, for it was made to analyze verbal texts. As Thierry Groensteen has it: "[...] no extrapolation from literary narratology can be envisaged unless the concepts are revised" (Groensteen 2013, ch. 5.1).

Therefore, I shall eventually drop the focalization concept from classical narratology in favor of François Jost's ocularization/focalization paradigm (see below, chapters 4.3.1.2 and 4.8). For the time being, however, I am keeping the focalization concept from classical narratology in order to problematize its use on graphic novels.

4.2 The Pictorial Track and Problems Concerning 'Focalization'

In comics images, showing is narrating.[15] This is why silent graphic novels like Peter Kuper's *The System* (1997) or Shaun Tan's *The Arrival* (2006) achieve their

---

14 From a transmedial vantage point, Karin Kukkonen writes: "In multimodal media like comics, [the verbal and visual] modes work together in their storytelling, and this suggests that they are perceived in a dynamic process of narrative cognition, rather than in a piecemeal combination of non-commensurable semiotic resources. [...] It is thus useful to analyze multimodal narration not by breaking it down into its components, but by considering how those modes dynamically interact [...]" (Kukkonen 2011: 39/40).
15 Groensteen writes that "the *shown* is itself a *told*" (2013, ch. 5.1.1, italics in the original). 'Telling' here must be taken as a metaphor of 'narrating,' not as a narratological term.

goal without speech balloons or narrative captions (see chapters 4.4.2 and 4.4.3). The mere definition that comics consist of images in a sequence – which many comics scholars regard as quintessential – implies this thesis. Narratorial caption script certainly is a core but not an absolutely necessary feature of graphic novels. In principle, however, it is a characteristic feature of graphic narratives that the verbal-narratorial and the (verbal-)pictorial track are jointly involved in meaning production and should therefore be considered as one.

Let me make a necessary terminological addition. When I speak of the pictorial track, I generally include thought and speech balloons because
a) they are pictorial containers (although they contain text), and
b) to a certain extent, those words are again pictorial, for they come as drawn or in semantically loaded typefaces and
c) they contain no narratorial voice, contrary to the writing in the captions.

Accordingly, I include sound lettering because its potential for showing is generally bigger than its potential for verbal signification. Certain critics, probably for similar reasons, prefer the term "verbal-pictorial representation" (cf. Thon 2013 and 2014). In some contexts, however, for systematic and analytical purposes, it may be adequate to subsume speech and thought balloons, and particularly the writing contained, under the category 'words' or 'text' (see chapter 4.4.3). The category 'verbal track' (or 'verbal narration') is somewhat blurry because of its overlap with 'pictorial track' in terms of the text in speech/thought balloons and sound lettering.

Strictly speaking, the pictorial and the verbal narration in comics cannot be simultaneously perceived (Schüwer 2008: 322). At a given point in time, we either read the writing or look at the image(s) so that text and image are not seamlessly integrated (ibid. 323); at best, the verbal and pictorial track are received in *virtual* simultaneity (ibid. 399). This, of course, is obvious, and apart from the differences in the reception of, and the radical semiological difference between, verbal text and images,[16] the question rather is whether or to what extent the narratorial caption script impinges on single images or (an) image sequence(s) in the process of meaning production. By narratorial caption script, I mean the enunciation or voice that usually comes in a caption box or is presented as a discernable block of text, framed or unframed.[17]

---

[16] This is in strong opposition to McCloud, who believes words and images differ only gradually (see ch. 3.4.2).
[17] In works like Spiegelman's *Maus* or Sacco's *Palestine*, intradiegetic narrating characters may initially narrate in speech balloons; yet as soon as the narration continues for longer, the narrating utterances usually come in a caption box.

Since comics have been said to be a predominantly pictorial medium,[18] the most discussed and contentious narratological concept has been focalization, which in Gérard Genette's narratology has been defined as the perception (including the cognition) of a character (internal focalization) or a minimally shaped perceiving consciousness (external focalization, cf. Genette 1972: 203, 206–208). Schüwer claims with regard to Alan Moore, Stephen Bissette, and John Totleben's *Saga of the Swamp Thing* (1983–1984) that verbal and pictorial narration correlate and that they produce focalization together (ibid. 392); Mikkonen holds that this is due to "focalization markers at these two levels of narration" (Mikkonen 2013: 103). On the other hand, as in James Vance and Daniel E. Burr's *On the Ropes* (2013) and in many other works, the verbal and pictorial narration seem to produce contrasting 'focalizations' in several episodes, which the readers ultimately have to resolve. Here, the question is what type of 'focalization,' or simply point of view, we are dealing with.

On the Ropes is a historical graphic novel set against the backdrop of New Deal politics and the projects of the Works Progress Administration. There are episodes that appear as 'focalized' either from inside, by the character Fred Bloch, speaking in the first person, or from outside, depicting for example the doings of the two thugs Virgil and Chase, or of Gordon Corey, Fred's mentor and antagonist, or of certain strike breakers. In all these episodes, there is no caption script, and the 'focalization' can be attributed neither to Fred nor to any other character who could have witnessed the happenings.[19] – If I conceived of Fred as the narrator because he speaks in the caption script at the beginning and at the end of this work, I would have to postulate a drawing (or showing) narrator besides the narrator speaking in the captions (as does Thierry Groensteen, who adopts Philippe Marion's terms 'reciter' and 'monstrator,' see below, chapter 4.5). This, however, seems rather implausible since in comics and graphic novels, there is no mediating/transmitting communication system and thus no fictional narrator who could bring forth both the verbal and the pictorial track (see above, chapter 4.1). The narrative captions as well as the images are finished givens and subject to the external communication system. They are produced by one instance: the *artist-writer*, a term I have chosen to account for the dual modality of the discourse in graphic novels and the fact that often more than one creator is involved in the making of a graphic novel (see chapter 4.5).

---

18 Cf. Eisner 2008: 2, 8; cf. McCloud's renowned definition of comics as "juxtaposed pictorial and other images" (McCloud 1994: 9) as well as his likening of words to images (ibid. 48); cf. Groensteen 2007: 3, 8, 9). – In the meantime, the tenet has been contested (see, for example, Miodrag 2013: 11).
19 See also the episode in which Gordon gets into a row with his co-workers from the migrating circus (cf. Vance/Burr 2013: 59–64).

Fig. 4.2: Vance/Burr 2013: 244, change of point of view

The problem with the focalization concept from classical narratology is that it accounts only for one fictional entity, the narrator, being solely responsible for the whole (verbal) narrative discourse – except in cases where there are multiple narrators/focalizations, as for example in William Faulkner's 1929 novel *The Sound and the Fury*. In the bimodal comics narrative, however, the voice speaking in the narratorial captions neither generates the images in general nor the disparate 'focalizations' in particular, represented in single images or whole image sequences. This is why, from now on, I shall replace 'focalization' by the pictorial *point of view*.

The switching from attributable to non-attributable points of view is nothing unusual in graphic narratives; and neither is the switching from one subjective point of view to another – despite a narratorial caption voice, as in the final sequence of *On the Ropes*, in the first person. Fred's mentor and antagonist Gordon Corey is dying from the knife wounds inflicted by Virgil, a thug (Fig. 4.2); lying on the ground, Gordon is looking up to Fred through the trap door of his prop gallows on which he used to perform his circus escape routine. In the fifth panel, in which his vision blurs, we find a wavy balloon, containing the verbal utterance "Gordon?," produced by Fred. The fact that the balloon has no appendice and that its outline is wavy suggests that Fred's utterance is already fading out in Gordon's perception. In the last panel, everything turns black, signifying that Gordon has died.

Apart from one reaction image (or counter shot, see panel #4), this sequence consists of genuine POV images in which the observer adopts Gordon's point of view; in the sequence following his death, the point of view immediately switches to Fred's, and the panels of that sequence bear narrative captions with a first-person voice, commenting on the preceding events and the conclusion of the story (cf. Vance/Burr 2013: 245). – Considering the manifold episodes of the work presenting various points of view, I infer that Fred is a *narrating character* (not a narrator, as this has been proven above as implausible), whose caption utterances as well as the pictorial representations accompanying them are brought forth by the artist-writers. As mentioned before, alternating points of view are nothing unusual in graphic novels and unless analytically scrutinized, they will very probably even go unnoticed.[20]

The case is different, however, when there is a narrator with a spatio-temporal identity distinct from the intradiegetic story, not just a narrating character (see below, chapter 4.5). In Mana Neyestani's autobiographic *Une métamorphose iranienne* (2012), which is about the eponymous newspaper editor's flight from Iran to Kuala Lumpur, one subplot is found in which a Chinese immigration officer fails to recognize that Mana's and his wife's pass-

---

20 In verbal narrative fiction, by comparison, a homodiegetic voice combined with (an) unattributable 'focalization(s)' is rather unusual, yet to be found in the *jeunes auteurs de Minuit*, as in the works of Jean-Philippe Toussaint (cf. Schneider 2008) and Patrick Deville: "the jeunes auteurs de Minuit's novels feature narrative situations which for the reader inevitably convey the impression that something actually impossible is going on. Unlike an authorial narrator, a first-person narrator 'cannot' know about the intimate thoughts of other characters, nor 'can' he or she convey what other characters have done, thought or said while geographically in a different location" (Rajewsky 2009: 148). In verbal narrative fiction, such an 'omniscient first-person' or 'focalizing narrator' seems logically implausible because their uniformly verbal-monomodal discourse lacks the mode of pictorial showing (which must be clearly distinguished from the metaphorical *showing* vs. *telling* opposition, used on verbal narrative fiction and brought about by Henry James [1884] and Percy Lubbock [1922]).

ports have been forged. Despite the fact that their actual encounter at the airport is incredibly brief and formal, the extradiegetic narrator[21] presents a whole subplot including the officer's nightmares and hang-ups, which probably are as fictive as the officer's name ("Tang Lu"). After all, it seems very unlikely for the narrator to have come to know about all this (cf. Neyestani 2012: 140, 178–181, 186, and Hescher 2014b). Yet in this case, contrary to *On the Ropes*, the panels of the subplot are accompanied by (unframed) narratorial captions so that what is presented in the images can be attributed to Mana the narrator's *imagination*.

Apart from several, rather text-oriented, graphic memoirs and the rare instances of fictional biography (as Posy Simmonds' *Gemma Bovery*, 1999), narratorial caption script is often minimalistic, restricted to 'telegraphic' information about time and place, if there is caption script at all.[22] The rare case of a narratorial voice using a third-person pronoun can be found in certain sequences of Ware's *Jimmy Corrigan* (2000) and *Building Stories* (2012) or Carey and Gross' *The Unwritten* (2010).[23] This is why I would endorse the claim that "[t]raditionally, graphic narratives are relatively independent of narrator figures in third-person narration, in which narrators appear only intermittently or not at all" (Mikkonen 2013: 120).

To sum up: if the verbal and the pictorial track are considered as one (cf. Baetens/Frey 2015: 165), 'focalization' can neither account for one nor for the other because no fictional entity from the mediating/transmitting communication system generates both tracks, that is the narratorial script as well as the images (including the speech/thought balloons). Consequently, 'focalization' cannot be made to account for unattributable and/or switching *points of view* and even less so for the cases in which the narratorial caption script is mostly or completely absent. In this sense, *point of view* does not actually replace 'focalization' (the latter having been proven an implausible concept for graphic novels to begin with) but stands for what is presented in an image or an image sequence with regard to composition and perspective construction. The 'point' of *point of view* thus is not 'who perceives' (as in classical narratology, concerning verbal narrative fiction) but the pictorial side of the images, what is *shown*.

---

[21] For a detailed description of the story's framing and the pictorial presentation of the extradiegetic narrator in Mana Neyestani's *Une métamorphose iranienne*, see Hescher 2014b: 62.
[22] Jan-Noël Thon writes that "non-narratorial representation" is "verbal-pictorial representation in panels or sequences of panels, which is evidently also the result of a process of creation but whose 'source' is usually not – or at least not explicitly – represented and whose multimodal configuration prevents us from attributing it to a 'speaker' as [in] verbal forms of narration" (cf. Thon 2013: 70–71).
[23] The rare case of a (character-)narrator and biographer telling about a historical-empirical person, as in Mary M. Talbot's *Dotter of Her Father's Eyes* (2012), here is exempted.

4.3 Showing and Seeing in the Pictorial Narration

How can images narrate when they lack grammatical markers like personal pronouns, as they are found in narrative discourse (cf. Jost 1987: 16, 17)? It appears as if verbal text is more easily related to a subjective instance than an image because of the latter's 'impersonality,' that is the fact that no script of a narrating 'voice' is invoked (cf. Currie 1995: 108 qtd. in Kukkonen 2011: 38). In addition, nothing in verbal narrative fiction tampers with what readers construe as seeing or seen, as perceiving or perceived, or as thinking or thought because there is no pictorial representation. In graphic narratives, however, readers do see given images on the page in which

- what characters see is often different from what the image shows. *Seeing* in this approach is restricted to visual (or other) perception and does not connote cognition, like thinking or knowing (which is a crucial concept of focalization according to François Jost, see chapter 4.8). Although this might seem restrictive, in graphic novels, as in graphic narratives in general, the tension building from where characters look or what they look at – as opposed to what the image shows – is important for the production of meaning from a recipient-oriented view (let's not forget that since showing is the dominant mode in graphic narratives, reader-reception should also be taken into consideration, see above, p. 115). What the image shows I have called *point of view*. Yet what characters visually perceive must be inferred: it often cannot be made out exactly or at all (I shall come back to this point below).

- In addition, what is supposed to be seen from the *projection center*, or the *implied observer*'s point of view, is not necessarily what the empirical reader perceives. Martin Schüwer explains how comics must project three-dimensional space on a two-dimensional surface. As in every perspectival image, the projection rays run from the points in the image space to the projection center, which equals the eyes of the (implied) observer, which again are abstracted to one single geometrical point (Fig. 4.3, "PZ," cf. Bärtschi 1976, qtd. in Schüwer 2008: 524–525). Yet not all projection rays converging in the projection center are equally important. One among them, the main visual ray, intersects the image surface at a 90-degree angle and indicates the general direction of the implied observer's gaze. Every perspective construction is oriented on precisely one main visual ray departing from the eyes of the observer, who (theoretically) fixes the gaze on one single point of the image surface. The point at which the main visual ray hits the projection surface is the *perspective center* (Fig. 4.3, "ZP," ibid.). Sometimes, however, in an "excentric" image composition, the perspective center is at odds with the projection center so that observers have the feeling that they are seeing an 'impossible space' (cf. Schüwer 2008: 100). Unless such a constellation is a coherence mistake, it should be important for the meaning building through the empirical observers with regard to what they see presented in the image (or possibly in the image sequence) and with regard to the way the image appeals to them as recipients (see my analyses of a sequence from *V for Vendetta*, ch. 4.3.1, and from *Ghost World*, ch. 4.3.1.2, for illustration). This is also why it is not enough, as brought up in the recent research, to posit only a "perceptual source" or "center" for what images show (Groensteen 2013, ch. 5.1.1, np., borrowing from Mikkonen 2008) because that would preclude effects of a projection center jarring with a perspective center.

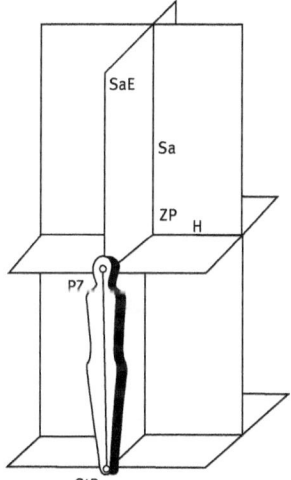

Fig. 4.3: Bärtschi 1976: 41, projection and perspective center, qtd. in Schüwer 2008: 525

As opposed to readers of verbal narrative fiction, who imagine one more or less consistent point of view (occasional paralepsis and multiple point of view construction notwithstanding), readers of graphic narratives see images in a sequence representing – on the whole – diverse points of view and perspective constructions that they cannot always attribute to a character or a narrator. They see what, in film theory, Deleuze called subjective and objective images (Deleuze 2009, V). Yet subjective images should not be reduced to mere POV or "gaze images."[24] In the renowned

---

24 Kai Mikkonen, who follows François Jost's ocularization concept, which he calls "perceptual focalization," distinguishes "the point of view (POV) image (the impression that the reader shares the point of view with a particular character), the gaze image (showing a picture of a character looking at something), the eye-line image/match cut (a combination of a gaze image

trauma episode from Frank Miller's *The Dark Knight Returns* (2002: 22–24), for example, it is obvious that the young Bruce's emotions during his parents' assassination could not be conveyed if the sequence only consisted of POV images (cf. Schüwer 2008: 170–177); also, a genuine POV sequence could not possibly show Bruce's facial expressions, and we would paradoxically be further removed from the action if we saw it only through the boy's eyes (ibid. 177). As François Jost writes about film: "A quite common error consists in the belief that internal focalization is inevitably conveyed by a subjective camera" (Jost 1987: 71, cf. ibid. 73, point 1) – or, respectively, by POV images in graphic narratives. The POV image is the only truly subjective image in which the positions of the empirical readers and the implied observer fully overlap; this makes it a special type of image representing what a character perceives (cf. Schüwer 2008: 177). However, genuine POV images are rather scarce in quantity and usually link up with images showing different points of view – the pictorial co-text – often in the form of reaction images or shot-reverse shots, as they are called in cinematic discourse. Let's look, for example, at the following sequence from Jason Lutes' *Berlin, City of Stones* (2001, Fig. 4.4):

Fig. 4.4: Lutes 2011: 136, POV and reaction images

The index that the episode is principally seen through the eyes of the journalist Kurt Severin – and not of his lover, the art student Marthe Müller – is found in the second panel: the fact that the image here appears grainy and blurry is an index of Kurt's screwing up his eyes because he is not wearing his thick glasses.

---

that is preceded or followed by a point of view image), the over-the-shoulder image, and the reaction image (a character reacting to what he has just seen)" (Mikkonen 2013: 103). Jost writes that generally, depending on the context, "every photograph can be called objective or subjective. A photograph of a landscape can be related to the landscape itself (the referential function) or to the photographer (expressive function). [...] And that is why any shot from any film can be transformed into a look simply by juxtaposing it with an image of someone looking" (Jost 2004: 74).

In the subsequent images, the viewers are offered other points of view, such as over-the-shoulder shots or frontal views.[25] In this 56-panel episode, only ten genuine POV images are found – which is comparatively many and certainly due to the action and the setting of the episode: Kurt and Marthe have fallen in love and spent the night in Kurt's apartment.

In general, most images are what Jean Mitry (1965) called *half-subjective*: Mitry coined this term for the perception image in film on the grounds that cinematographic perception incessantly goes from the subjective to the objective. Gilles Deleuze took this up and condensed it in the formula, "[the camera] no longer mingles with the character, nor is it outside: it is with him. It is a kind of truly cinematographic *Mitsein* [...,] the anonymous viewpoint of someone unidentified amongst the characters" (Deleuze 2009: 72). However, as I pointed out above, the comparison of film to comics images is not without problems. The cinematic image depicts movement within one shot, that is camera movement (panning or tracking shots, for example) as well as character movement. Also, the perspective center in cinematic images is generally situated in the middle of the frame (Schüwer 2008: 198) and, therefore, it is not as salient as in comics images, in which it may be removed from the implied observer.[26] I would hold that the still or comics image is more dominated by the perspective construction than the cinematic shot. To put it differently, comics artists are more concerned with perspective construction.

As for the above sequence from Lutes' *Berlin, City of Stones*, nothing seems to speak against the thesis that the whole episode is focalized through Kurt Severin. But this is not the whole truth. The episode is in fact introduced by a high-angle view over the housing unit, followed by three small panels depicting detailed views of the street and one view of the dormer to Kurt's apartment (Lutes 2011: 135, see below, Fig. 4.12); accordingly, the sequence closes with an oblong horizontal panel displaying a straight-on angle of the housing unit's rooftop (ibid. 139). This underscores the principle stated above: comics images usually show more than what is seen by the characters. The sequence from *Berlin, City of Stones*, is ambiguous with regard to point of view because of the mix of objective images in the opening and closing sequences, which cannot be attributed to any consciousness within the *diegesis*, and the subjective images in the middle; it is ambig-

---

[25] Thon would call this a "(quasi-)perceptual point of view sequence," Jost a "secondary internal ocularization" (Thon 2014, ch. 3, np., and Jost 2004: 75).
[26] Schüwer refers to the differentiation in film theory between the frame and the cache (Bazin 1985: 188, qtd. in Schüwer 2008: 186). The film image has a movable and moving border, and when the action happens beyond that border, it is called cache. This distinction is, with some restrictions or modifications, also applicable to comics images.

uous also because, in the context of the whole work, this sequence is one instance of multiple subjective points of view combined with non-attributable sequences.

4.3.1 What Is Shown and What Is (not) Seen: Mise en Scène vs. Character Vision

Showing is the overall dominating mode of representation in graphic narratives. I have claimed above that comics images normally show more than what the characters see. Only in POV images does what is shown exactly coincide with what is seen. A near-POV variant is the more frequent over-the-shoulder image, which presents almost but not quite what a character sees. Usually, what is shown is rather not, and sometimes not at all, what is seen. Also, the implied observer's view, or the center of projection, is often incongruent with the vision of a character or a perceiving consciousness. What exactly a character sees or perceives is rarely optically visible, or at least difficult to make out (genuine POV images being the exception rather than the rule). Therefore, I have rejected the focalization concept and associated *point of view* with what is shown, or the perspective construction, and not with what is seen.

As for film, François Jost distinguishes focalization from ocularization[27] and says that "*ocularization* has to do with the relation between what the [image] shows and what the characters are presumed to be seeing; *focalization* designates the cognitive point of view adopted by the narrative" (Jost 2004: 74, cf. ibid. 1987: 18). What a character knows ("the cognitive point of view"), however, cannot reliably be inferred from one or diverse ocularizations. In graphic novels, I must eventually rely on the verbal track (balloon speech and/or narrative captions, if there are any). In analyses of actual image sequences or episodes, however – and, eventually, of the graphic work as a whole – cognition or perception are often difficult to make out because there might be no narratorial script. Since comics images are, above all, made to show, the question is whether focalization as character knowledge related to reader knowledge (Jost) is a rewarding paradigm to start with or whether what is shown does not provide the vaster resource with respect to possible image interpretations or analytical approaches.

Let's look at representative image sequences and episodes from diverse graphic novels. In Alan Moore and David Lloyd's *V for Vendetta*, for example, we find V on the brink of blowing up the Statue of Justice on the Old Bailey court house in London (Fig. 4.5):

---

[27] I shall elaborate on ocularization below (see ch. 4.3.1.2).

4.3 Showing and Seeing in the Pictorial Narration — 127

Fig. 4.5: Moore/Lloyd 2005: 40, mise en scène: showing vs. seeing

In a mock farewell address, V addresses the statue, which used to be his 'love' until he chose 'Anarchy' over her because Justice 'betrayed him' (an allusion to the fascist leader Adam Susan, who rules the country with the aid of the super computer Fate). In the first two panels of this mock episode, we observe V, depicted from a high angle, as he is talking to Justice, his face slightly tilted down (Fig. 4.5, panel #1). The second panel shows Justice's face in a close-up from a low angle. Obviously, this is rather not a point-of-view image since the physical distance from V, standing distinctly lower on the rooftop of an adjacent building (cf. Moore/Lloyd 2005: 39), to Justice's face is simply too large (see panel #3); as readers, we might of course imagine V looking up and imagining, in turn, Justice's face from close by. A similar discrepancy of what is shown and (what can be) seen is depicted in panels #4 and #5, the difference being that panel #4 shows a slanted perspective with physically distorted relations of size and space. Thus, neither of the panels #2–5 actually show what V is actually seeing.

What then are we to make of this? Possibly that what is shown (and seen, like in genuine POV images) is related to the mise en scène – which pertains to the external communication system and for which the artist-writer team is responsible. The term mise en scène has been employed in theatre performance contexts and in drama and film analysis, while it has rarely been used on comics. Thierry Groensteen writes:

> [...] the hierarchy of information conveyed by the image is assured by its intrinsic organization, that which obeys the instance of the mise en scène. [...] this concept can be meaningfully extended to comics [...] In the case of the ninth art, we must rigorously distinguish at least two components to this organization of representation: the framing (*mise en cadre*) and the drawing (*mise en dessin*). [...] The mise en scène, therefore, organizes the different parameters of the image (framing, choice of point of view, composition, "actions" of the characters, lighting, etc. in accordance with the internal dynamic of the sequence, to produce an aesthetic or dramatic effect [...] (Groensteen 2007: 120)

I would add to the definition of mise en scène the perspective construction (see above), angle, coloring, in short: everything that can be seen in the images, except their ordering or sequencing on the page (layout). Thus, in graphic narratives, showing is the mode of representation of the mise en scène and its diverse components.

In the above example from *V for Vendetta*, the mise en scène defamiliarizes what at first glance might appear as subjective images: in the course of this sequence, we even find a panel with another implausible view, this time over Justice's shoulder down on V (Moore/Lloyd 2005: 41, panel #2). Although this episode seems at first to be V's point of view, the defamiliarization techniques (in the sense of *showing*) reveal it to be non-attributable in terms of point of view, if not to the mise en scène and the external communication system. In fact, the whole sequence is designed as a mock episode, a mock 'perspective' or view, and as if V himself were to comment on the mise en scène in these images, he says: "I used to wonder why you could never look me in the eye" (ibid., panel #3). He has a point here, indeed.[28]

From a cognitive point of view, one could argue with Pascal Lefèvre that these work-specific differences between seeing and showing, between character vision and mise en scène, "are not even perceived or considered as troubling

---

[28] Hannah Miodrag criticizes Moore for his way of telling instead of showing; his dialogues are supposedly "too palpably manufactured and constructed" (Miodrag 2013: 63). But V's 'theatricality,' for which Moore is blamed in the first place, seems intended and perfectly fits the make-up of the plot and its characters. Therefore, V's language is simply comical.

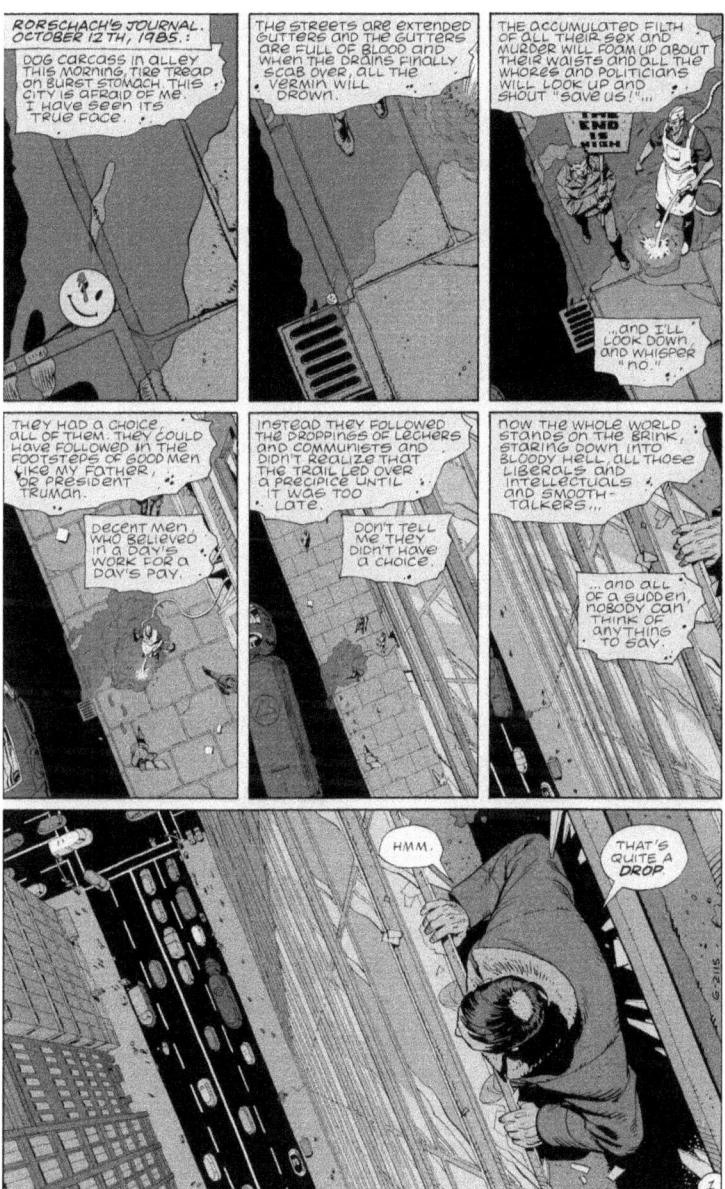

Fig. 4.6: Moore/Gibbons 2008: I, 1, zooming (mise en scène)

by the reader" (Lefèvre 2000, np.). In fact, "the degree of coherence of the fictive world," albeit "crucial for the acceptance by the reader" (ibid.), is by definition much more flexible in the comics medium than in verbal narrative fiction, without disturbing the readers' overall perception of the fictive world. Comics predominantly show (or give as a kind of 'ready-made') what in verbal media depends on the effort of the readers' imagination – which may fail to render the story world as coherent while it is constructing mental images from words.

If we consider such gaps of incommensurability between what is seen and shown to be continuity errors (while arguing in favor of an overall subjective point of view on V's part), we cannot possibly ignore similar instances from other graphic works – which clearly are not continuity errors but instances of the mise en scène. The often-referred-to opening sequence to chapter one from Alan Moore and Dave Gibbons' *Watchmen* (Fig. 4.6), for example, depicts from above a close-up of the blood puddle and the smiley button with the metaphorical hour/minute hand, which belongs to Edward Blake, 'the Comedian,' who has been thrown from the nth floor of his New York highrise apartment by the narcissistic and egomaniac Adrian Veidt.

The seven-panel sequence displays a continuing zooming away from the blood spot and the button until, in the seventh and last panel on that page, we are looking over the head and shoulders of a police detective, who is looking down from a few hundreds of meters above at the sidewalk with the blood spot. The zooming depicted in the first five panels cannot be accomplished by the detective (since firstly, he is simply too far away in altitude from the blood spot and secondly, characters are by definition incapable of zooming in on objects, unless they use a viewing device), and is a clear example of mise en scène, eventually attributable to the artist-writer team and the external communication system. Here, as in the example from *V for Vendetta*, the mise en scène encroaches upon point of view. What is shown is clearly no subjective image, despite the fact that the image is shot from a high angle over the detective's shoulders (Fig. 4.6, panel #7). – Although this section is not about verbal narration, let me briefly refer to the verbal track in this sequence. It is cross-cut with the homodiegetic 'voice' from Rorschach's journal in the yellow captions, commenting on the deplorable state of a world on the eve of destruction. Towards the end of this episode, we find a panel that, as in *V for Vendetta*, reveals the sequence as mockery, as an ironic comment from the artist-writer team: when the two detectives leave the crime scene, the elevator attendant asks them what floor they intend to go to. The next image shows Edward Blake as he is thrown out of the window by Veidt (who cannot be seen but whose hands protrude into the panel from the top left), falling down, the scene heavily tinted in red. It is obvious that this image is neither a flashback nor a point of view image but a sarcastic comment cued by the elevator man's utterance in the caption: "Ground floor coming up" (Fig. 4.7). The extreme angles of the mise en scène shape what is shown in this episode as non-subjective, which is starkly

Fig. 4.7: Moore/Gibbons 2008: I, 3, non-subjective mise en scène

contrasted by the homodiegetic, framing voice of Rorschach, a constellation (homodiegetic voice plus unattributable point of view) that would be implausible, following classical narratology, in verbal narrative fiction.

Other examples of showing as a part of the mise en scène are, with certain restrictions, pictorial metaphors or allegories such as the anthropomorphic figures in Spiegelman's *Maus*: as opposed to Orwell's *Animal Farm*, for example, in which the characters are animals and perceive each other as such, the characters in *Maus* perceive each other as human beings. A rather specific case of showing detached from character vision is found in the latest issue of Marc-Antoine Mathieu's *Julius Corentin Acquefacques, prisonnier des rêves: Le décalage* (Fig. 4.8):

Fig. 4.8: Mathieu 2013: 29, illustrated speechboxes (mise en scène)

Here, Hilarion Ozéclat, the twin brothers Dalenvert, and the professor Ouffe are wandering through space in search of Julius, who has become invisible because he has gone ahead of the story world time. Besides verbal speech, the speech boxes contain illustrating images of different degrees of iconicity, and it is obvious that the characters do not see these images. Many other examples of showing, owed to the mise en scène and the external communication system, could be brought up, for example non-diegetic pictorial elements with rhetorical and/or stylistic functions (see chapter 4.9.5).

4.3.1.1 Showing Taken to the Extreme: Cross-Cutting Strands of Action/*Montage*

The cross-cutting of two different narrative strands represents an extreme case of pictorial narrative ambiguity and complexity. Generally, cross-cutting and *montage* are actualized in two parallel strands of action or in two strands of action of which one is delayed in time; in this case, the other strand anticipates the upcoming events. – In Alan Moore and Eddie Campbell's *From Hell* (1999), there is no narratorial caption script, and the numerous instances of cross-cutting in this work connect strands of action that happen either consecutively (ch. IV) or simultaneously (ch. V). In chapter IV, the panels in the middle and bottom tier depict Queen Victoria as she is sending for Sir William Gull, the royal physician, to order him to silence a group of prostitutes who have conspired to blackmail a friend of her infamous grandson Prince Albert, who married a shop girl and fathered a child with her. The oblong horizontal panel on the top shows in silhouette the lower rear of the coach driven by Netley, Gull's simple-minded stooge, who assists him in the slaughterings (Fig. 4.9). This layout is repeated on the following page, only with the top panel displaying a medium shot of the horse as it is drawing the coach (Moore/Campbell 2006: IV, 3).

Chronologically, the action in the middle and bottom tier happens before Netley's driving the coach to Dr Gull's house in the top panel. As it is laid out on the page, however, the top panel anticipates the action following Queen Victoria's clandestine plotting and thus underscores the inevitability of the Whitechapel murders. – But what is actually seen on these two pages? And what is shown? In this instance of *montage*, the showing clearly is more salient than the seeing, and this is why point of view here is not at stake. Because of the stark contrast in the pictorial semantics of the different parts of the layout and because of the overly large continuity gap between the images on the top and the lower tiers, the narrative becomes more 'showy,' its driving force bigger, building momentum from one page to the next. – Martin Schüwer points out that all comics panels may in principle be looked at in terms of *montage*, for movement and action always 'happen in between the panels;' in other words, there is always a local and/or temporal leap between one and the following panel (Schüwer 2008: 271–273). Yet the contrast in the pictorial semantics (or the content) of the panels is not the only factor in the meaning production effected through *montage*. In the above example, the position, size, and form of the panel play an important role: that the top panel overarches the two lower tiers puts the emphasis on Dr Gull's killing spree, which starts with the depicted coach ride and which is the novel's point of convergence.

Little has been written on cross-cutting in complex graphic narratives. Originating in cinematic discourse, cross-cutting and its transposition on comics are worthy of comment. Both *montage* and cross-cutting are forms of editing to be seen against the backdrop of continuity editing, as it has been employed in Hollywood productions for more than half a century. Whereas *montage* signifies the putting together of extremely heterogeneous images, the context of which may not be clear immediately (Fig. 4.9), cross-cutting usually means the presentation of two strands of action the context of which is clear as they happen more or less simultaneously.

Fig. 4.9: Moore/Campbell 2006: IV, 2, montage

Schüwer aims at bringing cross-cutting in comics into line with cross-cutting in film theory by narrowing it down to the transition from one panel to the next[29]: if the local-temporal leap between the panels is so big that observers can no longer synthesize a continuous movement through time and space, the result is what he calls a "decentering [*Dezentrierung*] of the implied observer" (Schüwer 2008: 273). This, of course, is a matter of degree, as Schüwer holds – a thesis I totally endorse; I would add, however, that the transition may not only concern the next panel in line but possibly a whole image sequence in which the departing panel and the next panel are embedded, as in the above example.[30] The cardinal (and necessarily metaphorical) question therefore is: how big is the gap between the images or image sequences concerned? If it is too disproportionate, too wide to be synthesized into "a continuous movement through time and space," the images or image sequences qualify as *montage* (this does not apply to the field of abstract or experimental comics, where images are not necessarily sequential with respect to action, cf. Groensteen 2013, ch. 1). Yet I would like to point out one comic-specific restriction to Schüwer's approach: in a graphic novel, as opposed to film, cross-cut images or image sequences exist in factual-physical simultaneity. In the reading process, however, their actual reception happens at least partly linearly (or according to the 'Z-path,' that is one image or image sequence after another) and partly tabularly (cf. Hatfield 2005, ch. 3). Thus, cross-cut images or image sequences are read in virtual simultaneity.

Nevertheless, these last reflections are of minor importance. Accordingly, it is secondary that *montage* and cross-cutting are attributed to the artist-writer. The cardinal point is that they represent a type of showing in which the gap between two panels or panel sequences has been made extremely wide or disproportionate. The effect brought about through this type prevails by far over point of view and character vision. This is best illustrated in another cross-cut from *From Hell* (Fig. 4.10).

In one narrative strand, the 16-year-old William Gull sets out to dissect a mouse which he has found dead in the grass out of doors (panels #1 and #3), while his mother is inside, talking to the head of Beaumont Rectory (panel #2: his father having recently died, William is supposed to attend this boarding school).

---

29 Jakob Dittmar uses a similar departing point but remains more narrowly bound to film theory and more directly compares the two media with respect to narration. In that context, he also elaborates on parameters like the frame, dramaturgy of the sequences, point of view, etc. (Dittmar 2008: 125–136).
30 For an example of cross-cut single panels, see Moore/Campbell 2006: V, 10–13.

Fig. 4.10: Moore/Campbell 2006: II, 6, cross-cut

Panels #1 and #3 are genuine POV images, whereas panel #2 depicts no subjective bending at all. The fact that what is seen in panels #1 and #3 represents William's limited subjective point of view is absolutely secondary to the effect achieved through the juxtaposition of the static panel, showing the head talking to his mother, and the action-oriented dissection panels. It would not be useful to specify the points of view, neither for each narrative strand nor for the sequence as a whole.[31] What counts is that the two narrative strands correlate and foreshadow William Gull's atrocious slaughterings of several prostitutes, which is emphasized in the last panel of this sequence, a close-up of his palm in which (the mouse's) blood is dribbling (Moore/Campbell 2006: II.6, panel #9). To sum up, cross-cutting and *montage* are first and foremost particular types of showing.[32] To what extent they imply breakdown and layout is subject to another chapter (4.10).

---

[31] The whole sequence spreads over two pages, and the pictorial representations of the mother and the head hardly differ (Moore/Campbell 2006: II.5–6).

[32] In Horstkotte/Pedri 2011, it is claimed that the twelve images of the blood-red murder sequence (see above, Fig. 4.7), which occurs three times in *Watchmen* (ch. I.2–4, ch. II.26–28, ch. XI.24–26), have narrator or character-specific focalizers. However, those images are cross-cut with the main narrative strand, and the *montage*, as in this case, of single images or image sequences is a matter of breakdown and layout in the first place and cannot possibly be imputed to a narrator or focalizer. And since breakdown and layout pertain to the external communication system, they are attributable only to the artist-writers and their function as showers or presenters. The varying pictorial points of view or ocularizations of the twelve images are partly attributable to Veidt, partly to no perceptive center at all in the diegesis. Yet cognitively, this is irrelevant

4.3.1.2 Mise en Scène and Ocularization

What is *shown* or presented in graphic narratives is first and foremost attributable to the artist-writer team,[33] pertaining to the external communication system, or to the more drawing-specific parameter of perspective construction, which I take to be subordinate to the mise en scène, including parameters such as angle, width of frame, color, foreground/background, design of characters, etc. *Seeing* in graphic narratives means above all character vision since, in contrast to verbal texts, the comics medium mostly represents thought and feeling through extra sets of signifiers, the verbal-pictorial (and iconic), extradiegetic, thought or speech balloons and the purely pictorial emanata, which represent emotions or emotional states (see chapter 4.9.5). These also distinguish comics from film, in which the characters' thoughts may be visualized – as in the case of memory sequences (which is also done in graphic novels) – or rendered in the audiotrack (cf. Jost 1987: 56–57, 63). What is seen in graphic narratives is principally attributable to
a) a character (of the story world),[34] and
b) to the empirical reader-observers, who see images and on this basis (re)construct and interpret the bimodal narrative.

What is shown in a single image usually is not the same as in another image in that sequence or in the episode as a whole. Episodes consist of different 'shots' from different angles with different widths of frame (medium shot, shot/reverse shot, high or low-angle shot, close-up, 'subjective camera, etc., to borrow from cinematic terminology) with different *implied observer* positions. Schüwer writes that "representations of space denying all possible implied observer positions have consequences for the narrative structure" (Schüwer 2008: 401). A character's position in a drawing may be – and in fact often is – at odds with or detached from the position of the implied observer, that is her/his position in the perspective construction of the image (due to parallel, two/three-point perspective, etc.). To illustrate this, let's look at the very first page of Daniel Clowes' *Ghost World* (Fig. 4.11):

---

because in the first murder sequence, the murderer's identity is obviously withheld from the readers – which fact is in no way imputable to Veidt, the character, nor to a narrator speaking in the captions. Even in the last of the three sequences, when Veidt pompously reveals his doings to Rorschach and Dreiberg, the blood-red images are cross-cut with the main narrative strand and represent no focalization but *showing* on the part of the artist-writers.

33 Seymour Chatman refers to a "presenter" (Chatman 1990: 113) and Gaudreault to a "monstrator" (qtd. in Groensteen 2013, ch. 5.1.2).

34 What characters (can) see is mostly subject to inference, with the exception of the POV or over-the shoulder image.

Fig. 4.11: Clowes 2000: 9, vectorization and defamiliarization

4.3 Showing and Seeing in the Pictorial Narration — 139

The first panel depicts a frontal view of a house and a garage door (with the non-diegetic heading "Ghost World"). The perspective center here is literally in the dark, and a tension builds between the garage door (the outer world), and the lighted window of the house on the top left (the inner world). As opposed to a conventional frontal projection, the gaze of the implied observer is here distracted from the perspectival center and sent into oscillation between the main character, Enid, behind the window and the garage door, that is between inside and outside. Panel #2 also is a frontal view from outside, yet zoomed in on the lighted window and the TV set as the perspective center, which is axially aligned with the implied observer position. The dominating presence in this panel, however, is Enid, who is framed by the left transom square, the transom dividing the panel into a larger (left) and a smaller (right) part; her position is clearly removed from the implied observer and, in addition, Enid looks to the outside left of the image. In a social semiotics approach, frontal views are usually connected with maximum involvement on the viewer's side (Jewitt/Oyama 2006: 135). Here, however, in the first two panels, the opposite effect is brought about through vectorization: in panel #1, the top left corner of the garage forms a vector, an arrow pointing at the lighted window in the top left of the panel. Viewer attention, therefore, is divided or sent into oscillation between the garage door, the outer "ghost world," and the inside world of the teenagers; the viewer is thus defamiliarized in the sense of being 'in between' two worlds. In panel #2, a similar effect is produced through vectorization: the perspective center (the TV set) is in the background, and Enid, who is foregrounded, looks down to the outside left of the window, her gaze forming another vector.[35] Here again, viewer attention is drawn away from the center to the periphery of the image. Also, it is noteworthy that Enid's girlfriend Rebecca is depicted metonymically (only one of her legs is visible) so that we do not see her face: however, the eyeline of the head depicted on the TV screen serves as a vector pointing at Rebecca's eyes outside the panel frame on the lower right. Consequently, as in panel #1, viewer attention is sent into oscillation between Enid's face and Rebecca's (invisible) face, implied beyond the panel border, between foreground and background.

Panel #3 represents a parallel projection, which totally suspends an implied observer position (cf. Schüwer 2008: 124) because of the absence of a vanishing point; this effect is amplified by the two main characters Enid and Rebecca, whose eyelines are in parallel alignment. Panels #4 and #5 again are frontal

---

[35] "The eyline, the direction of the gaze of represented participants (insofar as it is not directed at the viewer), is a special kind of vector" (Jewitt/Oyama 2006: 143).

projections which may be read as (half-)subjective images: panel #4 as a shot over Enid's and Rebecca's shoulders and panel #5 as a POV image. Despite the absence of edges or border lines, the last panel on this page is another parallel projection of Enid and Rebecca looking at the TV screen outside the panel frame, the girls' eyelines being parallels; here again, the implied observer position is suspended. In this panel sequence, at least, the implied observer position is dissociated from the characters so that Enid and Rebecca clearly see something different from what is shown in the images. Empirical reader-observers may feel shut out of the self-centered world of the two teenagers, which stands in sharp contrast to the outer "ghost world" and includes adults, friends, and acquaintances. Indeed, the story as a whole seems to confirm this point in the way Enid and Rebecca behave toward the other characters throughout the story.[36]

An efficient conceptual tool for pictorial track analysis should be *relational* in order to account for what is shown (point of view) as opposed to what is seen (character vision) in a sequential image. In addition, it should imply an assessment of the mise en scène. Jost's term *ocularization* seems to be the most suitable existing relational term for this, although it does not imply all the parameters just mentioned:

> To characterize the relation between what the camera shows [*montrer*] and what the hero is supposed to see [*voir*], I suggest we speak of ocularization: in fact, this term has the advantage of evoking the ocular and the eye which looks at the field that the camera is "taking" [*prendre*] (Jost 1987: 18).[37]

Jost's film-oriented ocularization concept, however, does of course not account for the mise en scène parameters that are relevant for comics images. To give one example: it is in the nature of the moving cinematic image that perspective construction is less eminent (except in still shots) than in the still comics image; principally, the diverse perspective constructions of the images on a comics page relate to each other simultaneously, which may create a tension between the vantage points of the implied observer and the empirical reader-observer (see my analysis of *Ghost World* above). Also, Jost relates ocularization to the "hero" and thereby excludes the possibility of a sequential image displaying more than one character. Yet in *Ghost World*, it is often important to note where the two main characters are looking because their eye lines constitute vectors

---

[36] It would be interesting to know if teenage readers of *Ghost World* experience a similar defamiliarization effect.

[37] To some extent, Mikkonen uses a similar approach including "the position, angle, field, and focus of vision" (Mikkonen 2013: 102).

that direct the empirical reader-observers' gaze away from the perspective center and thus produce what I have called above a defamiliarization effect.

In the following, I shall take *ocularization* to signify above all the optical perspective construction with the resulting attributable or non-attributable point of view: after all, ocularization can but "does not have to belong to anyone or any instance in the story world, or in the frame narrative; it can remain fully impersonal and hypothetical" (Mikkonen 2013: 106). In addition, I would extend the definitional scope of Jost's concept and include the other parameters of the mise en scène (framing, angle, color, etc., see Jost 1987: 69, 71, and above, chapter 4.3.1).[38]

To sum up: ocularization in graphic novels signifies the relation between what the single image shows (mise en scène, including point of view) and what the characters see (character vision). The fact that ocularization is a relational term will not reduce the complexity in assessing a whole image sequence or episode: normally, different types of ocularization are found in a sequence, which seem to 'contradict' each other with regard to point of view; and oftentimes, it is not obvious whose or what type of ocularization it is. As for the whole graphic work, I would claim that, in most cases, we find zero or secondary internal ocularization.

Considering the additions made to the superordinate term, let me now introduce the different types of ocularization, borrowing again from Jost:

- *primary internal ocularization* for images representing a genuine POV shot (Jost 1987: 18–19); what Jost calls *secondary internal ocularization* occurs "when the subjective image is constructed through editing (as in shot/counter-shot); that is, through contextualization of an image. Any image that is edited together with a shot of a person looking [...] will be 'anchored' in the visual subjectivity of that person or character" (Jost 2004: 75); and

- *zero ocularization* for "when the image is not seen by any entity within the diegesis. [I]t simply signifies seen by no one, 'nobody's shot,' [...] it is not possible to assign an image to any specific gaze. Most shots of most films use zero ocularization, even in the case of characters or narrators telling their own stories in flashback" (Jost 2004: 75–76).[39]

---

38 In ch. 3, I already expounded on the complexity of graphic novels, two types of which directly concern parameters of the mise en scène, i.e. color and panel design, the others may involve aspects of mise en scène indirectly.
39 "Jost's category of 'zero ocularization' does not refer to a missing point of perception but to a broad range of perspectival options where the focalizer remains impersonal" (Mikkonen 2013: 106).

I would endorse this last claim concerning films for comics and graphic novels. Also, I would hold that the ocularization types internal and zero can be used on sequential images without major problems. In my example from Lutes' *Berlin* (see above, chapter 4.3, Fig. 4.4), panel #2 is a primary internal ocularization, panels #1 and #3 are secondary internal ocularizations or reaction images (Lutes 2011: 136); the images preceding this sequence, which show Kurt's street from different angles, are zero ocularizations (Fig. 4.12).

No reason is given why there is no 'external ocularization.'[40] This, however, is quite obvious: images contain no grammatical markers and display no pictorial equivalent of a proper name or a personal pronoun (*he, she, I*). Therefore, such a concept is of no use. According to the above definition, it is impossible to pictorially distinguish 'external' from zero ocularization.[41]

Jost suggests two more ocularizations, which are, however, very specific and therefore only of secondary importance: the viewer-directed or *spectatorial ocularization*, which aims at giving the viewer a cognitive advantage over a character or any diegetic instance (Jost 1987: 24–25),[42] and the *modalized ocularization*, which represents a character's thoughts or imagination by means of a "modalisation operator" like a blur (*opérateur de modalisation*, cf. Jost 1987: 27–28). Transferred to comics images, a modalized ocularization could consist, for example, in a salient framing (including non-frames) or drawing style (a different pencil stroke, graininess or blur, cross-hatching, pixelating,

---

40 The closest Jost comes to an explanation is this: "As far as the problem of the localization of a visual point of view is concerned, there are only two solutions: either the camera stands for a gaze [*vaut pour un regard*] – and I am speaking of primary and secondary internal ocularizations – or it does not stand for a gaze of a diegetic instance (zero ocularization)" (Jost 1987: 69).

41 "[...] the distinction between external and internal ocularization is potentially misleading in comics because purely internal or purely external points of perception are usually short instances only in [the comics] medium. The crucial distinction, then, is [...] how and to what extent the image, and what is seen in the image, is subjectified by narrative conventions and context with the perception and consciousness of a character in the storyworld (Mikkonen 2013: 106)."

42 There are two problems involved in spectatorial ocularization: firstly, this concept fully overlaps another concept of Jost's (spectatorial focalization); secondly, the example he gives is too specific to generalize from: Jost elaborates on the framing device of the iris mask used in a scene of *The Night of the Hunter* (USA 1955, d: Charles Laughton). This iris mask is supposed to narrow viewer attention to the two children, John and Pearl, as they are spying at Harry Powell (impersonated by Robert Mitchum), who is approaching the house (0:43:20). However, even in 1955 this was not an often-used device anymore; continuity editing à la Hollywood had long since taken over. From then on, such framing devices were (and still are) restricted to comedy, pastiche, or to children's movies. In fact, a simple cut could have accomplished the same effect. All this considered, I would rather see the iris mask as a rhetorical, hyperbolic and/or ironic, means that fits in with all the other extravagant usages of framing and mise en scène that make up the originality of this movie.

etc.); then again, it might not differ at all from its immediate pictorial co-text so that readers have to rely on the semantic context of the sequence.

To take stock: as a first step, I compared graphic narratives to drama and established that they lack the mediating/transmitting communication system and the fictional entity ('narrator') that would be solely responsible for the bringing forth of the whole discourse, verbal and pictorial. This is even more plausible when the verbal and the pictorial track of a graphic narrative are considered as one, as being the specific (or core) feature of meaning production in graphic narratives. Consequently, I abandoned the focalization concept from classical narratology to focus on what comics images *show*, in terms of the pictorial point of view and mise en scène. Because of the inherent tension in comics images between what is shown (mise en scène, point of view) and what is *seen* (character vision), I introduced Jost's ocularization types to account for exactly this tension and extended their definitional scope by including the parameters of showing from the step before (mise en scène and perspective construction). In this line of thought, showing, the reification of the deictic value or excess[43] in graphic images, must be attributed to the creators themselves, the artist-writer (team), pertaining to the external communication system.

In graphic narratives, showing is narrating, and what is shown (the pictorial track) matters as much as what is told (the verbal-narratorial track, which I shall elaborate on in the following chapter 4.4). Ocularization accounts for the relation of what is shown and what is seen in a single image within a sequence of images. Rarely will one ocularization be made accountable for a whole sequence or episode, in which different types of ocularization occur, let alone for a whole individual work.

In this sense, the whole episode containing the above example from Lutes' *Berlin, City of Stones*, does not exclusively display 'Kurt's point of view' (see above, Fig. 4.4), for what is shown in the opening and closing sequences to this episode, he neither sees nor hears: in the first panel from the opening episode (Fig. 4.12), the high-angle street view is overlaid by speech balloons which represent radio talk and which emerge from different spots in the streets. This is a clear example of zero ocularization. What can be said of this episode as a whole is that it provides instances of zero, primary, and secondary internal ocularization. The conceptional tool to account for the ocularizations in a sequence, episode, or possibly the whole work and the ratios of knowledge is Jost's focalization concept (see chapter 4.8). But let me first elaborate on the verbal track.

---

[43] Commenting on François Jost's terminology, Kai Mikkonen writes that "the image has a certain deictic value in itself (as showing or pointing to something) and that the image implies a spatially determined point of perception" (Mikkonen 2013: 105).

Fig. 4.12: Lutes 2011: 135, zero ocularization

4.4 Words and Text as Showing and Narrating

What does the verbal track consist of? Generally, it includes alphabetic signs which are primarily symbolic or iconic or pictorial. The literature about comics also speaks of 'text' and divides it into different classes or types. Text can be looked at with regard to size, typeface, color, its position inside or outside of an image, across images, or on a page. Besides, and that is held to be typical of graphic novels, "words are not only meant to be read, but they must also be looked at, both in themselves and in relation to the place they occupy in the work" (Baetens/Frey 2015: 152).

In other words, this section is about how different types of *text* – not language[44] – relate to showing (see ch. 4.2) and narrating. Ann Miller distinguishes five types of text:
1) paratext (cover, copyright page, etc.),
2) the narratorial voice-over or *récitatif*, for which I have been using the term narratorial (caption) script,
3) dialogue, usually in the form of speech or thought balloons,
4) sound effects or lettering, and
5) any texts which exist in the fictional world (Miller 2008: 97).[45]

Let me add *tags* as a sixth type, which consist of verbal and pictorial elements and exist outside the fictional universe.

4.4.1 Paratext

To start with, one could distinguish verbal from pictorial paratext in graphic novels; yet that distinction is easily blurred by metafictional works like Chris Ware's *Jimmy Corrigan* (2000) or Marc-Antoine Mathieu's latest volume of the *Julius Corentin Acquefacques* series, *Le décalage* (2013), which employ instances of both verbal and pictorial paratext. In this chapter, I shall focus on the verbal paratext where it is possible and mention the pictorial paratext where it is indispensable. In point of fact, (verbal-pictorial) paratext is worth a book in its own right; accordingly, if outspokenly metafictional works[46] generally make ostenta-

---

[44] Certain critical works are concerned with 'language' and 'comics' in the sense of 'the language of comics' or 'language in comics,' cf. Miodrag 2013 and Cohn 2013.
[45] Actually, Ann Miller uses "peritext" instead of paratext. For Genette, *paratexte* is the sum of *péritexte* and *épitexte*, the latter implying all kinds of added material, often supported by other media (for example on DVD) or categorized according to genres (journal, private correspondence, etc.). *Paratext* is here employed to include all kinds of texts that are usually not directly integrated into the narrative (cf. Genette 1987: 11).
[46] Marc-Antoine Mathieu's *Le décalage* is an explicitly metafictional work. On the cover, instead of a title and the name of the series and the author, we find the 'first page' of the narrative. Around the album cover, there is a red band (as around the covers of the classic Gallimard edi-

tious use of (different types of) paratext is a question the answer to which, however, deserves scrutiny of a broader scope than this subchapter.

Let me here add two more distinctive categories: factual and fictional paratext. In Alan Moore and Eddie Campbell's historical graphic novel *From Hell* (1999), excerpts from authentic sources, that is from essays and treatises from several disciplines of the humanities through letters of historical persons, police reports, and authentic narrative fiction count as factual[47]; the extensive graphic schema of Jimmy's family history in Ware's *Jimmy Corrigan*, parts of which are found inside the narrative and the complete overview of which on the dustjacket to the hard cover edition, qualify as fictional in as far as they complete or comment on the fiction inside the narrative.

The paratext, Miller writes, is "the least integrated element of an album [and] remains outside the fiction" (Miller 2008: 97). This is only partly true: since we have known graphic novels to be complex long-form books of comics, one or the other remark seems worthy of note. – In Ware's *Jimmy Corrigan*, paratexts like the cover or the half title, imprint, copyright information, blurb, and short review comments are found either on the dust jacket (which unfolds to a broadsheet displaying, among other things, a schematic representation of Jimmy's and his ancestors' family history) or are strewn over the first 15 pages as instances of specially designed (metareferential) texts. This 'mixing or blending' of narratorial script, balloon speech, and verbal-pictorial paratext certainly is a salient feature of *Jimmy Corrigan* and a typical feature of the whole of Chris Ware's cartooning (cf. Baetens/Frey 2015: 155–160). Somewhat similarly, in Mathieu's *Le décalage*, paratext like the imprint, copyright information, and cover image are found inside the narrative, spread over several of its concluding pages.

A fair share of what is called paratext is actually graphic and metaphorical or symbolic in nature: in Mike Carey and Peter Gross' *The Unwritten*, for example, before the first page of the narrative, we find a pencil sketch of the protagonist, Tom Taylor, as he is sitting, holding a book in front of him, with a noose around

---

tions), which reads: "Caution: this album displays perfectly intended anomalies which even constitute the subject matter." In this story, not only the (anti-)hero and narrator but also the story itself gets lost in a (dreamed-up) time warp so that Julius finds himself behind and, simultaneously, ahead of (t)his story (*décalage*, or 'story lag').

47 Gérard Genette's rather blurry definition of paratext consists in "a fact whose mere existence, if known to the public, provides a type of comment on the text and encroaches on its reception" (Genette 1987: 13). Basically, every instance of paratext is reception-guiding, though not in the same way, factuality or fictionality notwithstanding. On the whole of Genette's nomenclature, factuality (and fictionality, which he does not further elaborate on) is of secondary importance.

his neck consisting of letters forming the word 'text.' More renowned are the chapter beginnings in Alan Moore and Dave Gibbons' *Watchmen*, which display a metaphorical clock starting a countdown by the minute at 11:48 hours in chapter one until in chapter twelve, 12:00 hours toll and the catastrophe takes its course (cf. Hescher 2013: 186). In addition, we find a graphic image, usually a blow-up or an extreme close-up of an image from inside the chapter, and a chapter heading, which is often a quote from a famous (inter)text. Therefore, I would modify Miller's thesis to the extent that in some graphic novels, the paratext is not "the least integrated element" but, on the contrary, is in close connection with the ensuing narrative, although it may not directly influence the verbal or pictorial narration. The examples given here usually function as a metaphor or allegory of the story content and certainly build expectations on the side of the readers.

Last but not least, the following case is as ambiguous as it is interesting. In Jason's outspokenly comical *The Left Bank Gang* (2005), which generally dispenses with verbal narratorial comment, we find four one-word 'captions' indicating the point of view (or focalization as according to François Jost, see chapter 4.8) of the following sequence. In this work, set in Paris in the 1920s, Ernest Hemingway, James Joyce, Scott Fitzgerald, and Ezra Pound, who have been turned into comics artists in the shape of dogs, conspire to rob a bank, for all of them are chronically short of money. The robbery, which is thwarted by Zelda Fitzgerald and her lover Edouard, a young French pilot, is at first told from an external point of view until the point of view switches, and we are given seven consecutive internal accounts of the hold-up (the four artists', Edouard's, Zelda's, and finally Hadley Hemingway's). Each internal account is introduced by a pitch-black panel displaying in small white upper-case letters the name of the respective partner in crime. – Indeed, rather than categorize these captions as narratorial comments (which I find they are not because of their similarity to chapter headings), I would classify them as paratextual headings to the point of view sequences. They belong, as does paratext in general, to the external communication system – like the switchings from one internal account to the other.

To conclude, the most adequate approach to paratext, it seems to me, would be a prototype approach, the categories of which are flexible and permit overlap (see chapter 3.3). This overlap is necessary to do justice to the complexity of the different types of paratext in graphic novels. For example, assignments to categories like factuality or fictionality are sometimes hard to make. Thus, a verbal text on the dustjacket to Ware's *Jimmy Corrigan* is hard to classify if not as a type of comment to the graphic schema and to the actual narrative ("Patient is 36-year-old male [...] Family history is very sketchy [...] Addendum: [...]," Ware 2000, dust jacket). Possibly, such cases could qualify as 'semifictional.'

4.4.2 Narratorial Captions

The verbal narratorial script usually comes in a caption box or in some kind of 'framing,' inside the panel or at its top or bottom, if it is not spread across the page as in Joe Sacco's *Palestine*; sometimes, it may also come as unframed, as a text written across an image or image sequence, like in some flashback sequences of Chris Ware's *Jimmy Corrigan*, "printed in cursive handwriting, which 'floats' in unadorned lexical units amongst panels on the page" (Kannenberg 2001: 187).

Indeed, typeface makes a difference in the semiosis of the narrative captions. It characterizes the narrator or commentator through its display of types characteristic of certain writing tools (felt pens or pencils, for example); thus, narratorial utterances in handwriting can be understood as independent reports or comments, whereas print types underscore the documentary, non-fiction or objective features of a text (cf. Dittmar 2008: 31).[48] In some cases, typeface and content may ironize each other (ibid. 105). Also, typeface comes in different sizes, in upper or lower case, or in horizontal or vertical arrangement. In *Jimmy Corrigan* and *Building Stories*, the conjunctions *and, thus,* and *but* serve as connectors between sequences, and they often come in vertical upper cases and/or in color. Thus, typeface in graphic novels is semantically and pictorially loaded.

Whatever the make-up of a narrative caption and its container, it is always more than just a verbal message; to a certain degree, it is always 'showy.' Even the most unobtrusive narrative caption or comment cannot avoid partaking in the showing of the narrative as a whole, be it just by its position on the page or in its relation to the image(s). In comics, all texts are *text-images* in principle (see above, ch. 3.3.4.6), not just those images showing textual media (like a panel displaying a letter or a page of a book, as found so frequently, for example, in Alison Bechdel's *Fun Home*). This must be accounted for in analyses of comics image sequences, although it might not always add to the production of meaning. To sum up, the verbal narratorial script, with or without caption box, tells and shows (and showing, as I would have it by definition, is narrating).

---

48 It is interesting in this context that in *Palestine*, a work of graphic journalism, Joe Sacco uses a typeface resembling print characters written by hand; this is used throughout the novel, in the narratorial (or commentary) captions as well as in the speech balloons – with the exception of those sequences in which there is an image of a printed text, for example, a newspaper page (see for example Sacco 2003: 132).

4.4.3 Balloons and Balloon Speech

What is true of the verbal caption narration also is true of the speech and thought balloon. It is a bimodal constituent of the comics medium consisting of words (the balloon script) and a conventionalized sign or symbolic form: the balloon outline (which in some cases may come in box form). The speech or thought balloon also functions as an index, in Peirce's sense (cf. Miller 2008: 98), of speech or speech sound, emanating from both human and non-human sources.

Unlike direct speech in verbal narrative fiction, balloon speech is not brought forth by a fictional narrator since it is part of the (verbal-) pictorial track, which, as a finished given, relates to the external communication system (see chapter 4.1 for the details on mediation and transmission in verbal narrative fiction, drama, and the graphic novel). Balloon speech is verbal (as speech or writing) *and* pictorial (in its outline or shape), and diegetic *as speech*; the balloons, in contrast, are non-diegetic (for the characters see no speech balloons floating around them). The drawn balloon outline with its tail, also called appendice or pointer, indicates the source and the type of the speech or sound: tails in the form of little balloons becoming successively smaller and balloons looking like clouds signify thoughts; dotted balloon outlines signify whispering, serrated or jagged outlines "a voice relayed electronically or with volume, which we deduce according to other picture elements" (Miodrag 2013: 100) – or, I would add, according to the verbal and pictorial co- and context. However, recent graphic novels go further than that: in *Asterios Polyp*, David Mazzucchelli uses character-specific, non-conventionalized speech balloons, identifying their sources even if the characters are absent from the image (cf. Miodrag 2013: 178); in books three and four of Frank Miller's *The Dark Knight Returns*, Batman's and Robin's thought balloons come in box form and use color to indicate their source. And some booklets contained in Chris Ware's *Building Stories* display (written) thought with neither framing nor appendice, in the images themselves (as far as they are framed) as well as in the inter-panel space.

As a conventionalized sign, the balloon is a symbol like the script it contains, the difference lying in its iconic shape, which indicates the speech source – unless the speech is cross-cut with a different strand of action. In such a case, it could appear in a caption box, as in the first volume of *The League of Extraordinary Gentlemen*, in which Wilhelmina Murry is briefing Alan Quatermain, Dr Jekyll, Captain Nemo, and the invisible Mr Griffin on board the Nautilus. On the second page of this chapter, we find Mr Griffin in front of a mirror as he is putting on makeup and a wig. On top of each panel in the three-by-three grid, Mrs Murray's speech, introduced by quotation marks, is framed by a light orange caption box (Moore/O'Neill 2000, ch. 3, np.).[49]

The balloon script can be compared to direct speech in a verbal narrative, which has been labeled 'showing,' by diverse critics, to underscore the similarity with the (scripted) utterances in a drama.[50] Considering that direct speech in comics is additionally linked to a genuinely pictorial entity (the balloon shape plus appendice), it is all the more an instance of showing than direct speech in a verbal narrative (see above, chapter 4.1). In the individual work, this becomes manifest on several planes: in *Asterios Polyp*, the balloon script is written in different letters to distinguish the two protagonists and male (upper case letters) from female discourse (lower case letters). Those writing styles "are fairly arbitrary, and so could properly be termed symbols" (Miodrag 2013: 178). Whether symbolic or indexical, balloon script partakes in the showing of the pictorial track; nevertheless, it is not the same type of showing as in the mise en scène. – Finally, it should be added that, depending on the argumentative context or the issue to be categorized, balloon script may also be referred to as text or writing or as pertaining to the verbal track.

4.4.4 An Excess of Showing: Sounds and Lettering

Sounds can be represented by words, non-mimetic (or symbolic, like 'sob') or onomatopoeic ('boohoo'), in speech balloons or free-floating in a panel or across panels or pages. As pictorial elements, sound representations are called icons in comics lingo, for example when little notes emerge from the loudspeaker of a radio. As icons, which is the more interesting case, the words often become pictorial themselves through the form or typeface of their letters, their color and size, their positioning in a panel or on the page.

What is generally known as sound lettering is a master example of showing: besides its semantic content, sound lettering tries to 'make sound visible' (see the numerous examples in Dittmar 2008: 113–114). Thus, sound lettering is part of the verbal as well as of the pictorial narration and like the speech balloon, it is a nondiegetic element. By trying to make sound 'audibly visible,' or 'visibly audible,' sound lettering can show more than it can tell. Unlike balloon script, there is a genuine pictorial quality to the words, which is both symbolic and

---

[49] Here I disagree with Thon, who construes Murray's voice as "secondary homodiegetic narrator" (Thon 2014: ch. 3, np.). I would hold that she is simply a speaking character whose speech is cross-cut with a proleptic strand of action.

[50] "[...] in direct speech, in the manner of a drama" (Genette 1972: 184).

iconic: if iconicity works through reduction of, abstraction from, or concentration on certain features, sound lettering often works through increase and repetition (or prolongation), the increase consisting in its 'excessive' formal design, which goes beyond the verbal semantics and produces meaning on several planes, as in *Logicomix* (Fig. 4.13):

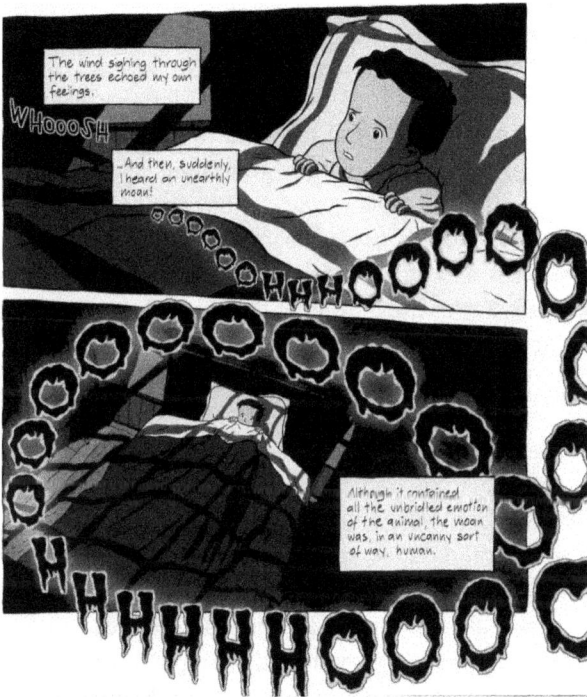

Fig. 4.13: Doxiadis/Papadimitriou 2009: 37, sound lettering

In this example, the child Bertrand "Bertie" Russell, who is raised by his grandparents, hears a frightening moan by night as he is lying in his bed. In these two panels, several of the points mentioned above are recognized: the pictorial prolongation of the moaning onomatopoeia is achieved through the repetition (and pictorial prolongation) of the letter 'o' (the /uː/ sound, that is); also, the letters have been rendered in black and yellow and in irregular outlines to make them appear more ghostly; finally, the sound-letter chain literally ensnares "Bertie" – and continues onto the top of next page (cf. Doxiadis/Papadimitriou 2009: 38). In so doing, it affects the intradiegetic narrator, professor Russell, who is giving a talk about his life before an academic audience. The form of the lettering adds to the semantics of the onomatopoeic word *hoo* through its length, its outline, and the way it is drawn across the panels and pages: the production of meaning on the pictorial plane of the narrative is therefore larger than on the verbal-semantic plane. This considered, the sound lettering shows more than it tells, here and in other works in which the pictorial semantics add to the verbal semantics, even if the design of the lettering is not as complex as above (Fig. 4.13).

4.4.5 Texts in the Fictional World

Texts "on décors or objects within the fiction" (Miller 2008: 98), for example signs or signboards, are part of the *diegesis* and intended to be acknowledged by the readers, rather than 'read,' because of their concision; their function usually is to enhance the plausibility of the story world. I have called them *text-images* (see above, ch. 3.3.4.6) because of their capacity to show. Sometimes, images show textual media such as letters or pages of newspapers or books which are supposed to be read. For example, Jimmy Corrigan's letter from his father, which triggers the plot of the work, is given to the readers as a POV image, showing the whole letter page in light blue with the father's handwriting on it (Ware 2000: np.). To know the content of the letter is essential for two reasons: firstly, we now understand why we saw Jimmy on a plane some few pages before (his long-absent father has invited him to meet up and included plane tickets in the letter); secondly, we would get confused by the following images in which Jimmy opens another letter, sent by his mother. This intradiegetic type of text demands to be read for the understanding of the plot.

Yet such text-images are not always designed to be read – or read in full, although they could be. Thus, in Alan Moore and Eddie Campbell's *From Hell*, detective Abberline receives a letter signed by a certain "Jack the Ripper," which he reads aloud to his colleagues; the last panel of this episode shows a POV close-up of the letter with the detective's hand touching it (Fig. 4.14).

Almost all the writing in the letter is quite realistic and, despite its small size, decipherable. Nevertheless, it is not intended to be read since the detective 'reads it out loud' in the preceding images, in which the balloon script, set between quotation marks, contains the exact wording of the letter (ibid. VII, 39, panels #5–9 and 40, panels #1–6). The reasons why the letter is shown anyway may be twofold: for one, the readers are meant to identify with the detective, through whose eyes they are looking at the letter[51]; for another, the attention is

---

[51] Sometimes, the reader-observer goes beyond the limits of his/her role: "He becomes a detective who must comprehend and question that which is shown" (Grünewald 2014: 474).

Fig. 4.14: Moore/Campbell 2006: VII, 40, text-image

drawn to the letter *as writing*, as a story made up (it has been faked by a journalist who wants to have a villain to write about). Until today, the Whitechapel murder cases count as unsolved, and the murders' value as stories is what set off other stories in turn, like *From Hell*.

Alison Bechdel's novel *Fun Home* teems with images of pages of letters and books, including many excerpts from 'high (verbal) literature' (see ch. 3.3.4.6), which are not intended to be read and whose function is more one of showing than of telling. Remarkable in this context is the extremely high degree of realism in the representations of the writings (see for example Alison's father's letters in Bechdel 2006: 63) as opposed to the rather cartoony representations of the characters and the setting. Readers get the impression that the writings are more 'real' than the actual protagonist, namely Alison's father, whose life and suicide (or accident?) she tries to make sense of. This is all the more plausible when we consider that literature actually was the channel through which Alison communicated with her father. The realistic representations of the letters and the literature are thus to be understood as metafictional references, accounting for the immense difficulty in the (re)construction of the artist-writer's own life and the way it is related to the life of her father.

On the third-last page of *City of Glass* there is a specific text-image: the form of the drawing – a sheet of script sticking out of an old-fashioned typewriter (Fig. 4.15) – suggests that it is a pictorial metaphor of the extradiegetic narrator, an unnamed (or covert) friend of Paul Auster's ('Paul Auster' figures as a minor character in the pictorial track of this novel), who sets out to tell the story of the writer Daniel Quinn on the very first page of *City of Glass*: there, the typewriter script is set in the middle of a pitch-black splash (Auster/Karasik/Mazzucchelli 2004, np.).

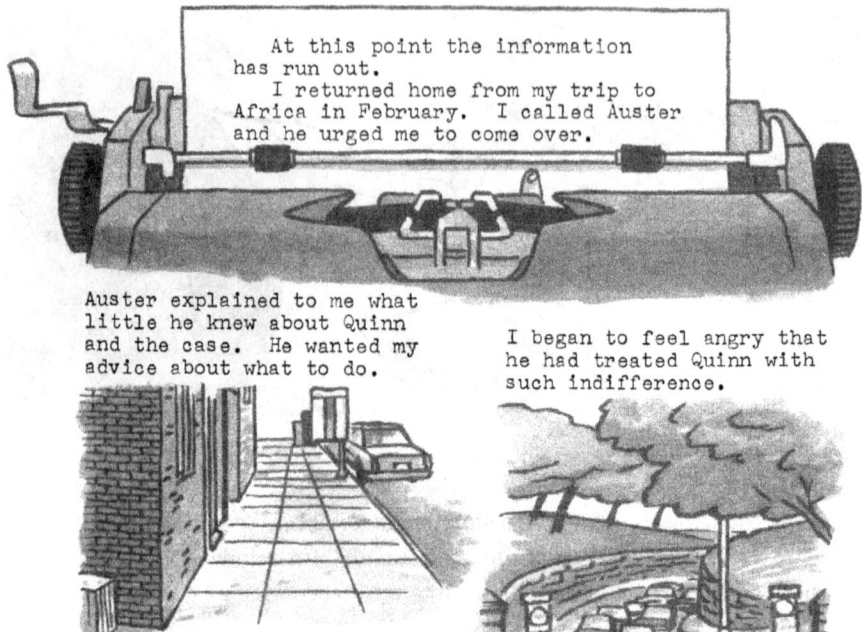

Fig. 4.15: Auster/Karasik/Mazzucchelli 2004, np., pictorial metaphor (text-image)

In the above spread (Fig. 4.15), the visual form of language has obviously been "exploited" with respect to typeface (Miodrag 2013: 105), but this is not all. In addition, the typewriter script connects to a rectangular outline which links up with the metonymical typewriter, under the top of which the ending of the novel unfolds through caption script and images. The verbal and pictorial signs together produce a complex signifier which reads as a metafictional reference, or a pictorial metaphor of metafictionality. This text is supposed to be read for the understanding of the plot on a superordinate level, that is how Quinn's story gets told in the first place. This text-image, therefore, tells as much as it shows, or shows as much as it tells.

In the end, it must be acknowledged that the showing of the verbal track is different from the type of showing in the pictorial track. Writing, of course, never wholly becomes a picture, although it may integrate pictorial elements. By linking up with or by referring to pictorial or other graphic elements like shape or color, writing can indicate or symbolize other graphic or semantic items in the bimodal comics narration. By doing so, it adds to the production of meaning and thus should be accounted for in comics sequence analyses.

4.4.6 Tags

In their form, tags resemble speech balloons and like them, they may not have a pointer or a 'framing' outline. Their verbal and pictorial components must be attributed to different instances of and in the narration. Like paratext, they partake of the external communication system, and I have categorized them as verbal-pictorial connectors and text-images (ch. 3.3.4.3, see also Hescher 2012: 347, 353). One function consists in rendering the plot and the pictorial narration more plausible by supplying essential or extra information, as it is the case in Joe Sacco's *Safe Area Goražde*. Also, they are employed by the artist-writer to – often ironically – comment on the pictorial narration. Alison Bechdel's *Fun Home* abounds with such ironic tags; and in Sacco's *Palestine*, we find a tiny tag commenting on the gesture of a wire service agent, who mockingly asks Sacco, "You the guy with the pictures of the 'violence'?" (Fig. 4.16) The tag reads, "Quote-unquote gesture," and ironizes the artist-writer's hyperbolic (and sarcastic) expectations regarding photographic prey, which are expressed in the captions above and to both sides of the agent.

Fig. 4.16: Sacco 2003: 57, ironizing tag

In general, the tag, that is the box with the appendice as well as the text, should be attributed to the artist-writer. Even if there is a narrator – which is not the default setting (see the following chapter 4.5) – the tags signify on another plane of meaning production: they represent a direct link to and a threshold between the verbal and the pictorial, unlike narratorial captions, whose pictorial design and arrangement do not directly refer to (a detail of) the drawings of the page. In the above example from *Palestine*, the narratorial captions are arranged into a curvy border line from the top right to the bottom left, dividing the page into two halves; they suggest a curtain drawn aside, giving a view of the new setting or reality; nevertheless, they do not directly explain or comment on any detail drawn in the four images on this page.

4.5 Of Authors, Artist-Writers, and Narrators

Showing is the dominant mode in graphic narratives, and the narratorial script is ineluctably connected to the pictorial narration. It often possesses pictorial elements itself or is pictorially designed. The pictorial elements of the narratorial captions are its typeface, (non)framing, including the background, its position inside or outside of an image or across images. In *Blankets*, Craig Thompson frequently exploits the showing potential of the narratorial script, such as in one panel in which it seems to support the 'falling' motion of Craig's girlfriend Raina, as she is falling asleep (Fig. 4.17): the script here shows as much as it tells, and the multiplication of Raina's body and the overlaid cloud shapes qualify the image as synchronistic (cf. Hatfield 2005: 52–58) and as indicative of time and space.

Fig. 4.17: Thompson 2003: 428, synchronistic panel

Graphic narratives always narrate, with or without narratorial script, and I endorse the claim that even in graphic novels, "much of the overall narrative is

4.5 Of Authors, Artist-Writers, and Narrators

usually conveyed via the verbal-pictorial mode of representation that defines the medium and that can – at least in fictional graphic narratives – usually be understood as a form of *non-narratorial representation*" (Thon 2013: 82, italics in the original). In fact, many graphic narratives do not use narratorial script and completely rely on the pictorial representation (images combined with speech or thought balloon script). Thus, the fact that there might not be caption script does not imply that a sequence does not narrate; it just lacks the mediating/transmitting communication system (see chapter 4.1).

In general, if narratorial script is not completely absent, it is often minimalistic (like the pictorially designed conjunctions in *Jimmy Corrigan* or the sparse information about time and place in *V for Vendetta*): nothing is narrated in these laconic utterances, which often consist only of a grammatical connective or of indicators of time and/or place. In examples of this kind, there is no reason to invoke a narrator. The minimalistic narratorial comments can and should be attributed (if one agrees with the theses I elaborated on in chapter 4.1) to what in the context of verbal narrative fiction is called the author and in graphic narratives to what I have above called the *artist-writer*, implying the possibility of more than one creator involved in the scripting, drawing, lettering, etc. of a single work.

What Franz K. Stanzel (1964 and 1979) termed figural narration (*die personale Erzählsituation*) is extremely rare in graphic narratives (cf. Groensteen 2013, ch. 6, np.). I know of only four examples with instances of third-person narration presenting an internal account: the already mentioned *Jimmy Corrigan* and *Building Stories*, by Chris Ware, *The Unwritten*, by Mike Carey and Peter Gross, and *Coraline*, by Neil Gaiman and P. Craig Russell. Yet even in these works, by far the largest proportion of the narrative is carried by the pictorial representation. Herein graphic novels differ essentially from verbal narrative fiction with figural narration: the latter cannot abstain from the use of the third-person pronoun or the proper name (given that the author has made the decision for this kind of perspective), for there is no other medium (or channel, like, for example, the images) to carry the narration. Neither is the increased use of dialogue a viable alternative: the capacity of dialogue to drive the action or push the plot in verbal narrative fiction is limited by default, and an extreme use of it at some point changes the representational mode of the text, which then mutates into something like a drama script (as in the often quoted example of Hemingway's story "The Killers").

There is another – general – problem to figural narration in Stanzel's approach: the ability to access a character's mind basically is a feature of omniscience. The function of a narrator, however, "is to allow the narrative to be read as something *known* rather than something imagined, something reported as fact rather than something told as fiction." Richard Walsh has it that omniscience is an "authorial imaginative act," not a narratorial act (Walsh 1997: 498, my italics, AH).

As a teacher of graphic literature, let me here open a parenthesis. To forestall interpretative blunders like intentional fallacy or biographical exegesis, critics have generally avoided attributing narratorial representation to an 'author' (or, as in this case, an artist-writer).[52] For three reasons, I do not see any danger of intentional fallacy or biographical interpretation of graphic novels:

1. authors often are a team of artists and writers – and not just one person; moreover, those creators are responsible for different specific jobs on the work so that potential intentionalistic or biographical attributions are difficult to make with respect to the individual creator or the whole team;
2. the images are cartoonistic (or iconic), which precludes an easy transfer of pictorial features to an empirical artist-writer personality; in other words, the distance between the (mental) image of an author and her/his cartoon figure/s is simply too big.
3. showing, that is the pictorial mode, dominates the work as a whole. Since the proportion of the narratorial script usually is distinctly small, it does not contain enough information to provide for the existence of an autonomous structural entity called narrator.

Moreover, for a character to be a narrator, s/he needs to possess a more or less fleshed-out spatio-temporal, that is pictorial and/or allegorical, identity, subsumable under the characters narrated in the story world (cf. Kablitz 2008: 29).[53] At the same time, such a narrator-character – as opposed to a merely narrating character – needs to be marked on both the narratorial (captions) and the pictorial plane (images) as an entity distinct from the intradiegetic story world. 'Marked on the narratorial plane' means that the caption script should not be

---

[52] For more than one and a half decades, there have been serious approaches in which narrators are dismissed in favor of the author (for example Walsh 1997, Kablitz 2008, see Margolin 2013 for an overview of approaches alternative to the positing of a narrator). These approaches, however, are oriented toward verbal narrative fiction although one or the other point made also applies to graphic narratives.

[53] Martin Schüwer gives an example from the 1950s EC horror comics series *The Haunt of Fear*, in which a visually designed, extradiegetic, narrator welcomes the readers at the beginning and bids them farewell at the end; they figure as an old witch or a vault or crypt keeper. However, these narrator figures "have no contour of their own" and serve as a mere story frame with a recognition value (cf. Schüwer 2008: 404–405). Therefore, they are not subsumable under the characters from the story world. In fact, since they neither narrate nor figure among the story world characters, they could be classified as pictorial 'paratext,' intended to shape the genre expectations of the readers.

4.5 Of Authors, Artist-Writers, and Narrators

limited to minimalistic adverbial phrases of time and/or place; it should contain personal pronouns and refer to the characters in the story world. 'Pictorial and allegorical' means that the narrator-character should be drawn in a way that it links up with the semantics of the caption script. Only then, I would hold, is there a plausible reason to speak of a narrator; nevertheless, the only difference between a narrator(-character) and a merely narrating character is that the former is marked as a narrator and that s/he may be on another diegetic plane.[54] – In practice, this almost exclusively applies to graphic memoirs (though by far not to all graphic memoirs): to "Artie" Spiegelman in *Maus II*, chapter two ("Time Flies"), who wears a mask at his desk and who consults his shrink to talk about his guilt complex; to Lynda and her demon in *One Hundred Demons* from the extradiegetic prologue; to David B., who, as an adult, argues with his mother about what stories to include in his graphic memoir *Epileptic* (B[eauchard]. 2005: 95–96); or in the fictional graphic biography *City of Glass*, in which the unnamed author-narrator is represented in a metaphorical text-image (or image-text: the script page sticking out of a typewriter, see above, chapter 4.4.5, Fig. 4.15). That all the narrators in these examples happen to be extradiegetic (and the narratives framed narratives) is not a *sine qua non*: in Shaun Tan's *The Arrival* as well as in Joe Sacco's *Safe Area Goražde*, we find marked intradiegetic narrators.

In all instances of minimalistic or absent narratorial script as well as in the case of (the extremely rare) third-person narration, I shall not invoke a narrator and attribute both the narratorial and the pictorial track to the artist-writer. – For didactic and/or methodological reasons, presupposed there is substantial narratorial script, one could alternatively refer to an "author-performer," or even better to an author-presenter, "merely feigning, pretending or playing the role of a reporter of facts, or a maker of true factual assertions, while in actuality he is their inventor" (Margolin 2013, par. 31). Indeed, the term *author-presenter* seems more appropriate with regard to showing, the dominating mode of representation in graphic narratives. For narratorial script, be it extensive or minimalistic, is not plain verbal or written narration (as in verbal narrative fiction): it comes as framed or unframed, in (a) certain position(s) on the page, in an image or across images, in one or several typefaces, or even in different colors or

---

54 The artist-writer Jean-Christophe Menu says: "If I represent myself, the image that springs from my pen is not one that has a real relationship with 'me,' it is more often a symbol, a hieroglyphic shorthand (even on the temporal level: it is a kind of synthesis of myself at different ages)" (qtd. in Groensteen 2013, ch. 5.2.1, np.).

against differently colored backgrounds.⁵⁵ Narratorial script in graphic narratives is inevitably bound up with pictorial elements. Thus, it is both verbal and pictorial, it tells and it *shows*, and for this reason it should be attributed to the external communication system (see ch. 4.1). To put it briefly: narratorial script or no narratorial script, the artist-writer or author-presenter has just one role or theoretical position in graphic narratives.

Last but not least, with an artist-writer or an author-presenter I can easily dispense with the extremely artificial construction of the "reciter," "monstrator," "overall narrator," and "fundamental narrator" (cf. Groensteen 2013, chs. 5 and 6; these terms having been borrowed from Marion 1993 and Gaudreault 1988).

That the artist-writer from the external communication system makes sense as an instance of attribution, bringing forth the narratorial script as well as the pictorial track, can be seen in the example of just one panel from Joann Sfar's *Le chat du rabbin* (2001–2006, Fig. 4.18):

Fig. 4.18: Sfar 2003: 2, panel #4, meowing and thinking cat as proof of the external communication system

---

55 *Jimmy Corrigan* contains examples of all the types of verbal-pictorial script mentioned above: in one spectacular case, 273 pages into the narrative, we find white first-person script against a blue background, white third-person script against a red background, and black first-person script against a grey background together on one tier (or strip). See also the narratorial script in the large caption "ANYWAY / Following a Taxiecab Ride [...]" with all its pictorial elements (187 pages into the narrative).

One is perhaps tempted to look at the cat as the story's narrator but actually, the cat is just a narrating character within the story, although it undoubtedly lends the narrative its leading commenting voice. In the above panel (Fig. 4.18), the cat is meowing and thinking at the same time – which is not plausible at all, or only under the condition that there is one instance behind what the cat is thinking and uttering: the artist-writer from the external communication system, bringing about both what a character sees and utters (here the shut door, which prevents the cat from getting to its mistress, and its animal utterance "Mraou!," in the speech balloon) and what it is thinking (the narratorial script): "What are you doing in there what I don't have the right to see?" On the opposite page, we see the cat's mistress in several panels as she is taking a bath (Sfar 2013: 109, panels #1–4) – something that the cat cannot possibly see, as it continues to meow in front of the shut bathroom door (there are several such instances in this work in which something is shown that the narrating cat cannot possibly see). In point of fact, the cat itself is nowhere pictorially marked as a narrator distinct from the intradiegetic story. Therefore, it cannot possibly bring forth the above sequence or any other image sequence from *Le chat du rabbin*.

Let me prove the importance of the marking of the narrator on both the narratorial and the pictorial plane with the example of a silent graphic narrative (coming with no verbal track at all). If the existence of narratorial captions alone were sufficient for the establishing of a narrator, there could be no narrators in silent novels – which is proven wrong in Shaun Tan's *The Arrival* (2006). When the young Asian refugee woman that the immigrant meets on board the air-borne steamer starts to narrate the story of her flight, not only the panels change into images resembling polaroids, the background color in the images also changes from sepia to grey. The polaroids seem to be laid out on a light-grey surface, imitating the pages of an old photo book, where there was no distinguishable background before (Tan 2006, np.). I here agree with Jan-Noël Thon that the young Asian woman is an intradiegetic narrator (Thon 2013: 86) because of the markers on the pictorial plane. A similar marking of another intradiegetic narrator occurs some ten pages later when the immigrant befriends the bespectacled family father, himself an ex-immigrant, whose narration is presented on pitch-black ground, the background colors of the images varying between light sepia and dark grey (Tan 2006, np.).

In any case, it takes more than a narratorial script with a pronoun or proper name to legitimize the existence of a narrator. A narrator-character with her/his own verbal and pictorial identity needs to be marked as distinct from or in the intradiegetic story world, verbally and pictorially. This cannot be taken for granted, yet is found in graphic memoirs like in Mary M. and Bryan Talbot's

Dotter of Her Father's Eyes (2012)[56] – and in the very sparse subgroup of fictional bio-graphical narratives (hyphen intended). One such fictional bio-graphical narrative is Paul Karasik and David Mazzucchelli's *City of Glass* (2004), a graphic adaptation of Paul Auster's eponymous novella from 1985, in which an unnamed extradiegetic narrator meets the writer-character Paul Auster, who, at the end of the story, hands him Daniel Quinn's notebook (the basis from which the narrator has been telling Quinn's story). Although the narrator's identity is not fully fleshed out – his existence being marked by the white typescript on black ground at the beginning and the metaphorical text-image of the typewriter with the inserted sheet at the end of the novel (see above, Fig. 4.15) – he persists as the antagonist to the character Paul Auster. In this role as an author-narrator(-character), he is solely responsible for the *verbal* track of the graphic novel – as every marked narrator – not for the pictorial track, for he does not create a graphic novel. In the end, the narration in *City of Glass* is not just a narration but a *representation* of a narration: the act of narrating here is explicitly marked as fictitious, which is why the narration is part of the narrated, fictitious, story world (cf. Kablitz 2008: 29 and Walsh 1997: 498). Therefore, it is legitimate in this case to speak of a narrator, not just of a narrating character.

4.6 Narratorial and Pictorial Representation in Graphic Memoirs and Fictional Biographies

Who (or what) is 'speaking' in the narratorial script of graphic memoirs and fictional biographies? The answer is: in most cases the artist-writer and in some cases the narrator. This depends, as I have shown above, on the markers on the pictorial plane and in the narratorial script.

Graphic memoirs represent a large group among the graphic novels. In Art Spiegelman's *Maus* and particularly in *Maus II* (chapter 2: "Time Flies"), the author is marked through a pictorial metaphor (or allegory), the anthropomorphic mouse "Artie," and as an extradiegetic narrator, who possesses the full identity as a would-be cartoonist and acts in his own spatio-temporal setting

---

[56] *Dotter of Her Father's Eyes* (Mary M. and Bryan Talbot, 2012) is, in fact, both autobiographical and biographical. The extradiegetic narrator Mary, wife of the don of British comics and graphic novels, Bryan Talbot, tells the story of her childhood and youth in parallel with that of Lucia Joyce, daughter of James Joyce. The three story planes (Mary in the present time and Mary and Lucia as children growing up) are color-coded and different in their drawing style: especially Mary's childhood and youth is presented in a drawing style resembling styles known from children's books.

(at his work desk or at his shrink's office); in the intradiegetic narration of both *Maus I* and *II*, Vladek, the father and holocaust survivor, narrates as a character. Artie's interruptions of Vladek's narrative occur in non-frames, often on top of the page, as opposed to the framed panels in his father's narrative (cf. Spiegelman 2003: 17), confirming Artie's identity as a narrator.

Fig. 4.19: Barry 2002, "Introduction," np., framed narrator(s)

In Lynda Barry's graphic memoir *One Hundred Demons* (2002, Fig. 4.19), the narrative is also framed, and the extradiegetic narrator is verbally and pictorially marked in her own spatio-temporal setting. In the unpaginated "Introduction" to this work, we find the grown-up artist-writer as she is drawing and thinking at her desk. The captions of the first two-panel spread read: "Is it autobiography if parts of it are not true?" and "Is it fiction if parts of it are?" The metafictional narratorial comment, the pictorial representation of the artist-writer at her desk, the bluish background to the author-character, the yellow tint of the legal-paper background to the captions (thoughts not contained in balloons) and the fact that the pages are not numbered mark the introduction as a frame and the character as an extradiegetic narrator. Another remarkable feature of the introductory frame is that Lynda, the narrator, from the third spread on, splits into two: the artist-writer herself and her demon, a narratorial *alter ego*, speaking of Lynda in the third person: "She was at the library when she first read about a painting exercise called, 'One Hundred Demons'! / The example she saw was a hand-scroll painted by a Zen monk [...] in 16th century Japan / I can assure you, it was not painted on yellow legal paper!" (Fig. 4.19, third and fourth spread, np., highlightings in the original). This verbal and pictorial doubling of the narrator underscores the status of the introductory frame as *doubly* extradiegetic. As soon as we pass over to the paginated intradiegetic narrative, Lynda the character, who happens to be a cartoonist, is speaking in the caption script (ibid. 16) about her childhood.[57] The change of narrative planes is indicated by a different background color in the panels: where there was legal-paper yellow, there now is light orange.

Fig. 4.20: Talbot 2007: 1–2, metareferential lead-in

An even more complex type of narratorial/authorial framing is found in Bryan Talbot's *Alice in Sunderland* (2007). This work comes across as playfully postmodern and simultaneously reads as a graphic autobiography, a metanarrative about the history of British comics, the history of the town of Sunderland, and as a biography of Lewis Carroll and the making of his *Alice* books. I attribute the narratorial script in the metareferential lead-in sequence ("Well, there's this guy, right...," Fig. 4.20) to the extradiegetic (artist-writer and) narrator Talbot, who makes his first pictorial appearance as a puppet player pulling the strings attached to his intradiegetic alter ego, who is wearing a rabbit mask (Fig. 4.21, a

---

[57] "The two intradiegetic classes [homo- and heterodiegetic narrators] are relatively straightforward. These narrators are simply characters, within a narrative, who relate a story in which (respectively) they are and are not themselves involved" (Walsh 1997: 497).

reference to the rabbit that Alice encounters in *Alice's Adventures in Wonderland* [1865] after she has gone down the hole).[58]

Fig. 4.21: Talbot 2007: 310, 'Talbot,' the narrator, as a puppet player

In the closing sequence of this graphic novel, Talbot wakes up from a dream – a dream in the medium of comics – which is nothing less than the (intradiegetic) narrative of *Alice in Sunderland* – and finds himself in the seat next to his wife, who reproaches him for having slept through *Swan Lake* and for having missed the show (Talbot 2007: 317).

---

58 For a detailed analysis of the lead-in and other metareferential sequences combining with numerous metalepses, see Hescher 2014c.

Here, Talbot is rendered in a somewhat photorealistic style, except for the rather screaming colors and the coarse grain, which in the last splash of the extradiegetic sequence has grown so large that it resembles an impressionist painting (Talbot 2007: 318). These defamiliarization techniques together with the typeface of the caption script in the lead-in sequence – which is nowhere as large as there – mark the artist-writer Talbot as a narrator. What is quite unique about *Alice in Sunderland*, among many other things, is the reappearance of the artist-writer in the intradiegetic narrative as a tripartite (narrating) character: the theater-goer (called the Plebeian), the Performer, a kind of master of ceremonies and stage manager, and the Pilgrim, the author and tour guide, leading the theater-goer and the readers through Sunderland and its surroundings. All three are intradiegetic embodiments of the extradiegetic narrator and comics artist. In fact, the embedded story is presented as a multimedia presentation or performance, hosted by the Performer (cf. Hescher 2014c: 232).

Le photographe, by Emmanuel Guibert, Didier Lefèvre, and Frédéric Lemercier, is one of the most extraordinary works among graphic memoirs[59] – which has also been categorized as graphic journalism or reportage comic. This widely discussed and appreciated work uses text, drawings, and photographs in the form of contact prints. They often come in whole series, attracting particular attention when single contacts occur as hand-framed with a red crayon. Occasionally, single contacts are blown up to regular panel size. It is exactly the use of the two pictorial media, drawings and photographs, that allows the creators to mark a narrator in the introduction to the actual narrative, in which a part of the paratext is integrated (Fig. 4.22).

The photographer, Didier Lefèvre, obtains his status as a narrator through the paratext on underexposed prints of the same motif, whose exposure time seems to increase as the sequence continues to the point where the main narrative starts (Fig. 4.22, panels #3–5 and #6). This extradiegetic narration, continuing over four pages, displays bright-yellow caption boxes, which will continue to frame the whole embedded narrative and which are indicative of no one else than the extradiegetic narrator (not a narrating character). An additional instance of narratorial marking occurs two pages earlier, where we see the narrator photographing himself in front of a mirror (ibid. 4, panels #4–5). This is the only time that Didier can be seen in a photographic image; in the embedded narrative, he figures as a drawn character.

---

[59] "Although the three work together to author the graphic narrative – orally, visually, verbally, and compositionally – *Le Photographe* tells one man's story, Didier's" (Pedri 2011: par. 8).

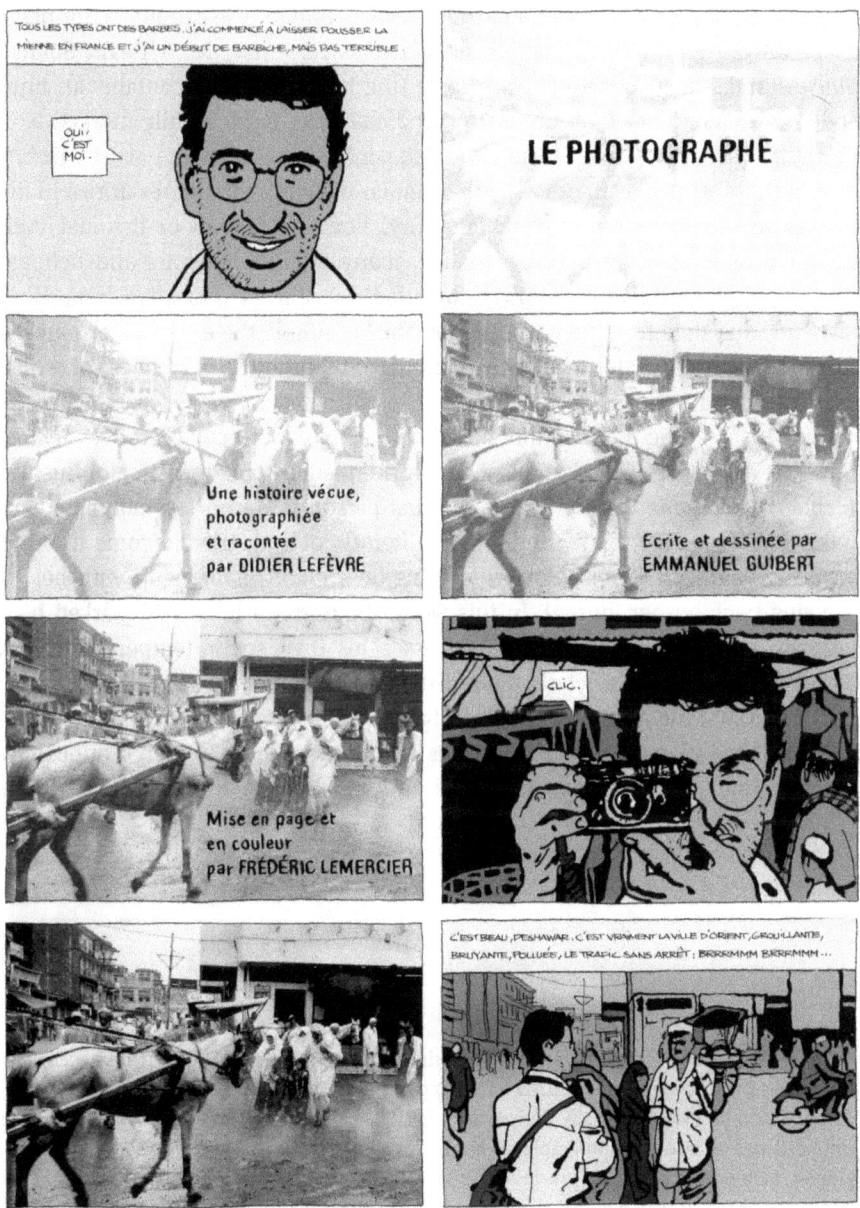

Fig. 4.22: Guibert/Lefèvre/Lemercier 2003, vol. 1: 6, narratorial marking

To sum up: a caption box with narratorial script alone does not make a narrator. It takes a *framing* in the form of verbal and pictorial markers to create an identity distinguishable from the character in the intradiegetic narrative. In this context, the pictorial representation of a narrator responsible for the caption script plays a crucial part. In several graphic memoirs, as for example in David Small's *Stitches* and Alison Bechdel's *Fun Home* (the latter of which contains an unusually large amount of caption script), no character is pictorially marked as a narrator. Therefore, each of the two protagonists speaks as the artist-writer.[60] And in these works, as in others with a similar makeup, the figures drawn in the images are (main) characters in the story, however factual or fictional their accounts of themselves may be. Indeed, many graphic memoirs and fictional bio-graphical narratives[61] (hyphen intended) employ no narrative framing of any sort, and therefore the narrating instance is simply the artist-writer – or the fictional main character (that is in fictional bio-graphical narratives, of which there are very few).

In this respect, Posy Simmonds' fictional bio-graphical narrative *Gemma Bovery* (1999) is an exception: in the freely adapted graphic rewriting of Gustave Flaubert's *Madame Bovary* (1857), the first-person narrator, Raymond Joubert, baker and associate (hobby) editor of a literary journal, tries to come to terms with the death of Gemma Bovery and his own illicit relationship with her by drawing back on her journal. In this work, the narrator is clearly marked both verbally and pictorially, and he possesses his own spatio-temporal identity. Moreover, *Gemma Bovery* tells the self-referential story of Joubert's own writing about Gemma: the numerous, unusually large, chunks of text, coming in different typefaces (Gemma's journal entries are juxtaposed to Joubert's publishing typeface) and enhanced by narratorial annotations, constitute a *textual* frame

---

[60] Therefore, I do not agree with Nancy Pedri that "Alison [...] functions as an extradiegetic narrator in the present who writes and draws of her past self" (Pedri 2013: 132).

[61] For example, I would classify Chris Ware's *Jimmy Corrigan* and James Vance and Dan Burr's *On the Ropes* as fictional bio-graphical narratives (they could also be made to count among graphic historical novels (see above, ch. 3.3.3, Fig. 3.3). In the three-page lead-in and in the closing sequence to *On the Ropes*, the old Fred Bloch speaks in the narratorial captions, of which the initial one reads, "Sometimes I'm asked to tell a story of the old days..." (Vance/Burr 2013: 1). This does not mean that the protagonist Fred Bloch is a narrator. He is nowhere marked as a narrator, neither pictorially nor in terms of a different story plane. That he only speaks at the beginning and closing of the narrative is not constitutive of a narrative framing. *On the Ropes* is a good example of my claim from above that in graphic novels, narratorial script is often minimalistic (on pp. 4–244 in this work, there is no caption script).

around the images and mark Joubert as a narrator.⁶² In this sense, *Gemma Bovery*, like *City of Glass*, is not a simple narration but a representation of a narration.

A rather unusual narrator is found in a very recently published bio-graphical novel about the blues legend Robert Johnson (1911–1938). *Love in Vain* (2014), created by the French Jean-Michel Dupont (script) and Mezzo (art,) figures no other narrator than the devil himself, speaking in serrated captions. He is not pictorially fleshed out, yet shortly before concluding the narrative after Robert Johnson's untimely death, the narrator sets out to build a full identity through the (audio)pictorial allegory of The Rolling Stones (besides Eric Clapton, Jimmy Hendrix, and Led Zeppelin the principal claimants to Johnson's musical legacy) and their 1968 song "Sympathy for the Devil," in which, as in *Love in Vain*, the devil 'speaks' in the first person. The Rolling Stones figure in the last four panels of the work during their performance at the 1969 Altamont Free Concert in Livermore, California. In the penultimate panel, the narrator says: "That night, I had invited myself to listen to the song they have kindly dedicated to me..." (Dupont/Mezzo 2014: 55), and in the last full-page splash, there is a serrated caption box at the bottom right with the incipit of the famous Rolling Stones song, translated into French: "Au fait, permettez-moi de me présenter [...] J'espère que vous avez deviné mon nom!" (Fig. 4.23). In the words and images of this graphic novel, the Rolling Stones and their song stand in as an allegory providing the spatio-temporal and verbal-pictorial identity specific of a 'full-fledged' narrator (– and obviously, the devil here is not a character that happens to narrate). Therefore, like *Gemma Bovery* and *City of Glass*, *Love in Vain* is a representation of a narration.

To sum up: calling the creators of graphic memoirs by the name of their *de facto* role as artist-writers (or authors) should not pose a serious problem, at least not with regard to (auto)bio-graphical narratives. In graphic memoirs, the identification of the artist-writer with the narrating persona or character – if this persona is not marked as a narrator – is willed and typical of the genre. In fictional or 'factual' biographies (the latter of which generally employ the same rhetorical and stylistic devices as their fictional counterparts), the existence of a narrator is not a default setting either unless her/his identity is marked on both the narratorial and pictorial plane.

---

62 "The visual apparatus categorizes typescript as narration and freehand as diary, and the correlative relationship (in the form of significant dissonance) between the two verbal components is blackly amusing" (Miodrag 2013: 72).

Fig. 4.23: Dupont/Mezzo 2014: 56, narrator as audio-visual allegory

4.7 Why the Narrating and Experiencing I Should Not Be Used on the Graphic Memoir

Franz K. Stanzel's "typical feature" of the first-person narration (1964: 31–39), the tension between the narrating and experiencing I, manifesting itself in verbal narrative fiction, has been used by contemporary critics on graphic memoirs in such a way that the narrating I is to correspond to the narratorial script and the experiencing I to the pictorial narration (cf. Watson 2008: 36, Herman 2011: 232–234). This is problematic for more than one reason. Firstly, in verbal narrative fiction (to which the paradigm originally applies), the tension between the narrating and experiencing I is purely linguistic, that is the temporal distance between the two constructs is cognitively inferred from lexical and grammatical features in the narratorial speech and its different modes of verbal narration. However, in bimodal graphic memoirs (and fictional auto/biographies, as in the case of Vance and Burr's *On the Ropes* and Simmonds' *Gemma Bovery*), the tension between the verbal-narratorial and the pictorial plane – if "tension" is the appropriate term at all – would be canceled out by the dominance of showing of the pictorial track. In practice, this means that the pictorial representation leaves a greater impact on the recipients than the narratorial script: the tension thus fails to build.

Secondly: if the narratorial script narrates, how can the pictorial plane *not* narrate? Generally, the lion's share of the narration in graphic narratives is carried by the images on the page, and this is why 'silent' works like *The System, The Arrival,* or *Here* can totally (or almost totally, as in *Here*) dispense with narratorial script (and balloon speech, as a matter of course). Thus, to equate the pictorial plane with an 'experiencing I' (as opposed to a verbal 'narrating' I) is simply a contradiction in terms – which is not ruled out by arguing that the images 'represent' an 'experiencing I': in graphic narratives, because of the sequential nature of the images, representation is inevitably bound up with narration.

Thirdly, in verbal narrative fiction, the first-person voice "personifies the agent of focalization, the overall position from which the story is rendered" (Schwalm 2014, par. 3). In graphic memoirs, as in graphic narratives in general, because of the two narrative modes (pictorial narration and narratorial script), there is no such things as an "overall position." And if there were one, it should be attributed to the pictorial narration – the 'experiencing I' – which, again, would be a contradiction in terms. Also, despite the presence of narratorial script, there is not necessarily a narrator (see ch. 4.1).

Last but not least, I hold that focalization as understood by classical narratology is a problematic concept to begin with (as shown in ch. 4.2). Focalization, if I borrow from François Jost, is a complex relational concept setting what images show (*ocularization*) against what characters and readers *know* (see ch. 4.8). Images or image sequences in graphic novels often show what is not (or not yet) focalized and whose focalization can only be accounted for by assessing a longer sequence or several sequences in a row – or even the whole work. Finally, if we acknowledge that many graphic novels narrate with no or just minimal narratorial script, the concept of the 'narrating I' (as represented by the narratorial script) is of no more use and the distinction between the narrating and experiencing I, as applied to verbal narrative fiction, has become pointless.

4.8 Focalization Revisited: What Is Known and What Is Shown

It is quite safe to say that there is not one concept or definition of focalization applied to graphic narratives that has received common approval or acceptance (cf. Thon 2014, np.). Of course, this is also due to the fact that research on this relatively new territory has just started. As far as can currently be assessed, the few approaches concerning focalization and narrative situation in graphic narratives are quite heterogeneous in nature, and practically all lack systematicness and breadth; most of them proceed from a rather limited body of single-case analyses from which they generalize. And often enough, they still struggle with narrator and focalization concepts from classical narratology (cf. Horstkotte/Pedri 2011).

I would side with Thierry Groensteen, who has expressed his doubts about transferring narrator and focalization concepts, forged to construe verbal narrative fiction, to graphic narratives (Groensteen 2013, ch. 5.1). Although, on the one hand, he constructs a highly artificial terminology in terms of a *"primary, fundamental* narrator [a term borrowed from Gaudreault 1988], a truly *supra-diegetic* (and always already *extra*-diegetic) narrator" (ibid., ch. 5.1.6, np.), a "monstrator" and "reciter" (ibid., ch. 6, np.), and although he attributes breakdown, page layout, and braiding to the narrator (and not the artist-writer/team, which would be more plausible), in the end, Groensteen totally dispenses with focalization and elaborates instead on the diverse representations of subjectivity (ibid., ch. 6).[63] Jan-Noël Thon (2013) also makes no mention of focalization and conceives of the narrator as a construct, often in the form of a character (borrowing from Jannidis 2006 and Walsh 1997), distinguishing narratorial from authorial and "non-narratorial representation" in his case analyses.[64] In the end, the question whether focalization is indeed indispensable in the context of graphic narratives is more than just rhetorical[65]: what critical pertinence does it have if, for example, it is redefined as an overall concept or umbrella term, containing parameters such as "optical perspectivation [...,] aspects of cognition, ideological orientation, and judgement" (Horstkotte/Pedri 2011: 331)? Does such a variety of parameters not diminish the concept's discriminatory power?

Let me come back to François Jost's cinematic terminology, whose ocularization concept I have adopted and extended (see ch. 4.3.1.2). In the first place, Jost's approach is appealing because it puts itself at a distance to theories whose subjects are linguistic representations of reality or monomodal narrative fiction (like cognitive grammar and cognitive narratology, cf. Herman 2009). Moreover, Jost's ocularization is a relational term that is needed to account for what is shown (mise en scène, including point of view) as opposed to what is seen, the two parameters fundamental to sequential images. The question now is if his focalization concept can adequately meet the demands of graphic narratives.

Focalization in Jost's sense seems to have little in common with classical or post-classical narratology. Focalization, contrary to ocularization, is "what a

---

63 Although subjectivity or subjective bending is often equated with focalization, Groensteen chooses not to bring up this term and instead extemporizes on numerous subjective devices: the use of the reciter and monstrator, pictograms, pictorial metaphors, drawing style, or the graphic line (Groensteen 2013, ch. 6).
64 "[...] verbal-pictorial representation in panels or sequences of panels, which is evidently also the result of a process of creation but whose 'source' is usually not – or at least not explicitly – represented and whose multimodal configuration prevents us from attributing it to a 'speaker' as [... in] verbal forms of narration" (Thon 2013: 70–71).
65 "The quasi-endless diversity of pictorial styles and techniques begs the question of how visual narrative marks off narration as opposed to focalization, and if this is, indeed, a helpful distinction for the analysis of graphic narratives" (Horstkotte/Pedri 2011: 331).

character knows" (Jost 1987: 18). Yet what a character knows is for the viewer, as Jost has it, "a more complex resultant" (ibid. 63–64). He argues that "the questions concerning focalization can only be solved, even in silent movies, if one includes the verbal dimension conveyed by the intertitles [*cartons*] and if one relates them to the contextual *ocularizations* [qu'on les articule aux...]" (ibid. 62, italics in the original). This claim has important implications:

a) focalization includes both the verbal and pictorial elements of a (silent) film[66]; transferred to graphic novels, this would be the caption and the balloon script as well as the images; and

b) more precisely, focalization results, at least in part,[67] from ocularizations, which in graphic novels would be the ocularization in the single image and in the co-text to the image, the image sequence.

Thus, if I transfer focalization from Jost's film theory to graphic narratives, I must keep in mind that it is a complex concept in itself, accounting for both what is known and what is shown.[68] Apart from that, and similarly to ocularization, it is a relational term, which adds to its complexity in that

c) character knowledge is assessed with respect to viewer knowledge and

d) the resulting disparity or equality of viewer and character knowledge is assessed with respect to its importance for the plot[69]; for example, the fact that the viewer perceives something that the character does not is possibly not at all important for the plot, neither does it inevitably give the viewer a cognitive advantage over the character (and vice versa).[70]

Thus, in the third chapter of *L'œil-caméra*, Jost derives three types of focalization from zero ocularization as a departing point:

---

66 "If ocularization can be inferred through the analysis of the visual track, one should not conclude [...] that the domain of focalization exclusively is the verbal track" (Jost 1987: 63).

67 "To the extent that what is perceived contributes to the diegetic knowledge, it is not absurd to form the working hypothesis that a part of the focalization results from the ocularization" (Jost 1987: 64). Markus Kuhn has it that focalization "can only be determined through the interplay of edited shots" (Kuhn 2009: 262).

68 This includes character vision since a large part of the images in a graphic narrative are half-subjective so that the extent of the character vision can only be approximated (see ch. 4.3).

69 "In order to deduce a cognitive attitude from an ocularization, one must account for the narrative pertinence of the perceived elements, that is their function for the plot" (ibid. 73).

70 "For the assessment of the focalization, the disparity between character and viewer vision is relevant only when those differences in the perception imply a cognitive heterogeneity of the narrative functions" (ibid. 65).

- in the case of an *external focalization*, the viewer ignores the thoughts or the knowledge of a character (or the characters), which entails a lack of knowledge about the character and about the actions s/he is taking; possibly, this again entails a cognitive disproportion with regard to the plot, to the disadvantage of the viewer (ibid. 67). In graphic narratives, an internal ocularization, thought balloon, or caption script would have to stand in for the viewer to possess all the narrative information. – A good illustration of external focalization are the blood-red murder panels cross-cut with the panels of the main narrative strand in the opening sequence to Alan Moore and Dave Gibbons' *Watchmen* (see ch. 4.3.1, Fig. 4.7): in the last panel of this sequence, especially, knowledge is visibly withheld by the artist-writer team,[71] for it is not (yet) known whose are the two hands protruding from the top left – and therefore the readers do not know who Blake's murderer is. And since there is neither caption script nor images revealing Blake's point of view, that is who is attacking Blake, the readers are made to wait until the last chapter for the *dénouement*;

- departing again from zero ocularization, a *spectatorial focalization*, in contrast, gives the reader-observers a cognitive advantage over the character, not necessarily in that they know the character's thoughts but that they perceive things that the character does not, at least not from her/his vantage point. This may also provide the viewer with a cognitive advantage concerning the plot (cf. Jost 1987: 68–71). – A good illustration of spectatorial focalization is the below nine-panel sequence from Alan Moore and Eddie Campbell's *From Hell* (Fig. 4.24):

Fig. 4.24: Moore/Campbell 2006: II, 4, panels #4–6, spectatorial focalization

---

[71] "In fact, the exteriority of the cognitive focus has its greatest relevance *when knowledge is visibly withheld*" (Jost 1987: 66, italics in the original).

4.8 Focalization Revisited: What Is Known and What Is Shown

The protagonist and future serial killer William Gull is 'shown' as a 16-year-old – actually, we can only see his hands protruding into the image from the lower right in three of the nine panels – as he is tampering with the corpse of his father, who has died from cholera. In the background, we can see William's mother and the physician, who has probably just pronounced the father dead. In the foreground, we are looking from close up at the father's head lying on a cushion, probably on a bier or in a casket. As William's mother is talking to the physician, her son secretly plays around with the father's left eyelid and opens it to the point that the eyeball grotesquely stands out. William obviously cannot stifle a laugh and is admonished by his mother, yet replies that he "just made a little sound" (panel #6 – in panel #8, William closes the eyelid). For viewers or readers, there is no doubt about whose hands we observe protruding into panels #4, 5, and 6, and we are given a cognitive advantage over the mother and the doctor, who are not aware of William's morbid doings. Neither is William aware that he is 'being watched:' the perspective construction is clearly oriented toward the implied observer, whom it grants a view from a spot outside the diegesis, despite the fact that the father's head is shown from close up. All nine panels of this sequence display a "mise en scène geared toward the depth of field" (Jost 1987: 68), and the reader-observers discern things happening in front of the background characters which they themselves ignore. Finally, the mother's (balloon) speech in the last two panels gives the readers another cognitive advantage over the doctor, the mother, and her son: she refers to bargees as "cold fish with no feelings at all" (her husband ran a small transportation business and used to take William on his barge) and with this foreshadows her son's future fate as a cold-blooded serial killer. To sum up, in spectatorial focalizations, the reader-observers gain a cognitive advantage over the character/s through the pictorial and the narratorial representation (if there is any);

- *internal focalization* also occurs most frequently in combination with zero ocularization: "a narrator (not necessarily a first-person narrator) tells how the character experiences a situation from the interior, and we watch it unfold on the screen" (ibid. 73); but it may also occur in combination with primary and secondary internal ocularization (cf. ibid. 72). In any case, internal focalization implies that the viewer knows as much as the character/s and that there is no cognitive disproportion between the two sides. – Nevertheless, the transfer of Jost's internal focalization concept to graphic narratives requires supplementary comment. In graphic novels, there may be neither a narrator nor caption script. In Daniel Clowes' *Ghost World*, for example, the verbal track merely consists of the balloon speech (the only exception being Enid's flash-back narration of her first sexual intercourse while she is talking on the phone with Rebecca, cf. Clowes 2000: 35–38, see my analysis in ch. 4.3.1.2, Fig. 4.11). Yet I would hold that the work as a whole as well as the single episodes are dominated by internal focalization, which will narrow down from Enid and Rebecca's to only Enid's focalization toward the end of the narrative. The great majority of the images are half-subjective and POV images, and what I get to know as a reader is all filtered through Enid and Rebecca's consciousness; nothing is withheld from my perception as I see (that is I know) the world through the minds of the two teenage girls.

Although Jost's focalization terminology nominally links up with Genette's,[72] the concepts of internal, external, and spectatorial focalization are radically removed from classical (and cognitive) narratology by the fact that they are applied to bimodal narratives. Nevertheless, Jost offhandedly reintroduces Genette's 'zero focalization' by including it in spectatorial focalization so that "'the reader becomes omniscient.'"[73] Yet nominally, there is zero *ocularization* (in which the camera, or what is shown in sequential images, has no vantage point in the diegesis) but no 'zero focalization.' All this considered, it is legitimate to generally doubt the cogency of zero focalization with respect to graphic narratives (cf. Groensteen 2013, ch. 5.1.1, np.), considering that this concept was forged to analyze verbal narrative fiction. Kai Mikkonen underscores the "distinct, spatially determined point of view of the image, the perspective from which the world is seen, whether this viewpoint is personal or impersonal" (2008: 309). Unlike verbal narratives, in which a narrator can look into the past and the future and survey a whole panorama, including the details, through nonfocalized (equal zero) focalization, graphic narratives do not allow for images with no point of view or perspective construction (that the point of view cannot be ascribed to a character or another diegetic instance is a different matter). In this regard, Jost's reintroduction of zero focalization from classical narratology is implausible and unnecessary.

Let me summarize the crucial points and bring up problems or spots of indeterminacy concerning focalization. According to Jost, a specific ocularization does not inevitably entail one certain focalization: as has been demonstrated above, zero ocularization (the most-used ocularization in film – as in graphic narratives, as I would hold) may combine with every type of focalization (cf. ibid. 65–73); the question here is if zero and internal ocularization combine with

---

[72] Tatjana Jesch and Malte Stein take up Genette's definition from *Nouveau Discours du Récit*, according to which focalization is "the author's temporary or definitive witholding of information from the reader" (Jesch/Stein 2009: 65).

[73] This quote by Genette is unproved, cf. Jost 1987: 71.

all focalization types – which Jost does not or only vaguely answer. As I have shown from Jason Lutes' *Berlin, City of Stones*, it is quite possible for (primary)[74] internal ocularization to combine with external focalization when I consider the opening and closing sequence to the above example (see chapter 4.3.1.2, Fig. 4.12, and the subsequent analysis). For the assessment of focalization, what counts in the end is how in an image sequence (or "succession of shots," cf. Kuhn 2009: 263) – and, ultimately, across sequences and in the whole work – the different ocularizations are set against each other (including the balloon speech) and the caption script; in other words: how the pictorial representation is set against verbal-narratorial representation.

From the preceding explications, it follows that focalization and ocularization overlap partly (cf. ibid. 63–64), or even to a considerable extent, and that focalization is grounded in the pictorial as well as in the verbal-narratorial representation. The overlap between the two concepts can even be full, as in the viewer-directed or "spectatorial ocularization" (see above, Fig. 4.24) which, however, is a very specific and quite rare case.

What generally matters as much for the assessment of focalization (in terms of knowledge relation) as of ocularizations in a sequence under scrutiny is the "textual" place of that sequence (Jost 1987: 66). If it is at the very beginning of a graphic narrative, the focalization most likely differs from the case in which that sequence is at an advanced stage or at the end of the narrative, at which the readers are (more) familiar with the plot. Take, for example, the prologue or lead-in sequence from *From Hell* (Fig. 4.25).

The first panel, overarching the other six panels on the page, is a straight-on extreme closeup of a seagull's carcass, lying on its back and marked by considerable decay. In the following six images, the vantage point of the ocularization moves up a bit so that we can see two elderly men as they continuously approach the dead bird from far off. In the last three panels we discern one of the work's protagonists, inspector Abberline, who sets out to prod the carcass with his walking stick. Although the point of view in this image sequence cannot be ascribed to a character in the story world, it guides the readers' perception and attention by providing a cognitive clue: the gull is obviously not just a random carcass that the characters happen to come across during their walk on Bournemouth beach. Readers are prompted to guess that it represents a link between

---

[74] A secondary internal ocularization normally combines with at least one primary internal ocularization.

Fig. 4.25: Moore/Campbell 2006: prologue, 1, focalization

the events in the prologue (or extradiegetic narrative), set in 1923, and what is to follow (Gull's killing spree, set in 1888) in the intradiegetic narrative. This is why I would here speak of a spectatorial rather than of a zero ocularization, even though the readers are by no means given a "cognitive advantage" (Jost 1987: 24) over the two characters.

In all the images of the prologue sequence, there is no question yet of focalization. What ex-inspector Abberline and Lees, the psychic, are saying as they approach the carcass is literally unrelated to Abberline's prodding it. From their foreknowledge, their genre expectations, the narratorial script (place and date), and the paratextual clues on the opposite page – every chapter in *From Hell* starts with a series of epigraphs from quite divergent sources – readers can infer that these characters must be related to the story about the Whitechapel murders (their suspicion will be confirmed on the following pages where more concrete allusions are made to the serial murder case). But their knowledge does not go any further. Since the readers here are obviously at a cognitive disadvantage, the focalization of this sequence as well as of the whole episode is external. If that same sequence appeared instead after the first half of the narrative or at the end (where this framing proleptic episode in fact is brought to a conclusion), the readers would be able to understand more of the paratextual allusions and the image of the carcass, which is an image-text (or pictorial metaphor, if you will): the gull connects to the author of the last paratextual epigraph to this chapter, "Sir William Gull," and his factual "notes and aphorisms." William Gull is the serial killer and monster hero of this graphic novel, and a similar metaphorical image-text is used one more time in another episode of this chapter, foreshadowing the lugubrious fate of a minor female character (cf. Moore/Campbell 2006: I, 7). Also, the carcass foreshadows the bleak fate of William Gull himself: he will die completely insane in a dungeon of a prison. The closing sequel to this episode at the end of the book, which frames the whole narrative, features no more an external but an internal focalization, whereas the ocularizations continue to be zero (Moore/Campbell 2006, epilogue, 1–10).

The problem spots in Jost's system: generally, with focalization being not just a complex category but a category overlapping with three other categories (ocularization, balloon speech, and caption script) from two different semiotic systems (verbal and pictorial), there is an imminent danger of blurriness and indeterminacy. As for character knowledge, the resultant of focalization, Jost himself admits that

> [...] this sometimes is for the viewer a more complex resultant than what a character saw, heard, or said [...] Contrary to ocularization and auricularization, focalization is a polymorphic phenomenon, an intersemiotic component, which is not defined in five lines nor in five minutes. (ibid. 63–64)

The problem thus is: how can I know for certain what the characters know? At times, this will have to remain approximate if unknowable, especially when there is little or no balloon or caption script. And speaking of characters: whose knowledge is it that matters? Jost designates the "hero" for ocularization and the "character" for focalization (ibid. 18 et passim), which is rather confusing. Regardless of focalization or ocularization, I would simply speak of the main or minor characters. Since ocularization relates to the single image rather than an image sequence or episode (see ch. 4.3.1.2), the differentiation between main or minor characters is of no substantial value. In the case of focalization, however, a sequence or episode may indeed be focalized by a minor character, especially in works with multiple focalization (as Jason Lutes' *Berlin* books) – to pick up a Genettean term. In *From Hell*, as a matter of fact, we find more than one episode (covering several pages) focalized through a prostitute, William Gull's would-be victim (cf. Moore/Campbell 2006: III, 3–7).

Also, what the characters see is sometimes hard to make out: firstly because the lion's share of the images is half-subjective, only approximately reflecting the characters' perceptions. The balloon and caption script can make up for this indeterminacy but does not necessarily have to. Jost adds that "[s]eeing is inferred from the image through the different subcodes of the shot and the editing" (Jost 1987: 63). Unless I am dealing with a genuine POV shot or with an image featuring vectorization,[75] it is only approximately possible to determine what exactly a character sees. In most cases, however, what a character *exactly* sees is not really important unless it directly concerns the plot – or, as Jost would put it, unless it has a narrative function. Therefore, the indeterminacy of what a character sees mostly is secondary in relevance.

Finally, in graphic narratives, everything narrates, the verbal and the pictorial elements, which I have compacted in the formulae 'showing is narrating' and 'verbal narration tells and shows' (see ch. 4.2). This is why showing cannot be separated from narrating nor narrating from showing. Focalization, as it has been redefined on the basis of Jost's terminology, is about the knowledge relation between characters – or possibly narrators – and readers. Knowledge, in turn, must be inferred from what is shown in the pictorial track (including the speech balloons) and from what is written in the narratorial captions. Therefore, focalization is a resultant or *second-order term*, as is narration: the latter must also be constructed or inferred from the verbal and the pictorial track. Ocularization, in contrast, directly concerns the finished given of an image and its pictorial composition and design. What is shown in the image can be described quite

---

[75] See my analysis of Daniel Clowes' *Ghost World* in ch. 4.3.1.2.

exactly, with only few spots of fuzziness or indeterminacy, whereas what is known, due to its complexity involving two semiotic systems, must be construed and therefore is sometimes vague. This is why I consider ocularization the more efficient and discriminate term for the analysis of graphic novels. In the above case of the gull's carcass (Fig. 4.25), for example, it is the ocularization and the mise en scène that comes with it, like its framing and viewing angle, that cater to construing the gull as an image-text, which links up with the paratext on the opposite page. As forms of construal, image-texts (and text-images) do justice to the double modality of the genre and thus represent an essential feature (see ch. 3.3.4, Fig. 3.5, and 3.3.4.6). On the other hand, they represent an enhanced means of showing, and in the above case from *From Hell*, this image-text also has a narrative function as it stirs the readers' anticipation of the plot – a major character will die – although only rudimentarily in this sequence. Contrary to focalization, ocularization is a *first-order term* that is directly connected to showing and thus to the dominating narrative mode in graphic novels (and graphic narratives in general).

4.9 Representations of Subjectivity

In graphic narratives, ocularization and focalization are only two aspects of subjective bending. Principally, subjectivity can be distinguished with respect to the artist-writer, characters, and the narrator (if there is one marked, with a spatio-temporal identity distinct from the intradiegetic story world). The following aspects and signs of subjectivy pertain to the (verbal-)pictorial track.

4.9.1 Styles and Their Makers

The subjectivity of the artist-writer is expressed in what is commonly called graphic or drawing style or styles, including the graphic line, use of color, degree of iconicity, or the lettering (the hand-crafted letters or 'typeface'). In graphic memoirs, "style actually presents readers with a particularly personal vision of what is remembered as having been experienced" (Versaci 2007: 44, qtd. in Pedri 2013: 145). Yet given the cartoonicity of the characters and the story world, the features or devices of a drawing style do rather not lend themselves to direct interpretations or conclusions about the artist-writer, which relativizes the claim quoted above. In non-autobiographical works, the relation of the style to its maker is certainly even more difficult to grasp (see also chapter 4.5).

Traditionally, as in Robert C. Harvey, the question of style can be made to embrace parameters like the narrative breakdown or layout (cf. Harvey 1996, ch. 7): if, for example, we compare the layout and the form of the panels in Craig Thompson's *Blankets* and *Habibi*, we shall find striking similarities.[76] French comics theory, in contrast, defines graphic style more narrowly in that it "does not extend to the broad functions of narrative organization, selection, and arrangement of words and images" (Mikkonen 2013: 111). As always, the actual scope of a concept like style depends on its definition; however, when the definitorial scope becomes too wide, the concept loses critical pertinence, and in that case, virtually anything could be subsumed under 'style.' For this reason, I would limit graphic style to the items outlined at the beginning of this section.

In theory, different drawing styles may coexist in one work. Thierry Groensteen has it that, besides the "tendency to include breaks in graphic style in mid-narrative," certain artist-writers from "the new generation" use a diversity of styles, be it in one and the same work or in different works, possibly of one series (Groensteen 2013, ch. 5.3.3, np.). Admittedly, artist-writers like Manu Larcenet use a drawing style in *Le combat ordinaire* (2003–2008) that is strikingly different from the one in his *Blast* series (2009–2014); this also applies to David Mazzucchelli, if I compare *City of Glass* with *Asterios Polyp*, or Bryan Talbot, in *Alice in Sunderland* and *Dotter of Her Father's Eyes*. Nevertheless, drastic changes in style usually do not happen within one individual work. Sweeping statements like the one above are often made of generalizations from a rather limited body of works.[77] The styles used in graphic novels from the beginnings until today are generally all typical of their makers, like the *ligne claire* in Jason Lutes and Rutu Modan, the touch of Crumbian underground in Joe Sacco, or the styles of Alison Bechdel, Marc-Antoine Mathieu, or Craig Thompson, which are difficult to label. Diversity of style, I would hold, is not a core feature of complexity to graphic novels as outlined in chapter 3.3.4 (apart from that, my prototype approach to graphic novels relates to the single work, not the whole body of works created by an artist-writer).

All in all, I see style as ultimately affecting the mise en scène, and therefore I have predicated it as artist-writer-specific. With certain restrictions, drawing style

---

[76] Compare ch. 3.3.4.4, Fig. 3.13, to Thompson 2011: 175, 455, et passim. Notice the small gutters combined with what could be called 'dynamic' panels, whose borders are curved for dramatizing effects.

[77] In fact, Groensteen's argument is constructed from basically one graphic memoir by Fabrice Neaud (*Journal*, 4 vols., 1996–2002, cf. Groensteen 2013, ch. 5.3.3, np.); the following examples he gives pertain to short- and long-form French and Italian books of comics, not graphic novels. Apart from that, his claim that there are different styles in the drawing of the two main characters in *Asterios Polyp* (ibid.) seems implausible to me: within one style, an artist may mark characters as pictorially different, while the overall style structurally remains the same.

and mise en scène can be seen as specific of a single work, artist-writer, genre, or period (cf. Mikkonen 2013: 113). Historically, it can be held that the emergence of the graphic novel has led to a caesura in both the assessment and marketing/marketability of individual styles: whereas in the big mainstream comic book companies, the artists had to more or less submit to the stylistic demands (i.e. uniformity) of the comic book series, nowadays, an artist's individual recognizable graphic style is looked at as a means to the "self-construction as a serious author to oppose the industrial principles underlying the production of comics" (Baetens/Frey 2015: 135).

4.9.2 The Subjectivity of Characters

The representation of character subjectivity is a more complex issue. To begin with, drawing style, that is the graphic line and color coding in particular, may underscore the subjectivity of characters, representing the way they perceive and think. Thus, the shape of David Mazzucchelli's protagonist Asterios Polyp is drawn in bright cyan geometrical forms when he is domineering, whereas his wife Hana is marked by magenta cross-hatching and round shapes when she is in a defensive position.[78] It goes without saying that these specificities in the drawing style generate meaning: in one way, they are pictorial metaphors or symbols of stereotypical masculinity and femininity; in another, they tell about the characters' mindsets and attitudes and, together with this, their perceptual and cognitive focus. An issue closely connected to drawing style is the characters' facial expression and body language, which, however, is highly dependent on the degree of iconicity of their design. Art Spiegelman's anthropomorphic mice, including the main and the minor characters, are rather incapable of facial expression and, a little less so, of body language (see chapter 3.2.3). In this sense, Spiegelman's characters hardly show the most basic emotions, such as joy and sadness, as are typical of even the most simple cartoon characters (– this, of course, must be seen as a strategic means on the part of Spiegelman the artist-writer through which he has successfully avoided the danger of an inappropriate rendering of the miseries and atrocities of WWII).

The most salient and, at the same time, unobtrusive way to represent character subjectivity in the medium of comics is through speech and thought balloons or captions, or through both. Comics usually favor direct speech and transform thoughts into words (cf. Groensteen 2013, ch. 6, np.). What characters typically say or think – if that can be generalized at all – is information of the

---

[78] See above, ch. 3.3.4.2, and Groensteen 2013, ch. 5.3.3, np., Miodrag 2013: 174–179, and Duncan 2012: 43–54 for closer analyses.

first order and, since it is written, does not have to be constructed by the readers (as opposed to the gap filling from panel to panel). This is equally true for the narratorial captions, if characters (or narrators) are made to speak through this device; caption speech, however, usually is less direct because of its use of pronouns and reporting clauses (the occurrence of 'figural verbal narration' being extremely rare, see ch. 4.5). Apart from that, the conventionalized design of the speech or thought balloons – including the writing contained, which primarily signifies as a verbal code – is ultimately also subject to showing: graphic narratives *show* what is being said. They also show what is said in the narratorial captions: being subject to layout, they cross-connect to the images.[79] Cross-referentiality, in turn, is constitutive of the complexity of graphic novels (see chapter 3.3.4). Thus, as far as the word/thought balloons and captions are concerned, they represent another instance of the dominance of showing over the telling mode.

4.9.3 Character Imagination

An interesting type of subjective showing with regard to the characters' perception, their mind states, and the plot is the representation of the characters' imagination. In one of the trailblazers of French alternative comics, Jean-Claude Forest and Jacques Tardi's *Ici Même*,[80] the protagonist Arthur Même, who has been dispossessed of his family's legitimate property and forced to live on top of the walls dividing the single lots, imagines the wall on which he is walking as well as his feet pricking their ears (Fig. 4.26).

Arthur is utterly lonely and regrets having to talk to the wall and his ears; in the preceding panel, he utters: "[...] I can hardly imagine my feet or the wall pricking their ears..." (Forest/Tardi 34, panel #3). He finishes his sentence in the following panel by saying "...and me overlooking it" (Fig. 4.26). The irony is that he is seeing it and, then again, that he is not: the ears of the wall and of his feet are indeed imaginary, yet he is seeing them anyway (in his mind's eye). In this type of subjective representation, seeing is imagining and/or contemplating, and such images or image sequences as they occur on several occasions in *Ici Même* are indexes of internal focalization, in which the readers know as much as the character (according to François Jost, see above, ch. 4.8).

---

[79] See Hanna Miodrag's analysis of Posy Simmonds' extensive "lexias" in Miodrag 2013: 65–78, Joe Sacco's salient use of diverse types of captions in *Palestine* (Sacco 2003: 1 and passim), or Alison Bechdel's use of captions in the gutters or inside the images in *Fun Home* (Bechdel 2006: passim).
[80] First serialized in the Franco-Belgian magazine *(À Suivre)* [parentheses part of title] in 1978, issued by the publisher Casterman.

Fig. 4.26: Forest/Tardi 2006: 34, comical imagination of the protagonist

Lewis Trondheim's graphic memoir *Approximativement* (1998) abounds with such imagination sequences, in one of which the much irritated protagonist Lewis turns into a superhuman who knocks out an imaginary kickboxing champion in a metro station, smashes his fist through a train window, and grabs another man who jostled him while he was waiting for the train (Fig. 4.27). Here too, the episode ends with an ironic twist: having finally gotten on the train, Lewis ends up sitting right next to the man he knocked out in his daydream (ibid. 5).

Fig. 4.27: Trondheim 1998: 4, hyperbolic allegory (comical)

In the first of the four volumes of Manu Larcenet's best-selling series *Blast* (2009–2014), the protagonist Polza Mancini, an ex-writer suspected of the murder of a woman, is looking at a huge Moai statue, as they are found on Easter Island (Fig. 4.28).

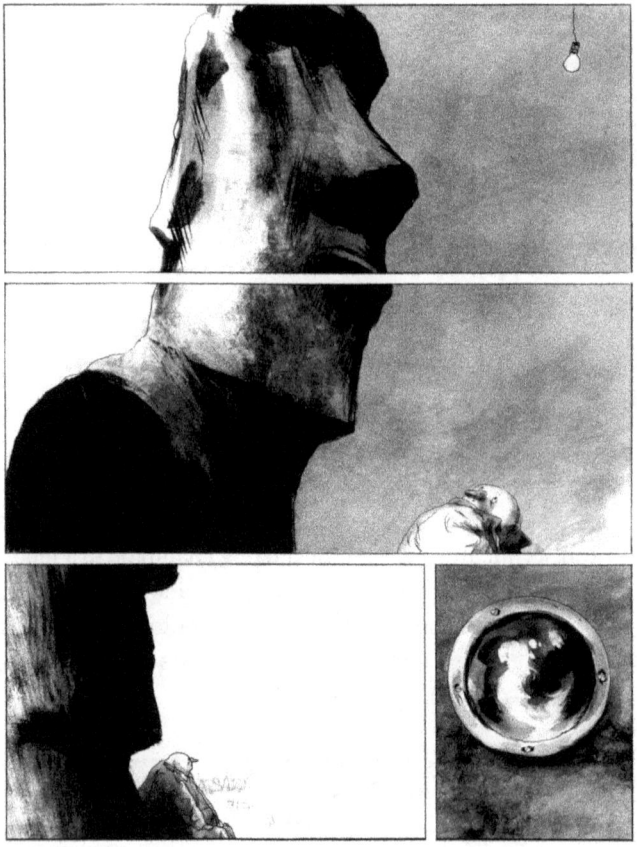

Fig. 4.28: Larcenet 2014: 9, character imagination (grotesque)

The split horizontal panel (Fig. 4.28, panels #1 and 2) is preceded by a full-page splash of a frontal projection of the Moai head (ibid. 8). The split panel and the following panel in which Polza is leaning with his back against the Moai statue actually show more than what is seen (by Polza), that is they show Polza contemplating and leaning against what he is imagining. Actually, Polza is not on Easter Island but in the detention room of a police station, from the antechamber of which two detectives are observing him through a bull's eye before they enter the room to question him (Fig. 4.28, last panel – also note the dangling light bulb, belonging to the detention room, in the upper frame of the split panel). According to Charles Hatfield, split panels "are often used to emphasize precise sequencing or deliberate rhythms," and they "stretch out the reading of single moment [sic] in time" (Hatfield 2005: 53/58). In this sense, the split panel reflects the deliberate rhythm of Polza's act of looking from the top to the bottom of the imagined statue. Then again, Polza's looking at the statue is non-diegetic, for it is very probably not observed by the detectives through the bull's eye in the door. As he is looking, Polza signals to the implied reader-observers that he is only in the image as an index of his own vision, and that they are actually seeing the Moai through his eyes. Polza's vision is mediated through his bodily presence and his looking posture in a half-subjective image – or, as Jost would call it, in a secondary internal ocularization. This is different in quality from the above sequences from Forest/Tardi and Trondheim, which, through their use of pictorial hyperbole and metaphor, can be relegated to the artist-writers as instances of comic – and 'dramatic' – irony. In the opening sequence of *Blast 1*, however, the focus is on the performativity of the protagonist's vision and his 'deliberate rhythm' of looking (Fig. 4.28). The reader-observers see (through) the character who is looking, and the Moai statue is a pictorial metaphor of Polza's mind, ever in search of an inner experience he calls "the blast" (Larcenet 2014: 43–44), which is rhetorically rendered in explosions of color in the style of children's drawings in otherwise black and white images (see also Mikkonen 2013: 116–117). The question that readers may ask with regard to Polza's and Arthur Même's figments of imagination is if the characters are not mad or mentally deranged.

In fact, madness is a highly interesting instance of subjectivity in graphic narratives. Besides the rhetorical devices of pictorial hyperbole and metaphor, we also find pictorial anachronisms or representations of objects, events, or conditions that are inconsistent with the story world. In a subjective sequence from Alan Moore and Eddie Campbell's *From Hell*, the protagonist William Gull looks through a window in an impoverished backyard of the Whitechapel district, where he is about to kill the prostitute Annie. As he is looking, Gull faces a man, who in turn looks back at him with surprise (Fig. 4.29).

Gull's vision leaves him wide-eyed and horrified: behind the man he discerns a running TV set (Fig. 4.29, panels #1 and 2) – which, of course, did not exist in 1888, the year in which that part of the story is set. As opposed to the first two POV images, the third panel is a reaction image (or a secondary internal ocularization), which creates an overall internal focalization together with the other subjective and half-subjective images of that eighteen-image sequence. Later on in the narrative, on another killing spree, we find Gull in a full-page splash, his back turned as he is raising his arms toward a twentieth-century

Fig. 4.29: Moore/Campbell 2006: VII, 24, Gull's hallucination

highrise, knife in one hand, both hands dripping with blood (Moore/Campbell 2006: VIII, 40). This splash ends a 23-image sequence displaying in great detail the extremely brutal killing of the prostitute Mary Ann Kelly. Since that slaughter sequence is more action-oriented than the sequence shown in Fig. 4.29, only four genuine POV images are found; in the rest, Gull is shown in half-subjective images as he is literally tearing up the prostitute's body (ibid. VIII, 37–39).

The use of objects, events, or conditions incompatible with the story world of the characters is typical of a technique called the grotesque, which can also be defined as a "*conflation of disparates*" (Thomson 1972: 20, italics in the original). Thus, images depicting the TV set and the highrise in William Gull's vision, the wall pricking its ears in Arthur Même's, and the Moai statue in Polza Mancini's vision produce a comical (Forest/Tardi), awe-inspiring, or terrifying effect (Larcenet) on the readers, or one which is both comical and terrifying (Moore/Campbell). The use of the grotesque through pictorial metaphor, hyperbole, or anachronism, however, does not automatically imply that the character they relate to is mad. Thus, the hyperbole of the superhuman used in Trondheim's *Approximativement* (Fig. 4.27) connotes the narrating character's feelings or thoughts,[81] not madness: Lewis, the protagonist, feels a deep unease and is

---

[81] Thierry Groensteen gives a similar example from a graphic memoir by Philippe Dupuis and Charles Berberian, *Journal d'un album* (1994), in which Charles, the narrating character, imagines himself as a Martian, having emerged from a flying saucer, as he is telling a taxi driver that he makes comic books for a living. This is to anticipate the reaction of the taxi driver, who, in the following, will make a deprecatory comment on comics (cf. Groensteen 2013, ch. 6, np.).

simply irritated by the daily banal events, wishing he could do away with them. And from another vantage point, William Gull's 'visions' may in fact be construed as "intimations" of the end of the Victorian age, which is a characteristic feature of neo-Victorian fiction, including *From Hell*: after his last murder, Gull says to Netley, his stooge: "It is [...] just the beginning. For better or for worse, the twentieth century. I have delivered it" (Moore/Campbell 2006: X, 33, qtd. in Domsch 2012: 111–112).

4.9.4 The Subjectivity of Narrators

To represent the subjectivity of a narrator – under the condition that there is a narrator marked with a spatio-temporal identity distinct from the intradiegetic plane – the artist-writer principally has the same verbal-narratorial and pictorial options as for the representation of character subjectivity. A narrator's subjectivity may appear as toned down until almost non-existent, like 'Paul Auster's friend' in Paul Karasik and David Mazzucchelli's *City of Glass*, or, on the other hand, it may come across as inflated or even neurotic, as with Spiegelman's narrator Art(ie), who, in *Maus II*, ch. 2 ("Auschwitz. Time Flies"), wears a mask – thereby drawing attention to the subject behind the mask, seemingly wanting to hide behind it – and consults a therapist to relieve him of his guilt complex and his worries about the legitimacy of his book in the making.

Not least, a narrator's subjectivity depends, of course, on the degree to which its persona has been fleshed out (realism) and the rhetorical or stylistic devices used in the representation of the persona, such as typescript and pictorial metaphor or others. In this sense, the narrator in *City of Glass* is not at all realistic (being virtually covert), for he is mainly alluded to by the verbal-narratorial type(writer)script and by the typewriter text-image (or image-text, the case being somewhat hard to decide); the narrator in *Maus* is not a realistic representation either, for Spiegelman uses pictorial metaphor, or allegory, to mask (and hide) his subjectivity. Apostolos and Christos, on the contrary, the extradiegetic self-reflexive narrators in Doxiadis and Papadimitriou's *Logicomix* (2009), occur as fully fleshed-out *personae*, who resemble their photographs on the inside of the back cover and who refer to their living conditions and their project laid out in that very novel. Although reduced through the cartoonicity of the drawings, the narrators appear as realistic, as a recognizable image of the real-life persons – not as an almost pure construct, like the narrator in *City of Glass*. The rather postmodern doubling and tripling of narrators in Barry's *One Hundred Demons* and Talbot's *Alice in Sunderland*, however, reduces the degree of subjectivity, Bryan Talbot's somewhat photorealistic images of himself notwithstanding, and seem to underscore that narrators are constructs, after all (see Fig. 4.21 as well as the closing sequence to the novel in Talbot 2007: 317–318).

4.9.5 Signs and Metaphors of Subjectivity

A not fully definable set of visual-pictorial signs representing subjectivity are 'emanata': "The term [...] was suggested by Mort Walker in his textbook *The Lexicon of Comicana* to designate the dashes, droplets, spirals, stars, and other graphic signs placed near a character's face in order to convey an emotion or physical state. The emanata reinforce the facial expression" (Groensteen 2013, ch. 6, np.). In addition, there are pictograms, like a heart with a dagger, signifying disappointed love, or an ice cube representing contempt. "Moreover, they are usually enclosed within the image, or a balloon, and considered to have been emitted by the character just as words would be" (ibid.). Thierry Groensteen claims that they are symbolic; I would hold that the heart with the dagger or the ice cube, for example, actually are pictorial metaphors or allegories.

Such emanata are typically found in traditional comic books rather than in graphic novels – in which other, non-conventional, signs occur that are not limited to reinforcing facial expressions and difficult to classify, such as the ones below (Figs. 4.30 and 4.31).

In the second volume of Joann Sfar's pentalogy *Le chat du rabbin* (2001–2006, Fig. 4.30), the character called Malka of the Lions is mad at the rabbi, who does not want his daughter to marry a rabbi from Paris. The black scribblings on red ground not only reinforce his facial expression but his whole emotional state; they are not conventional signs and do not belong to the comics lexicon. In Birgit Weyhe's family biography *Im Himmel ist Jahrmarkt* (2013), we find a structurally similar category of sign (Fig. 4.31), which could also be looked at as an image. The difference between the black scribblings on red ground in Sfar and what looks like a torn flower in Weyhe is that the latter stands for the emotional as well as for the physical conditions of the characters, the reconstruction of whose lives is subject to her graphic novel; also, Weyhe uses such images so frequently that they stand out as a typical feature of this particular work. To give one last example: Frederik Peeters' black and white graphic memoir *Pillules bleues* (2001) starts with a series of image-texts that depict shapes resembling atmospheric weather phenomena and solar eruptions, accompanied by various one-word captions starting with the letter *d* ("discern," "discipline," "discobolus," and "discordance", Peeters 2013: 2–4). These image-texts read as representations of Frederik's mixed emotions concerning his relationship with Cati and her little son, both of whom have tested HIV-positive. Pictorial creations of the above type are pictorial metaphors (or allegories, depending on their complexity) of mind states or emotional or physical conditions, as in Weyhe's case. They are neither icons nor conventionalized symbols but individual (verbal-)pictorial signs generating context- and work-specific meanings.

Fig. 4.30: Sfar 2002: 43, panel #3, context- and work-specific pictorial metaphor I

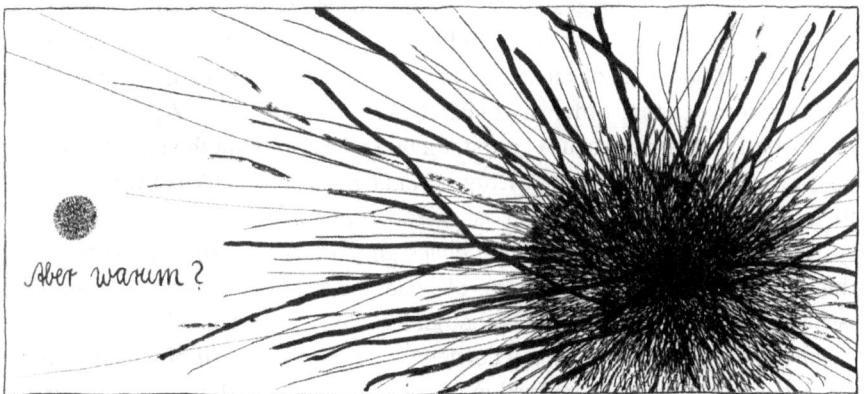

Fig. 4.31: Weyhe 2013: 31, panel #3, context- and work-specific pictorial metaphor II

4.10 Layout Revisited: Classification and Critical Efficiency

In their layout, graphic novels have been distinctly more experimental than other books of comics. This is especially eye-catching in all of Chris Ware's, Joe Sacco's, and Marc-Antoine Mathieu's works; besides, there are salient features of layout in single works like in Bryan Talbot's *Alice in Sunderland*, Charles Burns' *Black Hole*, Posy Simmonds' *Gemma Bovery*, or in Grant Morrison and Dave McKean's *Arkham Asylum*, to name but a few. In a prototype approach, I have elaborated on panel design and layout as one subcategory and distinctive feature of complexity, which in turn is a core feature of graphic novels (see chapter 3.3 and particularly 3.3.4.4). Layout in graphic novels is generally more complex than in other books of comics because the former have provided the freedom for the creators to go beyond conventionalized patterns.

In addition, I have elaborated above on *montage* or cross-cutting as a specific type of showing, in which point of view and character vision are of secondary relevance (see chapter 4.3.1.1). Apart from representing a type of showing, layout – or editing, to use a cinematic term – is a crucial parameter in the putting together of (usually not more than) two separately broken-down strands of action on a page. This is why *montage* and cross-cutting also increase the complexity of the layout, especially when one strand of action is constructed as a mise en abyme of the other, as in Moore and Gibbons' *Watchmen* (see my detailed analysis in chapter 3.3.4.7).

Basically, layout concerns the spreading out of the discrete pictorial panel units and chunks of text on the page (the latter primarily concerns the narratorial caption script, whereas balloon speech, tags, and sound lettering usually relate to the single images). The ordering or sequencing of the images and "lexias" (Barthes 1970), the chunks of text, directly affect the reading order and with it the production of meaning. When layout destabilizes the conventionalized western reading order of comics images (the so-called Z-path), meaning production increases because more than one way of linking the single images is possible, as is often the case in Ware's *Building Stories* (the title of which alludes to 'building stories' as much as to 'stories in or about a building').

Except for Hannah Miodrag's *Comics and Language* (2013), it seems to me that layout of *text*, or the placing of lexias on the page, has not been a big issue in the critical literature – although it is an important device in works like *Gemma Bovery, Palestine, Jimmy Corrigan* or *Fun Home*, in all of which it contributes enormously to the production of meaning across both the verbal-narratorial and the verbal-pictorial plane. Text layout analysis, I would assume, has rather been limited to single-work or single-sequence analyses because it is

4.10 Layout Revisited: Classification and Critical Efficiency

difficult to classify – unless one chooses to categorize it as a feature of individual style.

The case is different with images. The spreading of the panels across the page can and has been classified as early as 1983 by Benoît Peeters, who outlined four types of layout,[82] which have been referred to by critics such as Thierry Groensteen (2007, see below) and Jesse Cohn: 1) the regular type, that is three or four strips (*bandes*); 2) the decorative or creative type with often spectacular panel forms or arrangements, yet mostly without substance for the production of meaning; 3) the rhetorical type: here, the panel form serves the action, for example a large panel used for an important event, an oblong vertical underscoring the height of a building, etc.; and 4) the productive type, in which the panel form seems to "dictate the narrative" and produces meaning in its own right (Cohn 2009: 49, cf. Peeters 2007, par. 30). With the example of a page from Windsor McCay's *Little Nemo in Slumberland* (1908), Peeters explains how the oblong vertical panels seem to determine the growing and shrinking of the characters "to match the construction of the page" (Peeters 2007, par. 31, illustration #12).

Groensteen criticizes Peeters' typology for being partly blurry or ambiguous (cf. Groensteen 2007: 93–95). For my part, I think that there is considerable overlap between categories 3) and 4), the rhetorical and the productive, and I would simply include the productive in the rhetorical, or vice versa, given the difficulty of distinguishing the 'serving' from the 'dictating' in Peeters' examples.

According to Groensteen, layout belongs among what he calls the spatio-topical parameters (Groensteen 2007: 91, see my schema in chapter 3.4.4, Fig. 3.23). Moreover, he juxtaposes layout and what he calls "hyperframe"[83] and claims that the relation between breakdown and layout is not one of succession but of mutual determination (ibid. 92). Finally, he formulates three principles governing layout: 1) the principle of choice for each individual panel and the consequence that each such choice "restricts the range of possibilities for others"; 2) that a particular layout proposes a certain reading order, and 3) the principle of "global composition [...], which submits [the panels] to an aesthetic order" (ibid. 92).[84]

---

[82] Originally in "Les aventures de la page," *Conséquences* 1 (1983): 32–44, later integrated in Peeters 1993. The English translation of this article by Jesse Cohn was published as "Four Conceptions of the Page," *ImageTexT* 3.3 (2007), 66 pars., web.
[83] "[...] the hyperframe is to the page what the frame is to the panel. / [...] the hyperframe separates the useable surface of the page from its peripheral zone, or margin" (Groensteen 2007: 30/31).
[84] In his follow-up to *The System of Comics*, Groensteen elaborates on layout features characteristic of *shojo manga*, which must appear "unusual" to western European readers (Groensteen 2013, ch. 4.2). Considering the manifoldness of layout in Anglo-European graphic novels, however, it occurs to me that a lot of those features are not so "unusual" after all.

Recently, Neil Cohn (2013) submitted an approach inspired by linguistics (morphology) and cognitive science. Page layout here is subsumed under what he calls the "*external compositional structure* (ECS) of printed visual language" (ibid., ch. 5, np., italics in the original). In Cohn's recipient-oriented cognitive approach, there are four types of page layout: a) regular grids such as the two-by-two; b) the blockage type, in which one oblong vertical panel faces two panels half its size; c) the overlapping type, in which panels of different sizes intersect; and finally d) the "staggering" type, in which panels of different sizes prevent a continuous horizontal gutter "so that readers question the expected Z-path" (ibid.). In sum, Cohn's concern is how readers cognitively process panel sequences with regard to reading order, for example, what panels readers skip or the entry point they choose in a certain type of layout.

In principle, all these classifications are legitimate despite their ambiguity and reductiveness, owing to the degree of specificity in the approach in which they are embedded. Cohn's classification, for example, will fall short of pertinence when applied to (complex and experimental) graphic novels in which grids have more or less vanished. Maybe layout, much more than panels, is too complex a parameter to be reduced to a small set of categories – unlike ocularization, for example, which is specific enough in that it relates to the single image and the entity that sees what is shown (see chapter 4.3.1.2). Therefore, it is advisable to make the subcategories or types larger and to admit enough overlap among them. Such a (prototypical) system is stable enough to dispense with frequent readjustments or additions of categories over time. With respect to systemic stability, Peeters' four layout types (which I think could be reduced to three) can still be useful tools to analyze meaning production through layout – presupposed they provide enough categorial overlap to allow for 'both ... and' and 'more/rather ... than' relations (see chapter 3.3.4). In that case, types three and four could also be used on more experimental graphic works.

5 Taking Stock: The Graphic Novel as a Narrating Genre

Contextualization. – The beginnings of the graphic novel lie in underground comics in the 1960s and 70s: adult-oriented one-shots and magazines, developing into anthologies, sometimes with an autobiographical tinge (as with Robert Crumb and Aline Kominsky-Crumb), created by male and female artist-writers. They represent the early forerunners of the modern (long-form) graphic novel as far as subject matter, styles, and narrative structure are concerned. The works of Justin Green, Will Eisner, Harvey Pekar, and Art Spiegelman together with what comics critics labeled alternative comics grew in sophistication and in volume as their stories and narrations became increasingly multilayered, self-referential, and experimental in their verbal-pictorial form and their layout. In short, the graphic novel emerges with a changing, maturing, readership and a work-immanent increase in *complexity*.

More precisely, the graphic novel emerged in two *hypes*. The publication of *The Dark Knight*, *Watchmen*, and *Maus* in the late 1980s set off the first hype, which was ended by the comic book market crash of the early 1990s. The 'big three' are the first works that deserve the genre label 'graphic novel.' Whereas *Maus* was still influenced by underground comics, particularly by the works of Robert Crumb and Justin Green, *The Dark Knight* and *Watchmen* clearly relate to the tradition of youth-oriented superhero comics, albeit in a parodic or ironic-satirical manner, and with considerable innovation regarding the verbal-pictorial form (ch. 2). From 2000 on, with the second hype, those influences from underground and alternative comics had virtually disappeared, and a new (sub)genre emerged that nowadays is virtually equivalent to the graphic novel per se: the (auto/bio)graphic memoir, in more than one way anticipated by Spiegelman's *Maus*, and nowadays represented by works like Marjane Satrapi's *Persepolis*, David B.'s *Epileptic*, or Alison Bechdel's *Fun Home*. Today, the graphic novel has become even more diversified, comprizing subgenres like the (fictional or nonfictional) biography, reportage and science comics, historical novels, or steam punk.

Theses and approach. – The theory-based concern of this book has been threefold: firstly, to establish the graphic novel as a genre in its own right (ch. 3); secondly, to show that although graphic novels undeniably narrate – and despite the existence of narratorial caption script – there is not necessarily a narrator; thirdly, to argue that the focalization concept from classical narratology is not suitable for books of comics because it does not account for the relation between what an image *shows* and what characters *see*, which is paramount to meaning production (ch. 4).

To start with, I have opted for a medium-specific approach, asserting that 'comics' are not a historical text group (or genre) but a *medium* with material constraints that cannot be bypassed with its own medium-specific devices. This crucial presupposition makes graphic novels a genre whose rules, conventions, and expectations can be played with. And indeed, this has frequently occurred, which has led me to the conclusion that graphic novels have revived postmodernist verbal fiction, in which the play with genre boundaries was programmatic (see ch. 1).

To circumvent the aporias connected to genre classification, I have employed a prototype approach in which *complexity* occurs as a core feature of graphic novels: as a nominal kind category, 'complexity' is complex in itself, definable only in analytical terms, here 1) multilayered plot and narration, 2) multifunctional use of color, 3) complex text/image relations, 4) meaning-enhancing panel design and layout, 5) structural performativity, 6) multiplicity of references to texts or other kinds of media, and 7) self-referential or metafictional devices (ch. 3.3.4). These seven analytical features are subcategories resembling their superordinate category 'complexity' in *gradability*: a graphic work thus can be assessed in terms of 'a high, medium, or low degree of [feature 1–7].' In their sum, the gradable features are *differential* in that they permit assessments of the type 'X is both ... and ...' or 'X is ... rather than ... ,' thereby doing justice to the fuzziness of the category boundaries, which has generally been seen as an obstacle to classification. Thus, the focus on the *core* feature/s ('complexity' and its subcategories 1–7), as opposed to peripheral features (for example, the absence of a verbal track or the presence of a narrator), provides the necessary categorial stability needed in a systematic analytical approach. Such an approach allows for the subsumption of an unusual work like Chris Ware's *Building Stories* under an already existing category: *Building Stories* can be analyzed with the same complexity features as 'regular' graphic novels, despite the fact that it comes with a hitherto unprecedented (at least with regard to graphic novels) material layout (or format). Thus, if the focus is on the core category of complexity, *Building Stories* does belong to the family of graphic novels.

Thus defined, graphic novels appear as a twice-removed (sub)category of graphic narratives in a category tree (ch. 3.3.3, Fig. 3.2), distinct from the rather youth-oriented traditional comic books, which appear on the same hierarchical level and whose makeup is rather simplistic in comparison. This does not preclude the occurrence of a single instance of a complexity feature in a traditional comic book, as shown by Werner Wolf (2005) with an example of metalepsis from a Donald Duck issue or, more recently, by Jeff Thoss (2015) with examples from superhero, fantasy, and adventure comics. On the whole, however, metalepsis as one instance of complexity is not a core feature of traditional comic books. In this respect, it could be interesting for future research to find out whether or to what extent complexity is a core feature of graphic novels for children or adolescents, or of graphic adaptations of verbal narrative fiction or plays.[1] This, however, lies outside the scope of this book.

That graphic novels are distinguished from other books of comics through the prototypical feature of multilayered plot and narration has been given close attention in chapter four. It implies, among other things, that most but not all graphic novels have a multilayered plot and that although all graphic novels narrate (the possible absence of a verbal track notwithstanding), they do not necessarily feature a *narrator*, despite the existence of caption script. Therefore, I disagree with the claim that narrators are generally more present in graphic novels than in traditional comic books (cf. Baetens/Frey 2015: 10). In my opinion, the existence of a narrator is not a core feature of graphic novels, neither is it a cogent distinguishing feature of graphic memoirs and other subgenres which make a (more or less explicit) claim to factuality.

Narrator vs. narratorial script. – For the reason given above, I reject the concept of a narrator as a default assumption in books of comics. Although the possibility of "non-narratorial representation" in graphic novels was already hinted at (Thon 2013), the approach developed here goes much further: the existence of a narrator as the sole originator of the discourse of a whole work – a basic concept in Genette's narratology – can be logically excluded, at least from the vantage point of a communicative approach (Pfister 1977). Unlike verbal narrative fiction, graphic narratives have no mediating or transmitting communication system, reified in a 'fictional narrator,' that could be held responsible for the production of the whole verbal and *pictorial* discourse. Therefore, the pictorial track should be ascribed to the artist-writer in the external communication system. Only when there is a figure or character *marked* as a narrator on both the verbal and the pictorial plane (through narratorial script and a realistic or iconic shape, or through pictorial allegory), distinct from the intradiegetic story, should we speak of a narrator. In that case, however, which is found in some graphic memoirs, the pictorial track and layout continue to be attributed to the artist-writer. The marking of a figure or character as a narrator can be

---

[1] Examples of graphic works for children, adolescents, or students are Jennifer and Matthew Holm, *Babymouse: Queen of the World* (2005); Kazu Kibuishi, *Amulet* (7 vols., 2008–); Gene Luen Yang, *American Born Chinese* (2006); Neil Gaiman and P. Craig Russell, *Coraline* (2008), or J. McDonald's graphic textbook adaptation of William Shakespeare's *The Tempest* (2009). With respect to classification, it would be interesting to find out whether Shaun Tan's wordless *The Arrival* (2006) is a graphic novel for adults or children (see my classification of this work in ch. 3.3.4.7).

done in manifold ways: through framing or coloring, through the use of another medium (such as an authentic photograph, as in *Le photographe*), or through splitting of the narrator-character into two (or more) alter egos (as in *One Hundred Demons* or in *Alice in Sunderland*). To recapitulate: narratorial or caption script is not primarily connected to a narrator or a narrator figure; neither is it mere verbal *text*. Narratorial captions bear pictorial elements and therefore cannot solely be ascribed to a narrator (if there is one). This is why the first complexity feature has been called "multilayered plot and *narration*," not 'narrative situation' or 'narrator,' since both the verbal-narratorial and the pictorial elements narrate and should be considered as one with regard to meaning production.

The verbal-narratorial track. – Caption script is both verbal and pictorial, made to show and to be seen. Framed or unframed, positioned inside or outside a panel, caption script comes in a particular typeface and is possibly colored, or it appears on a colored background. Thus, it is always semantically, symbolically, or otherwise loaded, and it seems as if graphic novels, above all, have experimented with it, as seen in Posy Simmonds' *Gemma Bovery*, or the works of Chris Ware and Craig Thompson. As pictorially enhanced writing, caption script is nondiegetic, a feature it shares with other verbal track constituents.

Speech balloons pertain to the internal communication system. But whereas balloon speech is diegetic as speech, it is nondiegetic as a pictorial container, of which the different outlines are symbolically or otherwise loaded. In this respect, graphic novels have also been more experimental than traditional comic books: we find personalized or gender-specific speech balloons in different symbolic shapes, filled with different colors, and balloon speech with no surrounding balloon or with different typefaces as in *Asterios Polyp*, *The Dark Knight Returns*, or in *Arkham Asylum*.

Although they resemble speech balloons in their outward shape, the nondiegetic tags pertain to the external communication system and the artist-writer, who comments in them on the verbal-pictorial narration, be it for rhetorical or informative reasons. As connectors between the verbal and the pictorial, tags – even when they are unframed and have no appendice – 'point' at pictorial entities, similarly to speech balloons. We also find them in traditional comic books, yet some text-oriented specimens among the graphic novels, such as *Fun Home*, *Logicomix*, *Maus*, or *Safe Area Goražde* make more frequent use of them, especially in connection with maps or informative sketches.

Sound lettering is the verbal track component in which showing seems to outweigh the semantic content of the writing, in other words: it appears to be more pictorial than verbal. Formally, it works through increase, prolongation, or repetition of single verbal and/or pictorial elements (see ch. 4.4.4, Fig. 4.13). Sound lettering, or the representation of sounds in general, probably is the only one of the verbal track components here discussed that clearly occurs more frequently in traditional comic books, especially in action and horror comics.

Texts in the fictional story world (for example letters, pages of a book, signboards, etc.) divide into texts destined to be acknowledged (rather than intensively read) by readers and texts not destined to be acknowledged. Enhancing the plausibility of the story world and the coherence of the plot, texts destined to be acknowledged have an informative function. Texts not destined to be acknowledged are detached from their informative function and become *text-images* (or *image-texts*, see ch. 3.3.4.6) and as such draw attention to their mediality rather than to the semantic content of the writing. Finally, text-images are specific to graphic novels as they pertain to the sixth subcategory of complexity (references to texts/media).

Paratext belongs to the external communication system and, as all types of text in books of comics, contains pictorial elements. Verbal paratext is, of course, not specific to graphic novels. Some self-referential or metafictional specimens, however, present numerous occurrences, for example, of epigraphs preceding chapters (*From Hell*) or other original usage of verbal paratext, which often combines with pictorial paratext, as in *Julius Corentin Acquefacques: Le décalage*, on the dustjacket to *Jimmy Corrigan,* or in *Watchmen*, if we consider the epigraphic clock symbol together with the verbal literary quotes. As text outside the 'text,' it orients the readers' reception of the unfolding plot by providing clues or a framework to the subplots, like the sketch of the house on the bottom of the cardboard container in Chris Ware's *Building Stories*. As complex as it is – if only for its fictional and nonfictional variants – paratext should be a productive paradigm for future research on graphic novels, especially in view of classification.

The pictorial track: what is shown and what is seen (ocularization). – Narration, a prototypical feature of complexity, is independent of a narrator in the first place yet closely related to plot design. In the multiple strands of action or subplots, we observe the switching of different points of view, often without the presence of a narrator and with only minimalistic (or even no) caption script; in some cases, such sequences clearly seem to be presented from a 'biased' (or subjective) angle, the subjectivity of which cannot be pinpointed. Such points of view appear as unattributable, or attributable only to the artist-writer. In this context, it has been argued that the *focalization* concept from classical narratology cannot account for switching points of view in graphic novels, attributable or nonattributable, for there often is no character or diegetic instance to whom those images or sequences could be ascribed. Another big problem inherent in focalization as known from classical narratology is that it does not account for the relation of *what is shown* (point of view) to *what is seen* (character vision).

Like every image, a comics image is created on the basis of perspective construction, resulting in its point of view and oriented toward an implied observer or projection center. Yet what the implied observer 'sees' is not always identical with what empirical readers observe, which is key for the meaning production.[2] Apart from the point of view, this is also due to other parameters of the image, such as angle, framing, lighting, or coloring: in short, to the *mise en scène*. Certain defamiliarization effects produced in the empirical readers are grounded in the jarring of the character vision with the point of view and the mise en scène (see my analyses of examples from *V for Vendetta*, *Watchmen*, and *Ghost World*, chs. 4.3.1 and 4.3.1.2). All this, however, is far beyond the conceptional grasp of focalization as known from classical narratology.

To account for the *relation* – or the tension – of point of view and mise en scène to character vision, François Jost's concept of *ocularization* has been extended by the parameter of mise en scène so that it represents the relation between what is shown and what is seen in the comics image. As in Jost (1987), *primary* and *secondary ocularization* (genuine POV and half-subjective images, such as reaction or over-the-shoulder images) are distinguished from *zero ocularization*, which signifies a point of view unattributable to a gaze within the story world ('nobody's shot'). The concept of *spectatorial ocularization* can be used for images displaying a point of view unattributable to a consciousness within the story world, but from a salient, potentially subjective, angle. All in all, ocularization is suitable for the analysis of a single image or a short image sequence, not of a whole episode, which might contain several different ocularizations.

Character vs. reader knowledge (focalization). – Jost's concept of focalization has the definitional scope to account for the assessment of a longer image sequence, episode, or of the whole work.[3] Like ocularization, it is a *relational* term, yet with the difference that it is about cognition, not perception, and that it relates character to viewer (or reader-observer) *knowledge*. In Jost's cinematic approach, character knowledge implies both the verbal and the visual elements; in graphic novels this would apply to the images, to the balloon and to the caption script. Also, focalization results, at least in part, from the ocularizations in single images and image sequences. It is noteworthy in this context that only such knowledge counts which is relevant to the plot: in all objective and (half-)subjective images, readers gather information inaccessible to the characters,

---

[2] For example, with regard to focalization, which has been redefined on the basis of François Jost (1987), see ch. 4.8.
[3] See my assessment of the frame sequences in *From Hell* at the end of ch. 4.8.

as for example, when they see details of the story's setting behind a character's back. Yet this is usually irrelevant for the action in process or the plot in the process of unfolding. On the basis of Jost's approach, *external focalization* (in which readers know less than a character) is distinguished from *internal focalization* (in which readers know as much as a character). When readers are given a cognitive advantage over a character, we speak of *spectatorial focalization*. Both external and internal focalization may combine with or start out from internal as well as from zero *ocularization*. The drawback inherent in this concept of focalization lies in its categorial overlap with several other parameters of what is shown and seen, including ocularization, and a certain blurriness resulting from that overlap. And whereas focalization must be *inferred* from both the verbal and the pictorial track, ocularization concerns the finished given of the image and can be described and analyzed with great precision. In addition, ocularization pertains to showing, the dominant mode of representation in books of comics. Therefore, ocularization is a term of the first order, as it is the more discriminate conceptual tool and the greater resource with regard to the analysis of images or image sequences.

As has been shown, this approach rejects the use of the concepts 'narrator' and 'focalization' from classical narratology. Considering the publications on that subject from the last decade, I find that there is a general disparity among approaches despite – or because of – the fact that critics question the relevance of certain classical concepts and propose alternative or redefined ones.[4]

Subjectivity and layout. – By definition, comics images contain no linguistic markers of subjectivity like proper names or personal pronouns. As images in a sequence, however, and through their pictorial makeup (point of view and mise en scène), they can represent a subjective, or in a certain way biased, view (ocularization), which may not be personalized or attributable to a character or a consciousness in the story world. Readers establish knowledge relations by looking at single images, episodes, or a whole work (focalization). But this is not

---

[4] Miller (2008) and Mikkonen (2013) introduce Jost's concept of ocularization but hold on to the classical concepts of a narrator and of focalization. The problem spot in Horstkotte and Pedri's approach (2011) is that focalization is bound back either to a character or to a (classical) narrator. Although Thon (2013) allows for "non-narratorial representation" and a "narrator-as-narrating-character," he ultimately stays attached to a classical narrator and leaves focalization out of consideration. Borrowing from Mikkonen (2008), Groensteen (2013) gives up on focalization in favor of a "perceptual source" and proposes a rather extravagant typology based on Gaudreault (1988), Lejeune (1975), and Marion (1993), consisting in an "overall narrator," who coordinates a "monstrator" and a "reciter," a "fundamental narrator," an "autobiographical narrator," and an "actorialized narrator."

the only aspect of subjective bending. In fact, I observe a shift in focus on other aspects of subjective bending of the narrative, especially in the latest research (cf. Groensteen 2013 and Mikkonen 2013). These aspects concern the artist-writer, the characters, and the narrator (if there is one). Drawing style, for example, affects the mise en scène and is therefore artist-writer-, genre-, or period-specific. What is historically interesting about style is that with the advent of the graphic novel, style became the mark of an artist-writer's individuality and one 'unique selling point' of her/his works – contrary to the traditional main stream comic books, whose formal and content-related demands artists had to comply with. Pictorially, and besides the information transmitted through balloon speech, character subjectivity may be represented through the use of color, the graphic line, shape, and the degree of iconicity. Characters become most subjective when they imagine, daydream, or hallucinate, which may be represented in pictorial metaphor, hyperbole, or in the use of the grotesque. Some experimental graphic novels split, double, or even triple narrator figures in order to emphasize the constructedness of subjectivity (*One Hundred Demons*, *Alice in Sunderland*). Last but not least, subjectivity emerges as detached from characters or narrators when linked to simple graphic or pictorial signs functioning symbolically or metaphorically (emanata), or to more complex text-images. Such text-images acquire meaning from their verbal-pictorial co-text of the individual sequence or from the context of the whole work.

Finally, layout is a crucial parameter of narrativity in books of comics. The reason why this aspect is dealt with at the end of my chapter on narration is because layout, together with panel design, is a subfeature of the complexity of graphic novels – although *specific types* of layout are not. A number of attempts at classification of layout, bound up with partly very specific approaches, have been made, in broader or in narrower terms. Yet the narrower the category the less critically efficient it is for the manifold totality of graphic works to be scrutinized. Unless future research brings about more convincing classifications – or if one is not satisfied with Peeters' old but efficient 1993 typology – the meaning production through layout should be assessed in the context of individual sequences or the whole individual work.

6 Works Cited

6.1 Primary Verbal and Graphic Works

Abouet, Marguerite, and Clément Oubrerie (2005–2010). *Aya de Yopougon*. 6 vols. Paris: Gallimard Bayou.
Auster, Paul, Paul Karasik, and David Mazzucchelli (2004). *City of Glass*. New York: Picador.
Axe, David (2006). *War Fix*. New York: NBM.
Balbi, Amedeo, and Rossano Piccioni (2013). *Cosmicomic. Gli uomini che scoprirono il big bang*. Torino: Codice.
Barry, Lynda (2002). *One Hundred Demons*. Seattle, WA: Sasquatch Books.
Baru, Jean-Marc Thévenet, and Daniel Ledran (2010). *Le chemin de l'Amérique*. 1990. Brussels: Casterman.
Baum, Frank L. (1991). *The Wonderful Wizard of Oz*. 1900. Belmont, CA: Wadsworth.
B[eauchard]., David (2005). *Epileptic [Ascension du haut-mal]*. New York: Pantheon Books.
B[eauchard]., David (2010). *Journal d'Italie, Vol. 1: Trieste-Bologne*. Paris: Delcourt.
Bechdel, Alison (2006). *Fun Home*. Boston: Houghton Mifflin.
Burford, Brandon (2009). *Syncopated*. New York: Villard.
Burns, Charles (2005). *Black Hole*. New York: Pantheon Books.
Burns, Charles (2010). *X'ed Out*. New York: Pantheon Books.
Burns, Charles (2012). *The Hive*. New York: Pantheon Books.
Burns, Charles (2014). *Sugar Skull*. New York: Pantheon Books.
Carey, Mike, and Peter Gross (2010). *The Unwritten*. New York: DC Comics.
Carroll, Lewis (2012). *Alice's Adventures in Wonderland and Through the Looking Glass*. 1865 and 1872. London/New York: Penguin.
Cartier, Eric (1990). *Flip in Paradise*. Paris: Rackham.
Clowes, Daniel (2000). *Ghost World*. 1993–1997. London: Jonathan Cape.
Cortázar, Julio (1963). *Rayuela*. Buenos Aires: Editorial Sudamericana.
Crumb, Robert (1972). "The Confessions of R. Crumb." *The People's Comics*. San Francisco, CA: Golden Gate Publishing Company.
Davodeau, Etienne (2005). *Les mauvaises gens*. Paris: Delcourt.
Davodeau, Etienne (2011). *Les ignorants*. Paris: Futuropolis.
Delisle, Guy (2000). *Shenzhen*. Paris: L'Association.
Delisle, Guy (2003). *Pyongyang*. Paris: L'Association.
Delisle, Guy (2007). *Chroniques birmanes*. Paris: Delcourt Shampooing.
Delisle, Guy (2011). *Chroniques de Jérusalem*. Paris: Delcourt Shampooing.
Dinter, Tim, Jens Harder, Ulli Lust, Kathi Käppel, Mawil, and Kai Pfeffer (2001): *Altagsspionage: Comicreportagen aus Berlin*. Berlin: Monogatari.
Dinter, Tim, Jens Harder, Ulli Lust, Kathi Käppel, Mawil, and Kai Pfeffer (2004): *Operation Läckerli: Comicreportagen aus Basel*. Zürich: Edition Moderne.
Doucet, Julie (1996). *Ciboire de Criss!* Paris: L'Association.
Doxiadis, Apostolos and Christos H. Papadimitriou (2009). *Logicomix*. New York: Bloomsbury.
Drechsler, Debbie (2008). *Daddy's Girl*. 1996. Seattle: Fantagraphics.

Dupont, J. M., and Mezzo (2014). *Love in Vain. Robert Johnson. 1911–1938*. Grenoble: Éditions Glénat.
Dupuy [Philippe] and [Charles] Berberian (1994). *Journal d'un album*. Paris: L'Association.
Eisner, Will (2006). *A Contract with God*. 1978. New York: Norton.
Flaubert, Gustave (1973). *Madame Bovary*. 1857. Paris: Gallimard.
Forest, Jean Claude, and Jacques Tardi (2006). *Ici Même*. 1978/9. Brussels: Casterman.
Fowles, John (1969). *The French Lieutenant's Woman*. London: Jonathan Cape.
Gaiman, Neil (1988–1996). *The Sandman*. New York: Vertigo.
Gaiman, Neil, and P. Craig Russell (2008). *Coraline*. London: Bloomsbury.
Gloeckner, Phoebe (2000). *A Child's Life and Other Stories*. Berkeley: Frog.
Goodwin, Michael (2012). *Economix. How and Why Our Economy Works (and Doesn't Work) in Words and Pictures*. New York: Abrams.
Green, Justin (2009). *Binky Brown Meets the Holy Virgin Mary*. 1972. San Francisco, CA: Mc Sweeney's.
Gross, Milt (2005). *He Done Her Wrong. The Great American Novel*. 1930. Seattle: Fantagraphics.
Guibert, Emmanuel, Didier Lefèvre, and Frédéric Lemercier (2003). *Le photographe. Première partie*. Paris: Dupuis.
Holm, Jennifer L., and Matthew Holm (2005). *Babymouse: Queen of the World*. New York: Random House.
Hun, Jung Sik (2007–2013). *Couleur de peau miel*. Toulon: Editions Soleil.
Jason (2013). *The Left Bank Gang*. 2005. Seattle, WA: Fantagraphics.
Jensen, Thor K. (2007). *Red Eye, Black Eye*. Cupertino, CA: Alternative Comics.
Johnson, B.S. (1969). *The Unfortunates*. London: Panther Books.
Kibuishi, Kazu (2008–). *Amulet*. 7 Vols. New York: Scholastic.
Kleist, Reinhard (2012). *Der Boxer. Die wahre Geschichte des Hertzko Haft*. Hamburg: Carlsen.
Kleist, Reinhard (2012). *Havanna. Eine kubanische Reise*. Hamburg: Carlsen.
Kuper, Peter (1997). *The System*. New York: DC Comics.
Larcenet, Manu (2003–2008). *Le combat ordinaire*. 4 vols. Paris: Dargaud.
Larcenet, Manu (2014). *Blast 1*. 2009. Paris: Dargaud.
Lax, Christian, and Frank Giroud (1990/1, 2000). *Les oubliés d'Annam*. 3 vols. Paris: Dupuis.
Lust, Ulli (2009). *Heute ist der letzte Tag vom Rest deines Lebens*. Berlin: Avant Verlag.
Lutes, Jason (2011). *Berlin. City of Stones*. 2001. Montreal: Drawn and Quaterly.
Masereel, Frans (1961). *Die Stadt*. 1925. Berlin: Rütten & Loening.
Mathieu, Marc-Antoine (2004). *Julius Corentin Acquefacques, prisonnier des rêves. La 2, 333e dimension*. Paris: Delcourt.
Mathieu, Marc-Antoine (2013). *Julius Corentin Acquefacques, prisonnier des rêves. Le décalage*. Paris: Delcourt.
Mazzucchelli, David (2009). *Asterios Polyp*. New York: Pantheon Books.
McCay, Winsor (2014). *The Complete Little Nemo*. 2 vols. 1905–1911. Los Angeles: Taschen America.
McGuire, Richard (2014). *Here*. New York: Pantheon.
Menu, Jean-Christophe (2000). *Livret de phamille*. Paris: L'Association.
Meter, Peer, and Barbara Yelin (2010). *Gift*. Berlin: Reprodukt.
Miller, Frank (2002). *The Dark Knight Returns*. 1986. New York: DC Comics.
Miller, Frank (2011). *Holy Terror*. Burbank, CA: Legendary Comics.
Moore, Alan, and Kevin O'Neill (2000). *The League of Extraordinary Gentlemen. Vol.1*. New York: DC Comics.

Moore, Alan, and Kevin O'Neill (2007). *The League of Extraordinary Gentlemen: Black Dossier*. La Jolla, CA: WildStorm Productions.
Moore, Alan, Stephen Bissette, and John Totleben (2009). *Saga of the Swamp Thing. Vol. 1*. 1983–1984. New York: DC Comics (Vertigo).
Moore, Alan, and Dave Gibbons (2008). *Watchmen*. 1986–1987. New York: DC Comics.
Moore, Alan, and David Lloyd (2005). *V for Vendetta*. 1988–1989. New York: DC Comics.
Moore, Alan, and Eddie Campbell (2006). *From Hell*. 1989–1996 and 1999 (first collected edition). Marietta, GA: Top Shelf Productions.
Morrison, Grant, and Dave McKean (2004). *Arkham Asylum: A Serious House on Serious Earth*. 1989. New York: DC Comics.
Neaud, Fabrice (1996–2002). *Journal*. Angoulême: ego comme x.
Neufeld, Josh (2004). *A Few Perfect Hours*. Cupertino, CA: Alternative Comics.
Neyestani, Mana (2012). *Une métamorphose iranienne*. Paris: Éditions Ça et Là.
Peeters, Frederik (2013). *Pillules bleues*. 2001. Geneva: Atrabile.
Pekar, Harvey (1976–2008). *American Splendor*. Milwaukee, New York: Harvey Pekar, Dark Horse Comics, and Vertigo.
Prudhomme, David (2009). *Rébétiko*. Paris: Futuropolis.
Rabagliati, Michel (1999–2011). *Paul*. Montreal: La Pastèque.
Sacco, Joe (2000/2001). *Safe Area Goražde*. Seattle, WA: Fantagraphics Books.
Sacco, Joe (2003). *Palestine*. 1993–2001. London: Jonathan Cape.
Satrapi, Marjane (2000–2003). *Persepolis*. 4 vols. Paris: L'Association.
Schuiten, François, and Benoît Peeters (1983–2009). *Les cités obscures*. 12 vols. Brussels: Casterman.
Sfar, Joann (2002). *Le chat du rabbin 2. Le malka des lions*. Paris: Dargaud.
Sfar, Joann (2003). *Le chat du rabbin 3. L'exode*. Paris: Dargaud.
Simmonds, Posy (1999). *Gemma Bovery*. London: Jonathan Cape.
Small, David (2010). *Stitches: A Memoir*. 2009. New York: Norton.
Spiegelman, Art (2003). *The Complete Maus*. 1986/92. London: Penguin.
Spiegelman, Art (2004). *In the Shadow of No Towers*. New York: Pantheon.
Stassen, Jean-Phillippe (2000). *Déogratias*. Paris: Dupuis.
Talbot, Mary, and Bryan Talbot (2012). *Dotter of Her Father's Eyes*. Milwaukie: Dark Horse Books.
Talbot, Bryan (2007). *Alice in Sunderland*. London: Jonathan Cape.
Tanaka, Véronique [a.k.a. Bryan Talbot] (2008). *Metronome*. New York: NBM.
Tan, Shaun (2006). *The Arrival*. Melbourne: Arthur A. Levine Books.
Tardi, Jacques (1976–2007). *Les aventures extraordinaires d'Adèle Blanc-Sec*. 9 vols. Brussels: Casterman.
Tardi, Jacques (1993). *C'était la guerre des tranchées*. Brussels: Castermann.
Tardi, Jacques (2012/14). *Moi René Tardi, prisonnier de guerre au Stalag II B*. 2 vols. Brussels: Castermann.
Thompson, Craig (2003). *Blankets*. Marietta, GA: Top Shelf Productions.
Thompson, Craig (2006). *Carnet de Voyage*. Marietta, GA: Top Shelf Productions.
Thompson, Craig (2011). *Habibi*. London: Faber & Faber.
Trondheim, Lewis (2012). *Approximativement*. 1998. Bègles, France: Editions Cornelius.
Vance, James, and Dan E. Burr (2013). *On the Ropes*. New York: Norton.
Ward, Lynd (2010). *God's Man, Madman's Drum, Wild Pilgrimage*. 1929/30/32. New York: Library of America.
Ware, Chris (2000). *Jimmy Corrigan: The Smartest Kid on Earth*. New York: Pantheon Books.

Ware, Chris (2012). *Building Stories*. London: Jonathan Cape.
Weyhe, Birgit (2013). *Im Himmel ist Jahrmarkt*. Berlin: avant-verlag.
Yang, Gene Luen (2006). *American Born Chinese*. New York: Square Fish.

6.2 Secondary Works

Abell, Catharine (2012). "Comics and Genre." *The Art of Comics: A Philosophical Approach*. Ed. Aaron Meskin and Roy T. Cook. Malden, MA: Wiley-Blackwell. 68–84. Print.
Aristoteles (1982). *Poetik. Griechisch/Deutsch*. Stuttgart: Reclam. Print.
Arnold, Heinz L., ed. (2009). *Comics, Mangas, Graphic Novels*. München: Edition Text + Kritik. Print.
Baetens, Jan, ed. (2001). *The Graphic Novel*. Louvain: Leuven University Press. Print.
Baetens, Jan (2011). "Abstraction in Comics." *SubStance* 40.1: 94–113. Print.
Baetens, Jan, and Hugo Frey (2015). *The Graphic Novel: An Introduction*. Cambridge: Cambridge University Press. Kindle file.
Balzer, Jens (2007). "Hemd voller Hieroglyphen. Zur Revision der Bild-Text-Beziehungen im frühen Comic." *Bildtext – Textbild: Probleme der Rede über Text-Bild-Hybride*. Ed. Dirck Linck and Stefanie Rentsch. Freiburg i. Br.: Rombach. 117–54. Print.
Barthes, Roland (1970). *S/Z*. Paris: Seuil. Print.
Bärtschi, Willy A. (1976). *Perspektive. Geschichte, Konstruktionsanleitung und Erscheinungsformen in Umwelt und bildender Kunst*. Ravensburg: Maier. Print.
Baumgärtner, Alfred Clemens (1965). *Die Welt der Comics*. Bochum: Kamp. Print.
Bazin, André (1985). *Qu'est-ce que le cinéma?* Paris: Éditions du Cerf. Print.
Beaty, Bart (2007). *Unpopular Culture: Transforming the European Comic Book in the 1990s*. Toronto: University of Toronto Press. Print.
Beaty, Bart (2009). "Autobiography as Authenticity." *A Comics Studies Reader*. Ed. Jeet Heer and Kent Worcester. Jackson: University Press of Mississippi. 226–35. Print.
Becker, Thomas (2009). "Genealogie der autobiografischen Graphic Novel. Zur feldsoziologischen Analyse intermedialer Strategien gegen ästhetische Normierungen." *Comics. Zur Geschichte und Theorie eines populärkulturellen Mediums*. Ed. Stephan Ditschke, Katerina Kroucheva, and Daniel Stein. Bielefeld: Transcript. 239–64. Print.
Beebee, Thomas (1994). *Ideology of Genre: A Comparative Study of Generic Instability*. University Park: Pennsylvania State University Press. Print.
Bergson, Henri (1965). *Matière et mémoire*. 1896. Paris: Presses Universitaires Françaises. Print.
Bergson, Henri (1984). "L'évolution créatrice." 1907. *Œuvres*. Paris: Presses Universitaires Françaises. Print.
Blödorn, Andreas, Daniela Langer, and Michael Scheffel, eds. (2006). *Stimme(n) im Text: Narratologische Positionsbestimmungen*. Berlin, New York: De Gruyter. Print.
Bluhm, Lothar, Markus Schiefer, Hans-Peter Wagner, and Christoph Zuschlag, eds. (2013). *Untergangsszenarien: Apokalyptische Denkbilder in Literatur, Kunst und Wissenschaft*. Berlin: Akademie Verlag. Print.
Bredehoft, Thomas A. (2006). "Time: Chris Ware's *Jimmy Corrigan: The Smartest Kid on Earth*." *Modern Fiction Studies [MFS]* 52.4: 869–90. Print.

Breithaupt, Fritz (2002). "Das Indiz: Lessing und Goethes Laokoon-Texte und die Narrativität der Bilder." *Ästhetik des Comic*. Ed. Michael Hein, Michael Hüners, and Torsten Michaelsen. Berlin: Erich Schmidt Verlag. 37–50. Print.
Brooker, Will (2000). *Batman Unmasked: Analyzing a Cultural Icon*. London: Continuum. Print.
Burgdorf, Paul (1976). *Comics im Unterricht*. Weinheim: Beltz. Print.
Chandler, Daniel. *An Introduction to Genre Theory*. Web. 1 July 2012. http://www.aber.ac.uk/media/Documents/intgenre/intgenre.html.
Chaney, Michael A., ed. (2011). *Graphic Subjects: Critical Essays on Autobiography and Graphic Novels*. Madison: University of Wisconsin Press. Print.
Chatman, Seymour (1990). *Coming to Terms: The Rhetoric of Narrative in Fiction and Film*. Ithaca: Cornell University Press. Print.
Chute, Hillary L. (2010). *Graphic Women: Life Narrative and Contemporary Comics*. New York: Columbia University Press. Print.
Chute, Hillary, and Marianne DeKoven (2006). "Introduction: Graphic Narrative." *Modern Fiction Studies, MFS* 52.4: 767–78. Print.
Cohen, Ralph (1986). "History and Genre." *New Literary History* 17: 203–18. Print.
Cohn, Jesse (2009). "Mise-en-Page: A Vocabulary for Page Layouts." *Teaching the Graphic Novel*. Ed. Stephen E. Tabachnick. New York: The Modern Language Association of America. 44–57. Print.
Cohn, Neil (2010). "The Limits of Time and Transitions: Challenges to Theories of Sequential Image Comprehension." *Studies in Comics* 1.1: 127–47. Print.
Cohn, Neil (2013). *The Visual Language of Comics: Introduction to the Structure and Cognition of Sequential Images*. New York: Continuum. Kindle file.
Cohn, Neil (2014). "Building a Better 'Comic Theory': Shortcomings of Theoretical Research on Comics and How to Overcome Them." *Studies in Comics* 5.1: 57–75. Print.
Coogan, Peter (2012). "Reconstructing the Superhero in All-Star Superman." *Critical Approaches to Comics: Theories and Methods*. Ed. Matthew J. Smith and Randy Duncan. New York: Routledge. 203–20. Print.
Cook, Roy T. (2012). "Why Comics Are Not Films: Metacomics and Medium-Specific Conventions." *The Art of Comics: A Philosophical Approach*. Ed. Aaron Meskin and Roy T. Cook. Malden, MA: Wiley-Blackwell. 165–87. Print.
Crutcher, Paul A. (2011). "Complexity in the Comic and Graphic Novel Medium: Inquiry through Bestselling Batman Stories." *The Journal of Popular Culture* 44.1: 53–72. Print.
Currie, Gregory (1995). *Image and Mind: Film, Philosophy and Cognitive Science*. Cambridge [England], New York, NY: Cambridge University Press. Print.
Daniels, Les (1971). *Comix: A History of Comic Books in America*. New York: Mad Peck Studios. Print.
Davidson, Sol (2008). "Educational Comics: A Family Tree." *ImageTexT: Interdisciplinary Comics Studies* 4.2: 33 pars. Department of English, University of Florida. Web. 25 November 2014. http://www.english.ufl.edu/imagetext/archives/v4_2/davidson/.
Dean, Michael (2005). "The Pull of the Graphic Novel: Seven New Publishers on Why It's Going to Succeed This Time." *Comics Journal* 268: 18–22. Print.
Deleuze, Gilles (1983). *L'image-mouvement. Cinéma 1*. Paris: Minuit. Print.
Deleuze, Gilles (1985). *L'image-temps. Cinéma 2*. Paris: Minuit. Print.
Deleuze, Gilles (2009). *The Movement-Image*. Minneapolis: University of Minnesota Press. Print.
Devitt, Amy J. (2000). "Integrating Rhetorical and Literary Theories of Genre." *College English* 62.6: 696–718. Print.
Dirscherl, Klaus, ed. (1993). *Bild und Text im Dialog*. Passau: Wissenschaftsverlag Rothe. Print.

Ditschke, Stephan, Katerina Kroucheva, and Daniel Stein, eds. (2009). *Comics. Zur Geschichte und Theorie eines populärkulturellen Mediums*. Bielefeld: Transcript. Print.
Dittmar, Jakob F. (2008). *Comic-Analyse*. Konstanz: UVK-Verl.-Gesellschaft. Print.
Dittmar, Jakob F. (2012). "Die Vermittlung von Zusammenhängen von Handlungsfolgen mit Hilfe beweglicher Elemente." *Wissen durch Bilder: Sachcomics als Medien von Bildung und Information*. Ed. Urs Hangartner, Felix Keller, and Dorothea Oechslin. Bielefeld: Transcript. 301–16. Print.
Domsch, Sebastian (2012). "Monsters against Empire: The Politics and Poetics of Neo-Victorian Metafiction in The League of Extraordinary Gentlemen." *Neo-Victorian Gothic: Horror, Violence and Degeneration in the Re-Imagined Nineteenth Century*. Ed. Marie-Luise Kohlke und Christian Gutleben. Amsterdam: Rodopi. 97–122. Print.
Dröscher, Daniela (2007). "Punkt Punkt Komma Strich: Strategien der Visualisierung in Yoko Tawadas 'Bilderrätsel ohne Bilder.'" *Visualisierungen. Textualität–Deixis–Lektüre*. Trier: Wissenschaftlicher Verlag Trier. 215–234. Print.
Duncan, Randy (2012). "Image Functions: Shape and Color as Hermeneutic Images in Asterios Polyp." *Critical Approaches to Comics: Theories and Methods*. Ed. Matthew J. Smith and Randy Duncan. New York: Routledge. 43–54. Print.
Duncan, Randy, and Matthew J. Smith (2009). *The Power of Comics: History, Form and Culture*. New York: Continuum. Print.
Eco, Umberto (1976). *A Theory of Semiotics*. 1975. London: Macmillan. Print.
Eisner, Will (1985/2008). *Comics and Sequential Art: Principles and Practices from the Legendary Cartoonist*. 1985. New York: W.W. Norton. Print.
Eubanks, Adelheid R. (2011). "Logicomix: From Text to Image/From Logic to Story." *The Comparatist: Journal of the Southern Comparative Literature Association* 35: 182–97. Print.
Föckersperger, Wilhelm (1993). "Das Bild als Text." *Bild und Text im Dialog*. Ed. Klaus Dirscherl. Passau: Wissenschaftsverlag Rothe. 317–19. Print.
Fieguth, Rolf (1973). "Zur Rezeptionslenkung bei narrativen und dramatischen Werken." *Sprache im technischen Zeitalter* 47: 186–201. Print.
Fishelov, David (1993). *Metaphors of Genre: The Role of Analogies in Genre Theory*. University Park: Pennsylvania State University Press. Print.
Flood, J., S.B. Heath, and D. Lapp, eds. (2005). *Handbook of Research on Teaching Literacy through the Communicative and Visual Arts*. Mahwah, NJ: Lawrence Erlbaum. Print.
Fowler, Alastair (1982). *Kinds of Literature: An Introduction to the Theory of Genres and Modes*. Oxford: Clarendon Press. Print.
Frahm, Ole (2014). "Die Fiktion des graphischen Romans." *Bild ist Text ist Bild: Narration und Ästhetik in der Graphic Novel*. Ed. Susanne Hochreiter and Ursula Klingenböck. Bielefeld: Transcript. 53–77. Print.
Freedman, Ariela (2009). "Drawing on Modernism in Alison Bechdel's Fun Home." *Journal of Modern Literature, JML* 32.4: 125–40. Print.
Freedman, Ariela (2011). "Comics, Graphic Novels, Graphic Narrative: A Review." *Literature Compass* 8.1: 28–46. Print.
Fresnault-Deruelle, Pierre (1976). "Du linéaire au tabulaire." *Communications* 24: 17–23. Print.
Fricke, Harald (2010). "Definitionen und Begriffsformen." *Handbuch Gattungstheorie*. Ed. Rüdiger Zymner. Stuttgart: Metzler. 7–10. Print.
Fuchs, Burkhard (2006). "Narratives Bildverstehen. Plädoyer für die erzählende Dimension der Fotografie." *Bildinterpretation und Bildverstehen: Methodische Ansätze aus sozialwis-

senschaftlicher, kunst- und medienpädagogischer Perspektive. Ed. Winfried Marotzki and Horst Niesyto. Wiesbaden: VS Verlag für Sozialwissenschaften. 207–25. Print.

Gabilliet, Jean-Paul (2010). *Of Comics and Men: A Cultural History of American Comic Books*. Jackson: University Press of Mississippi. Print.

Gardner, Jared (2008). "Autography's Biography, 1972–2007." *Biography: An Interdisciplinary Quarterly* 31.1: 1–26. Print.

Gaudreault, André (1988). *Du littéraire au filmique: Système du récit*. Paris: Méridiens Klincksieck. Print.

Genette, Gérard (1972). *Figures III*. Paris: Seuil. Print.

Genette, Gérard (1979). *Introduction à l'architexte*. Paris: Seuil. Print.

Genette, Gérard (1983). *Nouveau discours du récit*. Paris: Seuil. Print.

Genette, Gérard (1987). *Seuils*. Paris: Seuil. Print.

Genette, Gérard (2004). *Fiction et diction: Précédé de Introduction à l'architexte*. Paris: Seuil. Print.

Genette, Gérard (2004a). *Métalepse*. Paris: Seuil. Print.

Gordon, Ian (2010). "Making Comics Respectable: How Maus Helped Redefine a Medium." *The Rise of the American Comics Artist: Creators and Contexts*. Ed. Paul Williams. Jackson: University Press of Mississippi. 179–93. Print.

Grünewald, Dietrich (2014). "Comics als eigenständige Kunstform und die Notwendigkeit den sachgemäßen Umgang mit ihr zu zu erlernen." *Bild und Bildung: Praxis, Reflexion, Wissen im Kontext von Kunst und Medien*. Ed. Barbara Lutz-Sterzenbach, Maria Peters, and Frank Schulz. München: kopaed. Print.

Groensteen, Thierry (1999). *Système de la bande dessinée*, Paris: Presses Universitaires de France. Print.

Groensteen, Thierry (2007). *The System of Comics*. Jackson: University Press of Mississippi. Print.

Groensteen, Thierry (2011). *Bandes dessinées et narration*. Paris: Presses Universitaires de France. Print.

Groensteen, Thierry (2013). *Comics and Narration*. Jackson: University Press of Mississippi. Kindle file.

Gymnich, Marion, Birgit Neumann, and Ansgar Nünning, eds. (2007). *Gattungstheorie und Gattungsgeschichte*. Trier: WVT, Wissenschaftlicher Verlag Trier. Print.

Hangartner, Urs, Felix Keller, and Dorothea Oechslin, eds. (2013). *Wissen durch Bilder: Sachcomics als Medien von Bildung und Information*. Bielefeld: Transcript. Print.

Hangartner, Urs (2013). "'Sequential Art to Teach Something Specific': Sachcomics – Definitorisches, Historisches, Aktuelles." *Wissen durch Bilder: Sachcomics als Medien von Bildung und Information*. Ed. Urs Hangartner, Felix Keller, and Dorothea Oechslin. Bielefeld: Transcript. 13–41. Print.

Harvey, Robert C. (1994) *The Art of the Funnies: An Aesthetic History*. Jackson: University Press of Mississippi. Print.

Harvey, Robert C. (1996). *The Art of the Comic Book: An Aesthetic History*. Jackson: University Press of Mississippi. Print.

Hatfield, Charles (2005). *Alternative Comics: An Emerging Literature*. Jackson: University Press of Mississippi. Print.

Heath, S.B., and V. Bhagat (2005). "Reading Comics, the Invisible Art." *Handbook of Research on Teaching Literacy through the Communicative and Visual Arts*. Ed. J. Flood, S. B. Heath, and D. Lapp. Mahwah, NJ: Lawrence Erlbaum. Print.

Heer, Jeet, and Kent Worcester, eds. (2009). *A Comics Studies Reader*. Jackson: University Press of Mississippi. Print.
Heider, Eleanor R. [= Rosch] (1971). "Focal Color Areas and the Development of Color Names." *Developmental Psychology* 4: 447–455. Print.
Heider, Eleanor R. [= Rosch] (1972). "Universals in Color Naming and Memory." *Journal of Experimental Psychology* 93: 10–20. Print.
Hein, Michael, Michael Hüners, and Torsten Michaelsen, eds. (2002). *Ästhetik des Comic*. Berlin: Erich Schmidt Verlag. Print.
Hempfer, Klaus W. (1973). *Gattungstheorie: Information und Synthese*. München: W. Fink. Print.
Hempfer, Klaus W. (2010). "Zum begrifflichen Status der Gattungsbegriffe: von 'Klassen' zu 'Familienähnlichkeiten' und 'Prototypen'." *Zeitschrift für Französische Sprache und Literatur (ZFSL)* 120.1: 14–32. Print.
Hempfer, Klaus W. and Jörg Volbers, eds. (2011). *Theorien des Performativen: Sprache– Wissen– Praxis. Eine kritische Bestandsaufnahme*. Bielefeld: Transcript. Print.
Herman, David (2009). "Beyond Voice and Vision: Cognitive Grammar and Focalization Theory." *Point of View, Perspective, and Focalization: Modeling Mediation in Narrative*. Ed. Peter Hühn, Wolf Schmid, and Jörg Schönert: De Gruyter. 119–42. Print.
Herman, David (2011). "Narrative Worldmaking in Graphic Life Writing." *Graphic Subjects: Critical Essays on Autobiography and Graphic Novels*. Ed. Michael A. Chaney. Madison: University of Wisconsin Press. 231–43. Print.
Hescher, Achim (1996). *Vom 'postmodernen Roman' zur postmodernen Lesart*. Essen: Die Blaue Eule. Print.
Hescher, Achim (2012). "Analyzing Graphic Novels in Terms of Complexity: A Typology." *Zeitschrift für Anglistik und Amerikanistik [ZAA]* 60.4: 335–60. Print.
Hescher, Achim (2013). "Schrecken ohne Ende: Apokalypse(n) in englischsprachiger Narrativik und der Graphic Novel Watchmen." *Untergangsszenarien: Apokalyptische Denkbilder in Literatur, Kunst und Wissenschaft*. Ed. Lothar Bluhm, et al. Berlin: Akademie Verlag. 167–94. Print.
Hescher, Achim, Anja Müller, and Anke Uebel, eds. (2014). *Representing Restoration, Enlightenment and Romanticism: Studies in New-Eighteenth-Century Literature and Film in Honour of Hans-Peter Wagner*. Trier: Wissenschaftlicher Verlag Trier. Print.
Hescher, Achim (2014a). "Classical Categories, Prototypes, and the Graphic Novel." *International Journal of Comic Art* 16.1: 384–402. Print.
Hescher, Achim (2014b). "Transgressing Borders in and with Comics: Mana Neyestani's Graphic Novel Une métamorphose iranienne (2012)." *PhiN [Philologie im Netz]* 70: 54–73. Web. http://web.fu-berlin.de/phin/phin70/p70t4.htm.
Hescher, Achim (2014c). "Metalepses, Mises en Abyme and Performativity in Bryan Talbot's Alice in Sunderland." *Representing Restoration, Enlightenment and Romanticism: Studies in New-Eighteenth-Century Literature and Film in Honour of Hans-Peter Wagner*. Ed. Achim Hescher, Anja Müller, and Anke Uebel. Trier: Wissenschaftlicher Verlag Trier. 229–50. Print.
Hühn, Peter, Wolf Schmid, and Jörg Schönert, eds. (2009). *Point of View, Perspective, and Focalization: Modeling Mediation in Narrative*. Berlin/New York: De Gruyter. Print.
Hillenbach, Anne (2013). "Authentisierungsstrategien in historischen Comics." *Wissen durch Bilder: Sachcomics als Medien von Bildung und Information*. Ed. Urs Hangartner, Felix Keller, and Dorothea Oechslin. Bielefeld: Transcript. 131–47. Print.
Hochreiter, Susanne, and Ursula Klingenböck, eds. (2014). *Bild ist Text ist Bild: Narration und Ästhetik in der Graphic Novel*. Bielefeld: Transcript.

Holbo, John (2012). "Redefining Comics." *The Art of Comics: A Philosophical Approach*. Ed. Aaron Meskin and Roy T. Cook. Malden, MA: Wiley-Blackwell. 3–30. Print.

Hoppler, Stephanie, Lukas Etter, and Gabriele Rippl (2009). "Intermedialität in Comics. Neil Gaimans The Sandman." *Comics. Zur Geschichte und Theorie eines populärkulturellen Mediums*. Ed. Stephan Ditschke, Katerina Kroucheva, and Daniel Stein. Bielefeld: Transcript. 53–79. Print.

Horstkotte, Silke, and Nancy Pedri (2011). "Focalization in Graphic Narrative." *Narrative* 19.3: 330–57. Print.

Häsner, Bernd, Henning Hufnagel, Irmgard Maasen, and Anita Traininger (2011). "Text und Performativität." *Theorien des Performativen: Sprache– Wissen– Praxis. Eine kritische Bestandsaufnahme*. Ed. Klaus W. Hempfer. Bielefeld: Transcript. 69–96. Print.

Hucheon, Linda (1988). *A Poetics of Postmodernism. History, Theory, Fiction*. London/New York: Routledge. Print.

Iadonisi, Richard, ed. (2012). *Graphic History: Essays on Graphic Novels and/as History*. Newcastle upon Tyne: Cambridge Scholars Publishing. Print.

Jahn, Manfred (1996). "Windows of Focalization: Deconstructing and Reconstructing a Narratological Concept." *Style* 30.3: 241–67. Print.

James, Henry (1957). *The Art of the Novel: Critical Prefaces*. 1884. Ed. R.P. Blackmur. New York: Scribner. Print.

Jannidis, Fotis (2006). "Wer sagt das? Erzählen mit Stimmverlust." *Stimme(n) im Text: Narratologische Positionsbestimmungen*. Ed. Andreas Blödorn, Daniela Langer, and Michael Scheffel. Berlin, New York: De Gruyter. 151–64. Print.

Thon, Jan-Noël (2014). "Subjectivity across Media: On Transmedial Strategies of Subjective Representation in Contemporary Feature Films, Graphic Novels, and Computer Games." *Storyworlds Across Media: Toward a Media-Conscious Narratology*. Ed. Marie-Laure Ryan and Jan-Noël Thon. Lincoln: University of Nebraska Press. Ch.3, np. Kindle file.

Jesch, Tatjana, and Malte Stein (2009). "Perspectivization and Focalization: Two Concepts– One Meaning? An Attempt at Conceptual Differentiation." *Point of View, Perspective, and Focalization: Modeling Mediation in Narrative*. Ed. Peter Hühn, Wolf Schmid, and Jörg Schönert. Berlin/New York: De Gruyter. 59–77. Print.

Jewitt, Carrey, and Rumiko Oyama (2006). "Visual Meaning: A Social Semiotic Approach." *Handbook of Visual Analysis*. Ed. Theo van Leeuwen and Carrey Jewitt. London: Sage. 134–56. Print.

John, Eileen, and Dominic McIver, eds. (2004) *Philosophy of Literature: Contemporary and Classic Readings*. Malden, MA: Blackwell. Print.

Jost, François (1987). *L'oeil-caméra: Entre film et roman*. Lyon: Presses universitaires de Lyon. Print.

Jost, François (2004). "The Look: From Film to Novel: An Essay in Comparative Narratology." *A Companion to Literature and Film*. Ed. Alessandra Raengo and Robert Stam. Malden, MA: Blackwell. 71–80. Print.

Kablitz, Andreas (2008). "Literatur, Fiktion und Erzählung– nebst einem Nachruf auf den Erzähler." *Im Zeichen der Fiktion: Aspekte fiktionaler Rede aus historischer und systematischer Sicht*. Ed. Ulrike Schneider and Irina O. Rajewsky. Stuttgart: Steiner. 13–44. Print.

Kannenberg, Gene (2001). "The Comics of Chris Ware: Text, Image, and Visual Narrative Strategies." *The Language of Comics: Word and Image*. Ed. Robin Varnum and Christina T. Gibbons. Jackson: University Press of Mississippi. 174–97. Kindle file.

Klauk, Tobias, and Tilmann Köppe (2013). "Telling vs. Showing" (rev. 2014). *The Living Handbook of Narratology*. The Interdisciplinary Center for Narratology, University of Hamburg. Web. 13 March 2015. http://www.lhn.uni-hamburg.de/article/telling-vs-showing

Kuhlmann, Martha B., and David M. Ball (2010). "Introduction: Chris Ware and the 'Cult of Difficulty.'" *The Comics of Chris Ware. Drawing Is a Way of Thinking*. Ed. Martha B. Kuhlmann and David M. Ball. Jackson: University Press of Mississippi. Print.

Kuhn, Markus (2009). "Film Narratology: Who Tells? Who Shows? Who Focalizes? Narrative Mediation in Self-Reflexive Fiction Films." *Point of View, Perspective, and Focalization: Modeling Mediation in Narrative*. Ed. Peter Hühn, Wolf Schmid, and Jörg Schönert. Berlin/ New York: de Gruyter. 259–278. Print.

Kukkonen, Karin (2011). "Comics as a Test Case for Transmedial Narratology." *SubStance* 40.1: 34–52. Print.

Kunzle, David (1973). *The Early Comic Strip: Narrative Strips and Picture Stories in the European Broadsheet from c. 1450 to 1825*. Berkeley: University of California Press. Print.

Labov, William (1973). "The Boundaries of Words and their Meanings." *New Ways of Analyzing Variation in English*. Ed. Charles-James N. Bailey and Roger W. Shuy. Washington, DC: Georgetown University Press. 340–73. Print.

Lacey, Nick (1998). *Image & Representation: Key Concepts in Media Studies*. Basingstoke, Hampshire: Macmillan. Print.

Lacey, Nick (2000). *Narrative and Genre: Key Concepts in Media Studies*. Basingstoke, Hampshire: Macmillan. Print.

Lakoff, George (1987). *Women, Fire, and Dangerous Things: What Categories Reveal about the Mind*. Chicago: University of Chicago Press. Print.

Leeuwen, Theo van, and Carrey Jewitt, eds. (2006). *Handbook of Visual Analysis*. London: Sage. Print.

Lefèvre, Pascal (2000). "Narration in Comics." 1.1: np. Web. 27 August 2014. http://www.imageandnarrative.be/inarchive/narratology/pascallefevre.htm.

Lejeune, Philippe (1975). *Le pacte autobiographique*. Paris: Seuil. Print.

Lejeune, Philippe (1989). *On Autobiography*. 1975. Minneapolis: University of Minnesota Press. Print.

Lewis, A. D. (2010). "The Shape of Comic Book Reading." *Studies in Comics* 1.1: 71–81. Print.

Linck, Dirck, and Stefanie Rentsch, eds. (2007). *Bildtext – Textbild: Probleme der Rede über Text-Bild-Hybride*. Freiburg i. Br. Rombach. Print.

Lopes, Paul D. (2009). *Demanding Respect: The Evolution of the American Comic Book*. Philadelphia: Temple University Press. Print.

Lubbock, Percy (1954). *The Craft of Fiction*. 1922. London: Jonathan Cape. Print.

Lutz-Sterzenbach, Barbara, Maria Peters, and Frank Schulz, eds. (2014). *Bild und Bildung: Praxis, Reflexion, Wissen im Kontext von Kunst und Medien*. München: kopaed. Print.

Man, Paul de (1979). "Autobiography as De-Facement." *Modern Language Notes* 94.5: 919–930. Print.

Margolin, Uri (1981). "On the Vagueness of Critical Concepts." *Poetics* 10: 15–31. Print.

Margolin, Uri (2009). "Focalization: Where Do We Go from Here?" *Point of View, Perspective, and Focalization: Modeling Mediation in Narrative*. Ed. Peter Hühn, Wolf Schmid, and Jörg Schönert. Berlin/Boston: De Gruyter. 41–57. Print.

Margolin, Uri (2013). "Narrator." 33 pars. *The Living Handbook of Narratology*. The Interdisciplinary Center for Narratology, University of Hamburg. Web. 13 March 2015. http://www.lhn.uni-hamburg.de/article/narrator.

Marion, Philippe (1993). *Traces en cases: Travail graphique, figuration narrative et participation du lecteur*. Louvain-la-Neuve: Academia. Print.
Marotzki, Winfried, and Horst Niesyto, eds. (2006). *Bildinterpretation und Bildverstehen: Methodische Ansätze aus sozialwissenschaftlicher, kunst- und medienpädagogischer Perspektive*. Wiesbaden: VS Verlag für Sozialwissenschaften. Print.
Matz, Chris (2009). "Supporting the Teaching of the Graphic Novel: The Role of the Academic Library." *Teaching the Graphic Novel*. Ed. Stephen E. Tabachnick. New York: The Modern Language Association of America. 327–32. Print.
McCloud, Scott (1994). *Understanding Comics: The Invisible Art*. 1993. New York: HarperPerennial. Reprint.
McCloud, Scott (2000). *Reinventing Comics: How Imagination and Technology Are Revolutionizing an Art Form*. New York: Perennial. Print.
McKinney, Mark, ed. (2008). *History and Politics in French Language Comics and Graphic Novels*. Jackson: University Press of Mississippi. Print.
Meister, Jan C., ed. (2005). *Narratology Beyond Literary Criticism: Mediality, Disciplinarity*. Berlin/New York: Walter de Gruyter. Print.
Merino, Ana (2009). "The Cultural Dimensions of the Hispanic World Seen through Its Graphic Novels." *Teaching the Graphic Novel*. Ed. Stephen E. Tabachnick. New York: The Modern Language Association of America. 271–80. Print.
Meskin, Aaron (2007). "Defining Comics?" *The Journal of Aesthetics and Art Criticism* 65.4: 369–79. Print.
Meskin, Aaron (2009). "Comics as Literature?" *British Journal of Aesthetics* 49.3: 219–39. Print.
Meskin, Aaron, and Roy T. Cook, eds. (2012). *The Art of Comics: A Philosophical Approach*. Malden, MA: Wiley-Blackwell. Print.
Mikkonen, Kai (2008). "Presenting Minds in Graphic Narratives." *Partial Answers: Journal of Literature and the History of Ideas* 6.2: 301–21. Print.
Mikkonen, Kai (2013). "Subjectivity and Style in Graphic Narrative." *From Comic Strips to Graphic Novels: Contributions to the Theory and History of Graphic Narrative*. Ed. Daniel Stein and Jan-Noël Thon. Berlin/Boston: De Gruyter. 101–23. Print.
Miller, Ann (2008). *Reading Bande Dessinée: Critical Approaches to French-Language Comic Strip*. Chicago: Intellect Books. Kindle file.
Miodrag, Hannah (2013). *Comics and Language: Reimagining Critical Discourse on the Form*. Jackson: University Press of Mississippi. Kindle file.
Mitchell, W.J.T. (1986). *Iconology: Image, Text, Ideology*. Chicago: University of Chicago Press. Print.
Mitchell, W.J.T. (2009). "Beyond Comparison." *A Comics Studies Reader*. Ed. Jeet Heer and Kent Worcester. Jackson: University Press of Mississippi. 116–23. Print.
Mitry, Jean (1965). *Esthétique et psychologie du cinéma*. Paris: Editions du Cerf. Print.
Moore, Alan (2003). *Writing for Comics*. Vol. I. Rantoul, IL: Avatar Press. Print.
Morgan, Harry (2003). *Principes des littératures dessinées*. Paris: L'An 2. Print.
Morin, Edgar (1986). *La méthode. Tome 3: La connaissance de la connaissance*. Paris: Seuil. Print.
Neumann, Birgit, and Ansgar Nünning (2007). "Einleitung: Probleme, Aufgaben und Perspektiven der Gattungstheorie und Gattungsgeschichte." *Gattungstheorie und Gattungsgeschichte*. Ed. Marion Gymnich, Birgit Neumann, and Ansgar Nünning. Trier: WVT, Wissenschaftlicher Verlag Trier. 1–30. Print.

Nünning, Ansgar (2007). "Kriterien der Gattungsbestimmung: Kritik und Grundzüge von Typologien narrativ-fiktionaler Gattungen am Beispiel des historischen Romans." *Gattungstheorie und Gattungsgeschichte*. Ed. Marion Gymnich, Birgit Neumann, and Ansgar Nünning. Trier: WVT, Wissenschaftlicher Verlag Trier. 73–99. Print.

Nyberg, Amy Kiste (1998). *Seal of Approval. The History of the Comics Code*. Jackson: University Press of Mississippi. Print.

Olson, Greta, ed. (2011). *Current Trends in Narratology*. Berlin/Boston: De Gruyter. Print.

O'Malley, Seamus (2012). "Speculative History, Speculative Fiction: Alan Moore and Eddie Campbell's From Hell." *Graphic History: Essays on Graphic Novels and/as History*. Ed. Richard Iadonisi. Newcastle upon Tyne: Cambridge Scholars Pub. 162–83. Print.

Packard, Stefan (2009). "Was ist ein Cartoon? Psychosemiotische Überlegungen im Anschluss and Scott McCloud." *Comics. Zur Geschichte und Theorie eines populärkulturellen Mediums*. Ed. Stephan Ditschke, Katerina Kroucheva, and Daniel Stein. Bielefeld: Transcript. 29–51. Print.

Pantaleo, Sylvia (2011). "Grade 7 Students Reading Graphic Novels: 'You Need to Do a Lot of Thinking'." *English in Education* 45.2: 113–31. Print.

Pearl, Monica B. (2008). "Graphic Language: Redrawing the Family (Romance) in Alison Bechdel's Fun Home." *Prose Studies: History, Theory, Criticism* 30.3: 286–304. Print.

Pedri, Nancy (2011). "When Photographs Aren't Quite Enough: Reflections on Photography and Cartooning in Le Photographe.." *ImageTexT: Interdisciplinary Comics Studies* 6.1: 26 pars. Department of English, University of Florida. Web. 25 November 2014. http://www.english.ufl.edu/imagetext/archives/v6_1/pedri/.

Pedri, Nancy (2013). "Graphic Memoir: Neither Fact Nor Fiction." *From Comic Strips to Graphic Novels: Contributions to the Theory and History of Graphic Narrative*. Ed. Daniel Stein and Jan-Noël Thon. Berlin: De Gruyter. 127–53. Print.

Peeters, Benoît (1991). *Case, planche, récit: Comment lire la bande dessinée*. Tournai: Casterman. Print.

Peeters, Benoît (1993). *La bande dessinée*. Paris: Flammarion. Print.

Peeters, Benoît (2007). "Four Conceptions of the Page." *ImageTexT: Interdisciplinary Comics Studies* 3.3, 66 pars. Web. 3 May 2015. http://www.english.ufl.edu/imagetext/archives/v3_3/peeters/.

Pfister, Manfred (1988). *Das Drama. Theorie und Analyse*. 1977. München: Fink. Print.

Pfister, Manfred (1993). "The Dialogue of Text and Image: Antoni Tapies and Anselm Kiefer." *Bild und Text im Dialog*. Ed. Klaus Dirscherl. Passau: Wissenschaftsverlag Rothe. 321–43. Print.

Platon (1990). *Werke. Politeia*. Vol. 4 (Ancient Greek – German). Darmstadt: Wissenschaftliche Buchgesellschaft. Print.

Platthaus, Andreas (2010). "Siegeszug unter falscher Flagge." *Frankfurter Allgemeine Zeitung*, 30 December 2010, 304: 29. Print.

Platthaus, Andreas (2015). "Zum Raum wird hier die Zeit." *Frankfurter Allgemeine Zeitung*, 17 April 2015, 89: 13. Print.

Raengo, Alessandra, and Robert Stam, eds. (2004). *A Companion to Literature and Film*. Malden, MA: Blackwell. Print.

Rajewsky, Irina O. (2002). *Intermedialität*. Tübingen: Francke. Print.

Rajewsky, Irina O. (2007). "Von Erzählern, die (nichts) vermitteln. Überlegungen zu grundlegenden Annahmen der Dramentheorie im Kontext einer Transmedialen Narratologie." *Zeitschrift für Französische Sprache und Literatur (ZfSL)* 117.1: 25–68. Print.

Rajewsky, Irina O. (2009). "Beyond 'Metanarration': Form-Based Metareference as a Transgeneric and Transmedial Phenomenon." *Metareference Across Media: Theory and Case Studies*. Ed. Werner Wolf, et al. Amsterdam: Rodopi. 135–68. Print.
Rhoades, Shirrel (2008a). *A Complete History of American Comic Books*. New York: Peter Lang. Print.
Rippl, Gabriele, and Lukas Etter (2013). "Intermediality, Transmediality, and Graphic Narrative." *From Comic Strips to Graphic Novels: Contributions to the Theory and History of Graphic Narrative*. Ed. Daniel Stein and Jan-Noël Thon. Berlin/Boston: De Gruyter. 191–217. Print.
Rosch, Eleanor, and Barbara B. Lloyd (1978). *Cognition and Categorization*. Hillsdale, NJ, New York: L. Erlbaum Associates; distributed by Halsted Press. Print.
Rosen, Elisabeth (2009). "The Narrative Intersection of Image and Text: Teaching Panel Frames in Comics." *Teaching the Graphic Novel*. Ed. Stephen E. Tabachnick. New York: The Modern Language Association of America. 58–66. Print.
Round, Julia (2010). "'Is this a book?' DC Vertigo and the Redefinition of Comics in the 1990s." *The Rise of the American Comics Artist: Creators and Contexts*. Ed. Paul Williams. Jackson: University Press of Mississippi. 14–30. Print.
Rousseau, Patrice, and Guillaume Gravé-Rousseau (2009). "Le 'roman graphique' francophone", in: *L'Ecole des lettres des collèges* 5–6: 103–110. Print.
Ryan, Marie-Laure, ed. (2004). *Narrative Across Media: The Languages of Storytelling*. Lincoln: University of Nebraska Press. Print.
Ryan, Marie-Laure (2004). "Introduction." *Narrative Across Media: The Languages of Storytelling*. Ed. Marie-Laure Ryan. Lincoln: University of Nebraska Press. 1–40. Print.
Ryan, Marie-Laure (2005). "On the Theoretical Foundation of Transmedial Narratology." *Narratology beyond Literary Criticism. Mediality, Disciplinarity*. Ed. Jan Christoph Meister. Berlin/New York: De Gruyter. 1–23. Print.
Ryan, Marie-Laure (2014). "Story/Worlds/Media: Tuning the Instruments of a Media-Conscious Narratology." *Storyworlds Across Media: Toward a Media-Conscious Narratology*. Ed. Marie-Laure Ryan and Jan-Noël Thon. Lincoln: University of Nebraska Press. ch. I.1, np. Kindle file.
Ryan, Marie-Laure, and Jan-Noël Thon, eds. (2014). *Storyworlds Across Media: Toward a Media-Conscious Narratology*. Lincoln: University of Nebraska Press. Kindle file.
Sabin, Roger (1996). *Comics, Comix & Graphic Novels*. London: Phaidon Press Ltd. Print.
Schikowski, Klaus (2009). "'Folks, I'm going to speak plain...' Robert Crumb und die Entwicklung der autobiographischen Comic-Erzählung." *Comics, Mangas, Graphic Novels*. Ed. Heinz L. Arnold. München: Edition Text + Kritik. 90–108. Print.
Schmitt, Ronald (1992). "Deconstructive Comics." *Journal of Popular Culture* 25.4: 153–161. Print.
Schnackertz, Hermann Josef (1980). *Form und Funktion medialen Erzählens. Narrativität in Bildsequenz und Comicstrip*. München: Fink. Print.
Schneider, Ulrike, and Irina O. Rajewsky, eds. (2008). *Im Zeichen der Fiktion: Aspekte fiktionaler Rede aus historischer und systematischer Sicht*. Stuttgart: Steiner. Print.
Schneider, Ulrike (2008). "Fluchtpunkte des Erzählens: Medialität und Narration in Jean-Philippe Toussaints Roman *Fuir*." *Zeitschrift für Französische Sprache und Literatur (ZFSL)* 118.2: 141–61. Print.
Schwalm, Helga (2014). "Autobiography." 28 pars. *The Living Handbook of Narratology*. Interdisciplinary Center for Narratology, University of Hamburg. 20 January 2015. Web. http://www.lhn.uni-hamburg.de/article/autobiography.

Schüwer, Martin (2008). *Wie Comics erzählen: Grundriss einer intermedialen Erzähltheorie der grafischen Literatur*. Trier: WVT Wissenschaftlicher Verlag Trier. Print.

Serles, Katharina (2014). "'Time in Comics Is Infinitely Weirder Than That'. Zooming/Folding/Building Time bei Marc-Antoine Mathieu und Chris Ware." *Bild ist Text ist Bild: Narration und Ästhetik in der Graphic Novel*. Ed. Susanne Hochreiter and Ursula Klingenböck. Bielefeld: Transcript. 79–96. Print.

Sinding, Michael (2002). "After Definitions: Genre, Categories, and Cognitive Science." *Genre: Forms of Discourse and Culture* 35.2: 118–219. Print.

Smith, Matthew J., and Randy Duncan, eds. (2012). *Critical Approaches to Comics: Theories and Methods*. New York: Routledge. Print.

Spengemann, William C. (1980) *The Forms of Autobiography: Episodes in the History of a Literary Genre*. New Haven: Yale UP. Print.

Stanzel, Franz K. (1964). *Typische Formen des Romans*. Göttingen: Vandenhoeck & Ruprecht. Print.

Stanzel, Franz K. (1995). *Theorie des Erzählens*. 1979. Göttingen: Vandenhoeck & Ruprecht. Print.

Stein, Daniel, and Jan-Noël Thon, eds. (2013). *From Comic Strips to Graphic Novels: Contributions to the Theory and History of Graphic Narrative*. Berlin/Boston: De Gruyter. Print.

Stoll, André (1974). *Asterix. Das Trivialepos Frankreichs. Bild- und Sprachästhetik eines Bestseller-Comics*. Köln: Dumont Schauberg. Print.

Swales, John M. (1990). *Genre Analysis: English in Academic and Research Settings*. Cambridge [etc.]: Cambridge University Press. Print.

Tabachnick, Stephen E., ed. (2009). *Teaching the Graphic Novel*. New York: The Modern Language Association of America. Print.

Tan, Ed (2001). "The Telling Face in Comic Strip and Graphic Novel." *The Graphic Novel*. Ed. Jan Baetens. Louvain: Leuven University Press. 31–46. Print.

Taylor, John R. (1989) *Linguistic Categorization. Prototypes in Linguistic Theory*. Oxford: Clarendon Press. Print.

Taylor, John R. (2003). *Linguistic Categorization*. 3rd ed. New York: Oxford University Press. Print.

Thomson, Philip (1972). *The Grotesque*. London: Methuen. Print.

Thon, Jan-Noël (2013). "Who's Telling the Tale? Authors and Narrators in Graphic Narrative." *From Comic Strips to Graphic Novels: Contributions to the Theory and History of Graphic Narrative*. Ed. Daniel Stein and Jan-Noël Thon. Berlin/Boston: De Gruyter. 67–99. Print.

Thoss, Jeff (2015). *When Storyworlds Collide: Metalepsis in Popular Fiction, Film and Comics*. Leiden: Brill/Rodopi. Print.

Thwaites, Tony, Lloyd Davis, and Warwick Mules (2002). *Introducing Cultural and Media Studies: A Semiotic Approach*. Houndmills, Basingstoke, Hampshire, New York, NY: Palgrave. Print.

Todorov, Tzvetan (1976). *Introduction à la littérature fantastique*. Paris: Seuil. Print.

Todorov, Tzvetan (1990). *Genres in Discourse*. Cambridge/New York: Cambridge University Press. Print.

Troutman, Phillip (2010). "The Discourse of Comics Scholarship: A Rhetorical Analysis of Research Article Introductions." *International Journal of Comics Art* 12.2/3: 432–44. Print.

Varga, Kibedi Aron (1989). *Discours, récit, image*. Liège: P. Mardaga. Print.

Varnum, Robin, and Christina T. Gibbons, eds. (2001). *The Language of Comics: Word and Image*. Jackson: University Press of Mississippi. Kindle file.

Versaci, Rocco (2007). *This Book Contains Graphic Language: Comics as Literature*. New York: Continuum. Print.

Wagner, Peter, ed. (1996) *Icons–Texts–Iconotexts. Essays on Ekphrasis and Intermediality*. Berlin/New York: de Gruyter. Print.
Walker, Mort (2000). *The Lexicon of Comicana*. 1980. Bloomington: iUniverse. Print.
Walker, Tristram (2010). "Graphic Wounds: The Comics Journalism of Joe Sacco." *Journeys: The International Journal of Travel and Travel Writing* 11.1: 69–88. Print.
Walsh, Richard (1997). "Who Is the Narrator?" *Poetics Today* 18: 495–513. Print.
Wartenberg, Thomas E. (2012). "Wordy Pictures: Theorizing the Relationship between Image and Text in Comics." *The Art of Comics: A Philosophical Approach*. Ed. Aaron Meskin and Roy T. Cook. Malden, MA: Wiley-Blackwell. 87–104. Print.
Watson, Julia (2008). "Autographic Disclosures and Genealogies of Desire in Alison Bechdel's Fun Home." *Biography: An Interdisciplinary Quarterly* 31.1: 27–58. Print.
Weiner, Stephen (2010). "How the Graphic Novel Changed American Comics." *The Rise of the American Comics Artist: Creators and Contexts*. Ed. Paul Williams. Jackson: University Press of Mississippi. 3–13. Print.
Whitlock, Gillian (2006). "Autographics: The Seeing 'I' of the Comics." *Modern Fiction Studies* 52.4: 965–79. Print.
Williams, Paul, ed. (2010). *The Rise of the American Comics Artist: Creators and Contexts*. Jackson: University Press of Mississippi. Print.
Wolf, Werner (1993). *Ästhetische Illusion und Illusionsdurchbrechung in der Erzählkunst: Theorie und Geschichte mit Schwerpunkt auf englischem illusionsstörenden Erzählen*. Tübingen: Max Niemeyer Verlag. Print.
Wolf, Werner (2002). "Das Problem der Narrativität in Literatur, bildender Kunst und Musik: ein Beitrag zu einer intermedialen Erzähltheorie." *Erzähltheorie transgenerisch, intermedial, interdisziplinär*. Ed. Vera Nünning. Trier: Wissenschaftlicher Verlag Trier. 23–104. Print.
Wolf, Werner (2005). "Metalepsis as a Transgeneric and Transmedial Phenomenon: A Case Study of the Possibilities of 'Exporting' Narratological Concepts." Ed. Jan Christoph Meister. *Narratology Beyond Literary Criticism: Mediality, Disciplinarity*. Berlin/New York: De Gruyter. 83–107. Print.
Wolf, Werner (2011). "Narratology and Media(lity): The Transmedial Expansion of a Literary Discipline and Possible Consequences." *Current Trends in Narratology*. Ed. Greta Olson. Berlin/New York: De Gruyter. 146–80. Print.
Wolk, Douglas (2007). *Reading Comics: How Graphic Novels Work and What They Mean*. Cambridge, MA: Da Capo Press. Print.
Zymner, Rüdiger, ed. (2010). *Handbuch Gattungstheorie*. Stuttgart: Metzler. Print.

7 Index of Primary Works

A Child's Life and Other Stories 25
A Contract with God 13–14, 17, 33–34, 87
A Few Perfect Hours 24
Alice in Sunderland 1, 24, 51, 63, 70, 164–66, 182, 189, 192, 198, 202
Alice's Adventures in Wonderland 70, 80, 165
Alltagsspionage 24
American Born Chinese 197
American Splendor 18
Amulet 197
Approximativement 2, 29, 51, 185, 188
Arkham Asylum 51, 63–64, 69–70, 80–81, 192, 198
Ascension du haut-mal, see Epileptic
Asterios Polyp 24, 33, 61–62, 64–65, 68, 94, 104, 149–150, 182–183, 198
Aya de Yopougon 29

Babymouse: Queen of the World 197
Berlin, City of Stones 51, 124–126, 142–143, 177, 180
Binky Brown Meets the Holy Virgin Mary 11, 13–14, 17–18, 34, 37
Black Hole 14, 24, 32, 50–52, 57, 64, 99, 104, 192
Blankets 23–24, 33, 35, 64, 66, 68, 156, 182
Blast 1, 29, 62, 182, 186–187
Building Stories 1, 70–72, 86, 121, 148–149, 157, 192, 196, 199

C'était la guerre des tranchées 29, 51
Carnet de Voyage 24
Chroniques birmanes 24, 29
Chroniques de Jérusalem 24
Ciboire de Criss! 2, 29
City of Glass 2–3, 52, 104, 153, 159, 162, 169, 182, 189
Coraline 157, 197
Cosmicomic 51
Couleur de peau miel 29

Daddy's Girl 25
Déogratias 29
Der Boxer 23, 33, 51

Die Stadt 8
Dotter of Her Father's Eyes 24, 63, 121, 161–162, 182

Economix 51
Epileptic 2, 23, 35–36, 57, 66, 159, 195

Flip in Paradise 93
From Hell 1, 5, 41, 51–52, 132–136, 146, 152–153, 174–175, 177–179, 180–181, 187–189, 199–200
Fun Home 2, 23, 25, 33, 35, 37–38, 51, 64, 66–68, 73–74, 77–80, 148, 153, 155, 168, 184, 192, 195, 198

Gemma Bovery 41, 51, 103–104, 121, 168–170, 192, 198
Ghost World 5, 24, 123, 137–140, 175, 180, 200
Gift 51
God's Man 8

Habibi 24, 33, 182
Havanna 51
He Done Her Wrong 2
Here 59–60, 110
Heute ist der letzte Tag vom Rest meines Lebens 2, 24
Holy Terror 24, 33

Ici Même 27, 184–185
Im Himmel ist Jahrmarkt 190
In the Shadow of No Towers 24

Jimmy Corrigan 23, 35, 37, 41, 50, 63–64, 70, 74–77, 86, 104–105, 121, 145–148, 152, 157, 160, 168, 192, 199
Journal (Neaud) 2, 29, 182
Journal d'Italie, Vol. 1 (David B.) 29, 52
Journal d'un album (Dupuis/Berberian) 29, 188
Julius Corentin Acquefacques, prisonnier des rêves 1–2, 29, 51, 182, 192
Julius Corentin Acquefacques, prisonnier des rêves. La 2,333^e dimension 75–77

7 Index of Primary Works — 219

Julius Corentin Acquefacques, prisonnier des rêves. Le décalage 131–132, 144–145, 199

Le chat du rabbin 160–161, 190
Le chemin de l'Amérique 29
Le combat ordinaire 29, 182
Le photographe 2, 23–24, 27, 29, 51–52, 78, 124, 166–168, 198
Les aventures extraordinaires d'Adèle Blanc-Sec 29
Les cités obscures 29
Les ignorants 29
Les mauvaises gens 29
Les oubliés d'Annam 29
Little Nemo 193
Livret de phamille 29
Logicomix 23, 33, 45–46, 51–52, 63, 112, 151–152, 189, 198
Love in Vain 24, 26, 29, 51, 169–170

Madame Bovary 168
Maus (The Complete) 1, 14–15, 17, 26–27, 31–33, 36–37, 50–52, 54, 56, 58–59, 64, 73–74, 77–78, 81–82, 117, 131, 159, 162–163, 189, 195, 198
Metronome 104
Moi, René Tardi 29

On the Ropes 4, 51–52, 118–121, 168, 170
One Hundred Demons 2, 23, 35–37, 61, 64, 159, 163–164, 189, 198, 202
Operation Läckerli 24

Palestine 1, 24, 48, 50–52, 54, 107, 111–112, 117, 148, 155–156, 184, 192
Paul 29
Persepolis 2, 23, 25, 27, 29, 35, 37, 50–51, 85, 195
Pillules bleues 29, 190
Pyongyang 24, 29

Rayuela 1
Rébétiko 29, 33, 83
Red Eye, Black Eye 24

Safe Area Goražde 24, 155, 159, 198
Saga of the Swamp Thing 118
Shenzhen 24, 27, 29, 51–52
Stitches 2, 168
Sugar Skull 11, 32
Syncopated 24

The Arrival 33, 83, 110, 116, 159, 161, 170, 197
"The Confessions of R. Crumb" 11–13, 17, 34
The Dark Knight Returns 15–17, 21, 26–27, 39, 51, 78, 104, 149, 195, 198
The French Lieutenants's Woman 1
The Hive 32
The League of Extraordinary Gentlemen, Vol. 1 43, 51, 56, 149
The League of Extraordinary Gentlemen: Black Dossier 56, 76
The Left Bank Gang 3, 147
The Sandman 15, 19, 21, 27, 51
The System 110, 116, 170
The Unfortunates 1
The Unwritten 51, 121, 146, 157
The Wonderful Wizard of Oz 74

Une métamorphose iranienne 1, 23, 27, 33, 51, 120–121

V for Vendetta 5, 123–124, 126–128, 130, 157, 200

War Fix 24
Watchmen 1, 2, 5, 15–17, 21, 26–27, 32, 43, 50–51, 54, 58–59, 63–66, 78, 82–83, 104, 129–131, 136, 147, 174, 192, 195, 199–200

X'ed Out 32

www.ingramcontent.com/pod-product-compliance
Lightning Source LLC
Chambersburg PA
CBHW050107170426
43198CB00014B/2495